Data Sources for Business and Market Analysis

Fourth Edition

by
JOHN GANLY

The Scarecrow Press, Inc.
Metuchen, N.J., & London
1994

The first edition of this book was issued under the title *Market Analysis: A Handbook of Current Data Sources.*

Data Sources for Business and Market Analysis, 2nd edition, published 1969.

Previous Scarecrow Press edition:

Data Sources for Business and Market Analysis, 3rd edition, by Nathalie D. Frank and John V. Ganly, 1983.

British Library Cataloguing-in-Publication data available

Library of Congress Cataloging-in-Publication Data

Data sources for business and market analysis / by John Ganly.   4th ed.
     p.   cm.
    ISBN 0-8108-2758-1 (acid-free paper)
    Prev. ed. cataloged under: Frank, Nathalie D.
    Includes bibliographical references and index.
    I. Marketing—United States—Information services. 2. United States—Commerce—Information services 3. Marketing—Bibliography. 4. Commerce—Bibliography. I. Frank, Nathalie D., 1918–   Data sources for business and market analysis. II. Title.
HF5415.124.F7   1994
016.56588'3973—dc20   93-23453

To William B. Stern

CONTENTS

Contents

Contents

Contents

Contents xiii

INTRODUCTION

It is a decade since the third, revised edition of *Data Sources for Business and Market Analysis* appeared. During that time technology, politics and economics (not necessarily in that order) exerted the force of change on the sources of data and upon access to data. New formats made their appearance and traditional sources of information either grew in importance or were superseded by newer or alternative sources.

In general three trends are clearly evident:

- Government agencies in the U.S. at the national or sub-national level have been pressured to reduce their information-related costs. This has resulted at the Federal level in a major shift to publish in nonprint formats such as microfiche and CD-Rom. In addition the pressure to privatize Federal information activities has resulted in the shifting of some publishing programs to private publishers or the cessation of some programs altogether. A related development is the effort to limit regional office activities by the Executive and independent agencies.

- At State level, publishing programs have been severely curtailed and informational units cut back or eliminated entirely. As a reflection of the Federal initiatives there has been a move to privatization within the States in the areas of directory and statistical publishing. An important development for the researcher is the move to copyright protection for their publications which many States are now reviewing.

- The introduction of CD-Rom technology and experiments with software for online databases which is "end-user friendly" has dramatically altered access to information for the researcher. Research which formerly required long periods of time and professional assistance can now be done quickly and with a minimal level of professional help. The further step of networking machine-readable information has made it possible to do a meaningful amount of research outside of the formal library setting.

The political restructuring of the world during the last decade has created a need for data that reflects the new paradigm. The European Communities, the Pacific Rim countries and the beginnings of a new Eastern Europe have generated new data sources and expanded existing ones.

The business researcher will continue to work in an ocean of information, an ocean made up of print as well as non-print data. The selection of sources for inclusion will reflect the current state of information. Where print sources continue to be important they will be identified; where machine-readable information has taken hold, as in the area of research sources, this will be indicated, and where they exist together this will be obvious.

Despite the changes indicated and a great number of other changes necessitated by the passage of years, *Data Sources for Business and Market Analysis* has retained the same format. Information is arranged by type of source so that the marketer, student, researcher or other user can locate specific titles, organizations, and other particular data resources and, at the same time, gain an understanding of the kinds of information most likely to be available from each of the broad source categories.

Because current, continuing information plays a primary role in business decisions, emphasis is on original sources of quantitative data, on useful secondary sources, and on keys to business facts. Coverage of non-statistical, non-marketing sources has been expanded to include such major support materials as directories, bibliographies and publications lists, technical indexes, and selected Federal, legal and regulatory titles, which the researcher may need to supplement and support his research. No attempt has been made to produce a definitive bibliography. Individual references have been selected on the basis of their general usefulness in researching economic conditions, business trends, and consumer and industrial markets. The emphasis is on serials, with monographs listed only if they provide needed time series data, function as major guides, or serve as examples of the area covered. Every effort has been made to cover the most recent sources available. The basic cutoff date was January 1992.

It is hoped that the arrangement by type of source, rather than by topic, will aid the user in identifying the major suppliers of information and the value of their product. Such orientation, although not infallible, transcends the vagaries of specific programs and publications; it provides more lasting guidelines to the origins of business data and, more importantly, to their underlying, unpublished strata.

John Ganly

INFORMATION AND ITS RETRIEVAL

The accessibility and use of information is a major concern of management. The widespread use of computers for the storage and retrieval of numerical and bibliographic data has expanded the potential for ready access to information, and the demand for ready access to this information has increased accordingly. The introduction of end-user technologies such as CD-Rom has accelerated this trend.

Marketing, with its emphasis on numerical measurement, has been in the forefront of the demand for current and accurate data. The great number of organizations which maintain libraries and information centers whose main function is the systematic accumulation, organization, and intramural dissemination of information applicable to current marketing data and long-range programs denotes the importance of marketing data to the overall management scheme. Despite the proliferation of these information centers and the development of sophisticated information retrieval systems, published and machine-stored facts still present an acute problem of inaccessibility to many marketers. Thus, researchers lacking organized facilities would benefit appreciably from a personal program of regular scanning, selection, and acquisition of source materials bearing directly upon immediate projects and foreseeable interests.

THE CLIMATE

Successful retrieval of available facts, either from an organized collection or from their scattered origins, depends not only on the individual but also to a large extent upon the climate within which he or she functions. Speaking from the vanguard of the information retrieval movement, one of its leading exponents, Calvin N. Mooers, states: " . . . for many people it is more painful and troublesome to have information than not to have it. . . . On the other hand, there are situations where the diligent finding and use of information is stressed and rewarded. . . . "*

Either approach may be detected in the posing of the question to one's self and to others. Under optimum conditions the searcher participates in the discussion of plans, goals, underlying assumptions, and end uses of the desired facts. He or she is briefed directly, thoroughly, and, if need be, continuously. Written requests for unrelated specifics produce, at best, "echo" results which many times are not representative of pertinent data available. Similarly, seepage and misinterpretation of purpose and direction may accompany the transmittal of an information call from person to person. Direct communication, on the other hand, engages the judgment, perception, and experience of the searcher. It hardly fails to produce related data and helpful intelligence. More often than not it precludes wasted effort and disappointing results.

THE PERSON

To achieve success, however, the fact-finder must contribute certain personal characteristics, knowledge, and search techniques.

Idle browsing, either in print or machine-readable sources, is the antithesis of the purposeful search. Concentrated, critical scanning with a sense of direction can be learned. More often, however, it is the sign of a naturally inquisitive and imaginative, as well as disciplined, mind productively at work. These characteristics, together with initiative, perseverance, understanding and insight, are fundamental to the application of knowledge and sound techniques.

Knowledge necessary to the successful search seldom lies in total recall of specific facts or specialized publications. More valuable is a broad acquaintance with the characteristics and behavior of information and its sources.

---

*Mooers, Calvin N. "Mooers' Law: Or Why Some Retrieval Systems Are Used and Others Are Not." *American Documentation,* vol. 11, no. 3, July 1960, p. [204].

THE INFORMATION

Familiarity with marketing facts, their types and nature, indicates that not all useful information is quantitative. Statements of experience and opinion, either individual or collective, offer a multitude of case histories, trends, forecasts, guesstimates and analyses in the solution of marketing problems.

When quantified and systematized, facts become statistics. Some represent the results of single research efforts. Others are collected and compiled continuously and issued regularly with varying frequency. Benchmark data published by the Federal government furnish the greatest amount of general purpose detail and serve as a basic reference. These are updated and supplemented by a large number of current statistics issued at more frequent intervals.

Not all the answers lie in published or recorded fact. An expert's voiced knowledge, experience, and opinion rank high as information, particularly in those areas that lack research effort or formal documentation.

THE SOURCE

So transient and mutable are information sources that knowledge, even of standard works past and present, quickly becomes obsolete. Moreover, the advent of the computer has given rise to a new and even more elusive source. Data banks and other sources of unpublished facts are growing in number and size at an accelerated rate and, through network connections, are becoming more available.

Current awareness of data collecting and producing sources, therefore, is more important than "knowledge." For continuous updating, both must rely on certain aids and on a method of evaluating current sources and their output. Guides, bibliographies, catalogs, checklists, as well as the literature of specific subjects and industries, provide current orientation and a basis for judging the adequacy of each source. This may be done principally in terms of its authoritativeness, scope, and timeliness.

Much of the validity of information rests on the authority of the source: the status and background of the individual or organization providing the information; methods of collection and compilation; and proximity of the source to the actual fact.

Primary sources, or those which originate the data, are preferable to secondary sources, or those which republish information produced by others. Many sources are secondary in their entirety. A large number are primary for some information and secondary for other information. Although often helpful because of their selection and arrangement, secondary sources frequently lack valuable explanatory material, detail, recency and proper documentation. On the other hand, precise identification of cited data, preferably in complete bibliographic form, enhances their usefulness as secondary sources and as guides to primary sources.

The adequacy of a source for any given purpose also depends on its scope and timeliness. The coverage, nature, detail, and preciseness of information are best judged from a study of its prefatory text, definitions, and annotations. Recency and frequency of publication are the main indicators of timeliness. Particularly important for statistical data, these are critical factors in the selection and use of a statistical source. Nor does recency of publication insure the location of only the latest information. Advance or preliminary releases, for example, often carry greater detail as well as revisions of data previously published in final form.

Standards used in mounting and evaluating field research have been promulgated by trade associations active in the various areas of marketing practice. Such associations in related areas should be consulted when standards are required for mounting and evaluating research in marketing disciplines.

THE SEARCH

Many a search for information is frustrated not so much by the obscurity of the fact as by the lack of systematic application of search techniques. Proper orientation should be followed by an analysis and definition of the problem. Complex projects need to be particularized and outlined. This may be done from the project's overall strategy or guided by an intramural or published model marketing plan. Such a procedure highlights the areas requiring information.

Habitual reliance on memory is often a shortcut to overlooking new data, new sources, even new features of standard works. When undertaking a project it is advisable to review the types and nature of marketing facts, their origin and sources. A thorough check of

pertinent catalogs, guide lists, and other bibliographic tools produces a current list of research material. This, if coded to the outline preferably as culled, creates a working plan with which to
expedite the assembly of necessary sources and gives direction to the
search. The use of an SDI system enhances the quality of ongoing
research.

Further application of the search technique may vary with the
problem, the individual, and the source. A few basic principles,
however, are universally applicable. A number of these are cited here
to serve as a guide to more productive effort:

- Consult the specific primary source.
- If unfamiliar with the original source, refer to secondary sources,
  compendia, indexes, and other bibliographic tools for guidance
  to the primary source.
- Start with the most recent source and work back to insure
  accuracy and recency, particularly of statistical data.
- Use the index, if one is available, checking under all terms from
  the most specific to the most general. Follow through on all
  page references and cross-references. With any machine-
  readable databases identify the fields indexed.
- Tables of contents are available in works that are not indexed.
  Mark likely references throughout and consult each in turn. A
  thorough check of related data often reveals unexpected detail.
  The availability of tables of contents in machine-readable
  format is a major advance.
- Consult the introductory text for terminology and methodology; footnotes for scope and bibliographic citation; the front and
  back of the work for errata, addenda, and appendixes. In case of
  continuing doubt, consult the technical personnel of the issuing
  body.
- Weigh each fact against the needs and goals of the project.
- Watch for trends; for related, supplementary, contradictory
  facts; for data that can be correlated, juxtaposed, projected.
- Recheck the original outline and work plan with persons
  concerned for policy and implications of supplementary or
  substitute information.
- Check each source through for all necessary facts before turning
  to the text.
- Note all sources consulted.

- Note all further sources to be consulted as they suggest themselves.
- Take notes or abstract data systematically, preferably verbatim, and in adequate detail.
- Identify each fact, citing the source in full bibliographic form: author, title, edition, publication date (month, day, and year where applicable), page number, table number, and column number, if need be.

From time to time, published sources fail to provide some or any of the needed information. Asking the person who knows is a delicate task and is best undertaken from a position of knowledge based on a thorough search. It is important to be specific and, insofar as possible, to supply him or her with the intended context for the required information. The expert's specialty is the obscure fact which, in itself, often contains broad implications, limitations, and complexities. Nothing discourages cooperation more effectively than an offhand request, muffled in secretiveness, for the obvious or for the limitless generality.

Although the principles highlighted here are familiar to many, it is surprising how often they are overlooked under the pressure of an immediate information need. The primary purpose for setting them forth, therefore, is not only to provide orientation and a critical approach to the sources which follow, but also to assist the literature search past the more common pitfalls to more frequent achievement of optimum results.

COMPENDIA

A number of single publications contain a large selection of basic economic and marketing data. Some of these are compiled from a multitude of original sources and are arranged for ease of access and ready reference. A few are also primary sources of data not published elsewhere. To these publications may be added compendia in electronic formats that provide online access to statistics gathered from a variety of sources, and research studies containing support data similarly compiled. This would include online databases and CD-ROM products. All are compact resources that may reduce research time.

Databases, proprietary and online, maintained by economic forecasting companies, demographic data firms, and other service organizations in support of their expertise are covered in the chapter on services.

GENERAL

Basebook. Cleveland: Predicasts, Inc. Annual.
Coverage worldwide for over 27,000 statistical series. Inclusion of data depends on the availability of information and, therefore, sources vary from edition to edition. Also available online.

CENDATA. Washington, D.C.: U.S. Bureau of the Census. [Online database].
A database of census and related statistical information. Updated as new information is made available.

Historical Statistics of the United States, Colonial Times to 1970 . . . (A Statistical Abstract Supplement.) Washington, D.C.: Government Printing Office. 1975. 2 vols. SuDoc: C3.134:
Contains over 12,500 time series covering all major phases of

7

business, economic, government, and social development. This edition contains some data below the national level and displays a sizable increase in social statistics coverage. A chronological index and a subject index are included. An appendix in the *Statistical Abstract . . .* relates these series to tables carrying comparable current data in the abstract. Last edition seen: 1975.

JCPS Congressional District Fact Book . . . Washington, D.C.: Joint Center for Political Studies. Irregular.
    A statistical analysis of each Congressional district which provides social, economic and political data.

National Trade Data Bank: the Export Connection. Washington, D.C.: U.S. Department of Commerce. Monthly. [CD-Rom]. SuDoc: C1.88:1CD.
    The National Trade Data Bank (NTDB) combines data from 15 Federal agencies and the Massachusetts Institute for Social and Economic Research (MISER). In CD-Rom format this product provides import/export statistics and narrative data on world market and economic conditions.

Predicasts Forecasts. Cleveland: Predicasts. Quarterly.
    Provides forecasts on products, markets, industry and economic factors for the U.S. and North America. The statistics which are included in this publication are derived from the trade and business press. A companion series of publications is known as *Worldcasts;* this is subdivided into two series identified as *World-Regional Casts* and *World-Product Casts.* These series provide forecast statistics for parts of the world other than the U.S. and North America. These publications are issued quarterly.

PTS System. Cleveland: Predicasts.
    PTS System, which is available online, provides access to 23,000 additional series not included in the printed version of Predicast's *Basebook.* The PTS system also includes approximately 15 years of data which are not included in the printed publication. PTS system includes *PTS Forecasts* which contains abstracts of published forecasts. The statistics included in this database usually provide historical data, a short-term forecast and a long-term forecast. The PTS

system also includes *PTS U.S. Time Series,* an online database which contains annual time series of United States historical data relating to demography, industry, finances, economics, and statistics of a variety of business activities. Each series includes an average of 20 years of statistical data and a calculated growth rate. The PTS system and the Predicasts printed publications form a particularly valuable source of information relating to industries, companies, and products.

PTS U.S. Time Series. Cleveland: Predicasts, Inc.

Data in this online database, ranging from 1957 (for some series) to date and updated quarterly, are contained in two files: Basebook contains key U.S. economic variable time series covering such major indicators as production, consumption, price, foreign trade, and usage for agriculture, mining, manufacturing, and services. Also included are national account and demographic statistics. Input is from Federal and specialized sources. Composites contain forecasts for key economic series for the U.S. and historical data from 1957 where available. Input is from published forecasts.

State and Metropolitan Area Data Book. (A Statistical Abstract Supplement.) Washington, D.C.: Government Printing Office. Biennial. SuDoc: C3:134/5:

Data from Federal and private agencies include land areas, population, vital statistics, housing, education, employment, social insurance, public assistance, hospitals and physicians, government employees and finances, banking, manufacturers, services, retail and wholesale trade. Over 2,000 items are given for each state, District of Columbia, census regions and divisions. Over 400 items are shown for MSAs by population-size categories for each census division, for individual MSAs and New England County Metropolitan Areas and their component counties. In editions of the *State and Metropolitan Area Data Book* issued prior to June 30th, 1983, the metropolitan areas were listed as SMSAs or New England County Metropolitan Areas. Data included in this publication are available on flexible diskette for IBM PC compatible microcomputers and on computer tape for larger computers. A related product, available on computer tape—County Statistics File 2 (CO-STAT 2)—presents for all counties the statistics included in the *State and Metropolitan Area Data Book* only for metropolitan counties.

Two Hundred Years of U.S. Census Taking: Population and Housing Questions, 1790–1990. Washington, D.C.: U.S. Bureau of the Census. 1991. 116p.

A compilation of data collection and instruction for enumeration forms, 1790–1990.

U.S. Bureau of Economic Analysis. *Business Statistics. (A Supplement to the Survey of Current Business.)* Washington, D.C.: Government Printing Office. Biennial. SuDoc: C59.11/3: ISSN: 0083–2545

Provides historical trend data for the "Current Business Statistics" tables in the *Survey of Current Business.* Data are derived from governmental and nongovernmental sources. Descriptive notes and source references are included.

U.S. Bureau of Economic Analysis. *Long Term Economic Growth. 1860–1970.* Washington, D.C.: Government Printing Office. ISSN: 0565–0976

Statistical compendium of the study of long-term economic trends. Includes series taken from both Federal and private sources. Areas covered include aggregate output, input, and productivity; processes related to economic growth; regional and industry trends; international comparisons; growth rate trends. Each volume begins with 1860. Last edition seen: 1973.

U.S. Bureau of Economic Analysis. *Survey of Current Business.* Washington, D.C.: Government Printing Office. Monthly/Weekly supplement. SuDoc: C59/11: ISSN: 0039–6222

A comprehensive source of information on the major business and economic indicators. Includes data on national accounts; income; business sales and inventories; manufacturers' sales, and orders (by industry group); business incorporations and failures; commodity prices; construction and real estate; domestic trade; labor force; finance; foreign trade; and specific industries. Each issue also contains important articles and features on a variety of economic topics. The articles and features are indexed in the December issue.

The "Current Business Statistics" tables in each issue update the identically numbered tables in the biennial supplement, *Business Statistics* (ISSN: 0083–2545). Time series data for its national income and product accounts tables are provided in another supplement, *National Income and Product Accounts of the U.S.: Statistical Tables*

(ISSN: 0361–3895), published irregularly. The weekly supplement presents selected data prior to its publication in the monthly.

U.S. Bureau of the Census. *County and City Data Book: 1988.* (A Statistical Abstract Supplement.) Washington, D.C.: Government Printing Office. 1988. xl, 797p + appendices. SuDoc: C3.134/2:C
   Most of the data are derived from the 1980 Census of Population and Housing, the 1982 Census of Agriculture, the 1982 Census of Governments, and a variety of the 1982 economic censuses. Data are included from other federal and private sources and provide information about states, counties, MSAs and other places in the U.S. New categories of data in this edition include infant deaths, housing units demolished or removed, Federal funds, grants for cities, and county seats. Available on 5–1/4 inch diskettes for use on IBM compatible microcomputers and on computer tape for use with larger computers.

U.S. Bureau of the Census. *Statistical Abstract of the United States.* Washington, D.C.: Government Printing Office. Annual. SuDoc: C3.134:
   Published annually since 1878, this standard statistical compilation provides charts and tables on social, political and economic topics. Its data are derived from government and private agencies and the documentation accompanying the tables and charts is an excellent reference guide to more current and detailed data available. In addition to a subject index, an appendix relates to the *Abstract* tables' comparable data in *Historical Statistics . . .* and in the *State and Metropolitan Data Book* series. Other appendices act as guides to sources of statistics, State statistical abstracts, foreign statistical abstracts, metropolitan area concepts and components, population of metropolitan statistical areas and statistical methodology and reliability. A new feature provides a list of telephone contacts within each department or independent agency which users of the *Statistical Abstract* may enlist to find more data and information.

U.S. Department of Commerce. *Economic Bulletin Board.*
   The Department of Commerce has created an online database of current statistical data which is referred to as a "bulletin board." This database, available to subscribers, contains the most current information and is updated as new data are released. Other Executive agencies of the Federal government are creating similar "bulletin boards."

AREA DATA

Canada. Statistics Canada. *Market Research Handbook.* Ottawa: Statistics Canada. Irreg.

A compendium of population, income, housing and household data for metropolitan areas, with national aggregates.

Canadian Markets. Toronto: Financial Post Information Service. Annual.

Provides up-to-date statistics on Canada's provinces, cities and towns, as well as a review of national economic and business indicators.

CANSIM (Canadian Socio-Economic Information Management System). Ottawa: Statistics Canada, CANSIM Division.

Online daily updated database. The various files provide access to 400,000 monthly, quarterly, and annual time series (1946 to date), covering the major economic variables, as well as population, welfare and health variables, for Canadian provinces and cities. Statistics correspond to those found in a number of Canadian government publications.

CRONOS. Luxembourg. Statistical Office of the European Communities. [Online database].

A time series database which includes the statistical series of the European Communities.

Current Economic Indicators. Paris. O.E.C.D. [Online database].

An online database which contains time series of economic indicators for the members of the O.E.C.D.

DRI Europe Data Bank. Washington, D.C.: Data Resources. [Online database].

Continuously updated online database supplies weekly, monthly, quarterly, semi-annual and annual time series covering key economic data for the European economies.

Economist Intelligence Unit International Statistics. London: Economist Intelligence Unit. [Online database].

A database available through Reuters Information Services which contains time series economic data for developed and developing countries.

Editor & Publisher Market Guide: The Fourth Estate. New York: Editor & Publisher Company. Annual.

Arranged by State and city. For each city, the *Guide* gives principal industries, number and sales of retail outlets, population and housing data, automobile registrations, and other data for market analysis. Provides data for U.S., Puerto Rico, and Canada.

European Marketing Data and Statistics. London: Euromonitor. Annual.

By a topical arrangement, this presents statistics for individual countries of Western and Eastern Europe on population; employment; production; retailing; trade; national income and product, and other economic factors; market sizes; standard of living; consumption; consumer expenditures; housing, health and education, communications; culture and mass media; travel and tourism. A separate section, arranged by country, gives population data for main urban areas and standard regions within each country.

International Marketing Data Statistics. London: Euromonitor. Annual.

Covers the Americas, Asia, Africa, and Oceania, but not Europe. Arranged by the following topics within which statistics are given for individual countries grouped by continent: population; employment; production; trade; and economy; standard of living; consumption; housing, health and education; communications; travel and tourism; retailing and consumption and market sizes. The statistics are taken from the publisher's own research and analysis, and from published sources.

Nomura Research Institute Economic. Tokyo: Nomura Research Institute. [Online database].

This continuously updated, online database provides access to over 5,400 weekly, monthly, and quarterly time series covering key economic and financial indicators, general industry indicators, and key indicators for specific major industries such as construction, transportation, and services. Annual data cover the last ten to thirty years. Quarterly and monthly data are from 1965 to date; weekly data cover 1980 to date.

OECD Annual National Income Accounts. Paris. Organization for Economic Cooperation and Development (OECD). [Online database].

Online database containing over 23,000 quarterly and annual time series. Data covers national accounts statistics for 235 individual countries and four aggregate totals. Coverage is from 1960 to date and data are updated semi-annually. This database, available from several online vendors, is only one of the OECD statistical databases.

Rand McNally Commercial Atlas & Marketing Guide. Chicago, IL: Rand McNally & Company. Annual.

Maps, tables, and charts provide economic and geographic market data for the United States. Categories covered include retail sales, agriculture, manufacturers, population, bank deposits, and automobile registrations. Unique source of city and town population figures not available elsewhere. Randata, which contains the geographic data files, is available on diskette for personal computer users and on magnetic tape for use on mainframe computers.

Sales & Marketing Management. Survey of Buying Power. New York: Bill Communications. Annual.

An annual survey issued in two parts as issues of *Sales & Marketing Management.* The first part of the survey, published in August, provides a geographic analysis of population, effective buying income, and retail sales for U.S. and Canadian markets in the preceding year. The second part, published in November, gives survey highlights and five-year projections. Includes data on merchandise line sales, metropolitan area market projections, newspaper and TV markets. A separate section is devoted to Canadian market projections.

Data based on latest available benchmarks are provided for States, cities, counties, and metropolitan areas on population; total retail, food, drug, general merchandise and other outlet sales; effective buying income; buying power and quality indexes.

The separate *Sales & Marketing Management Data Service* is an annual publication which provides ten-year forecasts.

Sales & Marketing Management. Survey of Industrial & Commercial Buying Power. New York: Bill Communications. Annual.

This survey appears each April as an issue of *Sales & Marketing Management,* serving as a guide for industrial marketing and giving data on manufacturing activity at the regional, State, and county levels. Provides data for four-digit SIC manufacturing industries. Highlight tables include listings of the 50 leading metro markets in manufacturing activity, profiles of the nation's 25 largest non-manufacturing industries and the top 50 counties in manufacturing shipments.

Standard Rate & Data Service: {Consumer Market Data}. Skokie, IL: Standard Rate & Data Service.

A series of statistical analyses presented in the appropriate editions, each of which covers a specific advertising medium. Areas represented are States, counties, cities and metro areas. Statistics include estimates (based on the latest official data) of population, households, consumer spendable income, retail sales, car registrations; metro area rankings for each of the preceding categories. Farm market statistics cover farm population, gross farm income and income by farm product category, total farms, and related data.

The statistics included in *Consumer Market Data* that appear in SRDS publications are provided by National Decision Systems in Encinitas, California.

INDUSTRY AND PRODUCT DATA

Market studies containing relevant industry, company and product data from various government and private sources are published by on-demand information services such as Packaged Facts and Find/SVP, and by other sources grouped in the following chapters.

A large number are issued by companies that specialize in the compilation and publishing of such works. Among these are the following:

Business Trend Analysts. Commack, N.Y.

Comprehensive statistical market reports, analysis and forecasts on all major U.S. industries. A customized marketing information service is available in the Contract Research Division. Publications include *Predicasts Industry Studies, WorldTech Reports,* and *Leading Edge Group Report Series.*

Frost & Sullivan. New York, N.Y.

Compiles and issues a great number of studies assessing individual industries and forecasting their markets. Published reports have covered all industries including chemicals, plastics and paper; communications and electronic components; leisure; retailing; building; data processing and office machines; defense, aerospace, and security; energy and power systems; financial business services; food, beverage and associated equipment; health; instrumentation and controls; machinery and materials; transportation. Custom reports are prepared by Frost & Sullivan Consultants upon request. Abstracts for reports from 1983 to date are available online.

Venture Development Corporation. Natick, MA.

Besides specializing in consulting to the electronics industry, the company issues studies that contain industry data, analyze the impact of technologies and trends, forecast markets for industry segments and products, and project market shares.

The company also publishes a series of data books, each of which covers an electronics product group, one devoted to European data, another to Asian data. These compendia present statistics and forecasts of production, sales, foreign trade and similar data abstracted from the technical and business press and other sources published in a stated year.

FEDERAL STATISTICAL PROGRAM

The greatest single supply of research data originates in the agencies of the Federal government. The implementation of computer technology on a wide scale throughout the Federal government has greatly expanded the amount of statistical data available and has promoted increased flexibility in the access and use of these data.

Along with mechanization and computerization, a major thrust has been toward coordination of the statistical policies and programs of the decentralized Federal statistical system, which consists of many agencies each with its own statistical responsibilities and activities. A number of different plans have been implemented at one time or another for placing the responsibility for statistical policy in the hands of one agency.

COORDINATING BODIES

Effective October 9, 1977, the statistical policy functions formerly exercised by the Office of Management and Budget (OMB) were assumed by the newly created Office of Federal Statistical Policy and Standards (FSPS) in the Department of Commerce. The Paperwork Reduction Act of 1980, effective April 1, 1981, reassigned these functions to the OMB, where they were to be delegated to a newly created Office of Information and Regulatory Affairs (OIRA). The reassignment and delegation were implemented effective August 23, 1981, and a new Statistical Policy Division (comparable to the pre-October 1977 Statistical Policy Branch) was established to perform the statistical policy functions of OIRA.

Regardless of these reorganizations in recent years the statistical policy functions have remained very much the same: the development and coordination of Federal statistical policy, programs and activities system-wide and across all subject areas. In implementation they have included reviewing all data-gathering proposals; evalua-

17

tion of statistical programs; coordinating the dissemination of statistical information; long-range planning of improvements in statistical activities; assistance to agencies in the establishment of methodologies and in the use of advanced statistical techniques; and, most significant in terms of general interest and user needs, the development and implementation of statistical standards and guidelines whereby consistency and comparability are achieved within the decentralized Federal statistical system. In addition, on the international level, the statistical policy unit has acted as central liaison on all statistical matters.

The unit's working tools of internal coordination and policy implementation have been such publications as the *Statistical Policy Handbook* and the *Statistical Policy Working Papers.* Communications were expedited by the statistical personnel.

GENERAL ORGANIZATION

The agencies of the Federal statistical system fall into three groups according to their statistical function:

> Administrative or regulatory agencies, which collect statistics as a by-product of their operations or to implement their programs and to provide a factual basis for their policies.
> Fact-producing agencies, whose primary function is the collection and dissemination of statistics for general use.
> Analytic and research agencies, whose statistical importance lies in the interpretation and analysis of data collected by other sources both governmental and private.

Since some agencies support more than one type of program, the categories are not mutually exclusive.

Fuller understanding of the functions, activities and organization of the Federal statistical program may be obtained from the following.

U.S. General Accounting Office. *Congressional Sourcebook Series.* Washington, D.C.: Government Printing Office. 3 reports. Irregular. SuDoc: GA 1.22: In 3/

This series, updated at intervals, is the product of a continuing program surveying for the benefit of Congress (and its budgetary function) the sources and systems, many of them statistical, maintained by the Federal government.

Requirements for Recurring Reports to Congress. Biennial. SuDoc: GA 1.22: R 29/

Entries for reports, listed under submitting agency arranged by government structure, include title, frequency, due date, availability, geographic coverage, content required by law, abstract, and other reference items. No title index but subject and agency name indexes are among the five indexes provided. Last edition seen: 1984.

Federal Information Sources and Systems. Irregular. SuDoc: GA 1.22: In 3/

This directory-type report covers program related, as well as fiscal and budgetary, sources and systems maintained by executive agencies and independent agencies, boards and commissions in support of their programs and responsibilities. Included are major information collection and dissemination facilities, and automated and manual data processing systems, among them many statistical data files, that generate recurrent reports. The entries describe the source or system and give program names, geographic coverage, abstracts or recurrent reports, availability of publications generated, agency contact. Contains a glossary and seven indexes providing access by subject, report title, various names and other information items.

Federal Evaluations: A Directory Issued by the Comptroller General. Annual. SuDoc: GA 1.22: P94/

Describes and abstracts program and system evaluations of programs and systems maintained by executive agencies, independent agencies or agencies in combination produced by private contractors and government bodies. Subject, agency and program name are three of the six indexes provided.

A parallel database, CISID (Congressional Information Sources, Inventories and Directories), consisting of four files on magnetic tape, is maintained and made available by the GAO. Currently it is accessible online via the Library of Congress SCORPIO Information Retrieval System.

U.S. Office of Federal Statistical Policy and Standards. *Revolution in U.S. Government Statistics. 1926–76.* Washington, D.C.: Government Printing Office, 1978. ix, 157p. SuDoc: C 1.2:St 2/10

Provides an historical overview of Federal government statistical policies, procedures, and activities, mainly for the years 1926 to 1976. Includes a bibliography, and a name and subject index. This report is the first part of a major study of the Federal statistical system. The second part is listed immediately below.

Framework for Planning U.S. Federal Statistics for the 1980s. Washington, D.C.: Government Printing Office. 1978. vii, 440p. SuDoc: C 1.2:F 84/2

An analysis and comprehensive review of Federal statistical programs along with recommendations for consolidation of these activities in the 1980s. The subject matter areas discussed are agricultural statistics; construction statistics; criminal justice statistics; economic statistics; education statistics; energy statistics; financial statistics; health statistics; housing and community development statistics; income maintenance and welfare statistics; income, wealth and consumption statistics; labor statistics; population statistics; price statistics; production and distribution statistics; science and technology statistics; and statistics on environment and occupational safety and health. Issues that affect all or many of these areas across agency lines are also discussed. Includes bibliography. This report is the second part of a major study of the Federal statistical system. The first part is listed above.

U.S. Office of the Federal Register. *United States Government Manual.* Washington, D.C.: Government Printing Office. Annual. SuDoc: Gs 4.109/

This official guide to the organization of the Federal government provides reasonably detailed and current information on the organization, functions, activities, and major publications of the legislative, judicial, and executive branches. Additional sections provide data on boards, committees, and commissions; quasi-official agencies; selected multilateral organizations; and selected bilateral organizations. Appendixes provide data on abolished and transferred agencies and functions; commonly used abbreviations and acronyms; agencies appearing in the *Code of Federal Regulations;* and information on Standard Federal Regional Councils and Federal Executive Boards. Includes an agency acronym list, a subject index, and an agency index. Inter-edition changes in agency policies, and procedures may be found in the *Federal Register.*

METHODOLOGY AND STANDARDS

The origin and techniques of preparation are of major importance in the proper interpretation and effective use of statistical data.

Federal government sources excel in providing explicit definitions, methodology statements and manuals. Over time, a number of generally applicable procedures and classification schemes of individual agencies and statistical programs have been coordinated, standardized, and published to ensure system-wide compatibility of series for the benefit of producers and users. More recently this work has progressed to the correlation of standards at the international level.

Other, more specialized methodologies and classifications are issued by individual agencies in conjunction with their specific programs, either separately or in the series to which they pertain. When such individual publications are lacking, primary sources for the particular statistical series generally carry ample annotations and references to pertinent explanatory materials available.

At intervals, evaluative studies appear that explore the scope and adequacy of basic data, governmental and private. Improvements in statistics are constantly being proposed, studied and effected by the Federal agencies concerned. Much of this work is done on an interagency level and in cooperation with industry. One such project to improve data and methodology, whose government-wide implementation impacted a number of agencies, may be seen in the following report.

U.S. Office of Federal Statistical Policy and Standards. *Gross National Product Data Improvement Project Report.* Washington, D.C.: Government Printing Office. 1979. xii, 204p. SuDoc: c 1.2: G 91/2
The first comprehensive evaluation of the underlying data used to estimate the national economic accounts. Content and timeliness are evaluated and recommendations are made for specific improvements.

Other products of central policy and planning are two organs of internal coordination that deal with data collection and compilation, including interagency guidelines and standards.

U.S. Office of Management and Budget. Office of Federal Statistical Policy and Standards. *Statistical Policy Working Papers.* Springfield, VA: National Technical Information Service. Irregular.

A series of reports prepared by special subcommittees of the Federal Committee on Statistical Methodology, this series includes reports dealing with the technical operations of statistical programs, the statistical methodology and various uses of Federal statistics.

U.S. Office of Management and Budget. Office of Federal Statistical Policy and Standards. *Statistical Policy Handbook.* Washington, D.C.: Government Printing Office. 1978. v, 85p. SuDoc: C1.8/3:St 2/2
Provides official Federal government directives on standards, regulations, classifications, and guidelines applicable to the development and coordination of Federal statistics.

Proposals for the revision of or for the introduction of new statistical procedures, guidelines or standards are published in the *Federal Register* to invite public comment. These revisions are issued as *OMB Circular.*
From the classification systems and methodology reports issued by the central statistical policy unit and individual agencies, the following were selected as most useful in the interpretation and application of some of the general-purpose business statistics. To find or to keep current on all Federal methodological publications, including classifications, the researcher can consult the monthly *American Statistics Index* and the *Federal Register.*

Classification Systems

Among the more developed standards is the Standard Industrial Classification System, which covers all units of economic activity by establishments, legal form of organization, and correlation with the international system.

U.S. Office of Management and Budget. *Standard Industrial Classification Manual,* Washington, D.C.: Government Printing Office. Irregular. SuDoc: PrEx 2.6/: In 27/
Popularly known as the SIC, this classification scheme provides two-, three-, and four-digit codes to be used in categorizing data on all kinds of business establishments (manufacturing and non-manufacturing) by type of activity as determined by principal product or service. The manual is revised periodically to reflect the

economy's changing industrial organization. Each new edition results in the addition, revision and deletion of codes and has an effect on SIC-based indexes produced by private publishers. The time lag is often compensated by supplements.

U.S. Bureau of the Census. *1987 Industry and Product Classification Manual.* Washington, D.C.: Bureau of the Census. 1987. 414p.

Intended to be used in the Census Bureau's economic programs for the classification of establishments by industrial activity. Based on the 1987 SIC, this manual follows the same organization and expands its classification scheme to a seven-digit code.

U.S. Office of Management and Budget. *Enterprise Standard Industrial Classification Manual.* Washington, D.C.: Government Printing Office. 1974. 26p.

This manual classifies business enterprises (i.e., legal entities such as companies, corporations, etc.) by type of economic activity using the SIC two-, three-, and four-digit codes, and is updated by the 1977 supplement to the *Standard Industrial Classification Manual, 1972.* Latest seen: 1974.

U.S. Office of Federal Statistical Policy and Standards. *Correlation Between U.S. and International Standard Industrial Classifications.* Washington, D.C.: Government Printing Office. 1979. 101p.

Provides a way of relating data collected in terms of the U.S. and international classification systems. Incorporates 1972 revisions to the SIC and updates earlier Census Bureau Publications. Latest seen: 1979.

Redefinition of Metropolitan Statistical Areas. Washington, D.C.: Office of Management and Budget. 1983.

A series of three press releases which detail statistical areas designated as Metropolitan Statistical Areas (MSAs). These MSAs, effective June 30, 1983, replace the former statistical area classifications called Standard Metropolitan Statistical Areas (SMSAs) which were in effect prior to that date. Each release includes MSA code number, new and previous title, population size group, component counties, and counties and places added or deleted. Also as part of the 1983 revision of its Metropolitan Area Classification, the Federal Government replaced the term Standard Consolidated Statistical Area (SCSA) with the term Consolidated Metropolitan Statistical

Area (CMSA). These CMSAs consist of Component Primary Metropolitan Statistical Areas.

U.S. Office of Federal Statistical Policy and Standards. *Standard
Occupational Classification Manual.* Washington, D.C.: Government
Printing Office. 1980. 547p. SuDoc: C 1.8/3:Oc 1/
Popularly known as SOC, this two- to four-digit classification
provides standardized descriptions and classification codes for all
occupations performed for pay or profit. It is compatible with the
nine-digit classification of the *Dictionary of Occupational Titles* and was
developed for use in Labor Department programs and the 1980
Census of Population.

U.S. Employment and Training Administration. *Dictionary of Occupational Titles.* 4th ed. rev. Washington, D.C.: Government Printing
Office. 1991. 2 vols. Supplements. SuDoc: L37.2.Oc 1/2/
Provides job descriptions and classifications for thousands of
occupations. Includes job titles, job tasks, industry, and nine-digit
code that indicates occupational group and level of competency.

U.S. International Trade Commission. *Tariff Schedules of the United
States Annotated.* Washington, D.C.: Government Printing Office.
Looseleaf/Supplement updates. Annual.
This classification of over 10,000 imported commodities gives for
each its seven-digit classification code, description, unit of measurement, applicable duty rate, etc. The commodities are grouped in
eight TSUSA schedules and follows:

Schedule 1. Animal and Vegetable Products
Schedule 2. Wood and Paper; Printed Matter
Schedule 3. Textile Fibers and Textile Products
Schedule 4. Chemicals and Related Materials
Schedule 5. Nonmetallic Minerals and Products
Schedule 6. Metals and Metal Products
Schedule 7. Specified Products; Miscellaneous and Nonenumer-
    ated Products
Schedule 8. Special Classification Provisions

These annotated schedules are based on the *Tariff Schedules of the
United States Annotated* (TSUSA), which give only commodity code

identifications. The 18th and final edition of TSUSA was published in 1986 and has been replaced by the *Harmonized Tariff Schedules of the U.S. Annotated for Statistical Reporting Purposes.*

U.S. International Trade Commission. *Harmonized Tariff Schedules of the U.S. Annotated for Statistical Reporting Purposes.* Washington, D.C.: Government Printing Office. Irregular. SuDoc: ITC 1.10
The first edition of this publication appeared in 1987 in looseleaf format and included duty rates on more than 10,000 items imported into the United States. The codes contained in this schedule may also be used in place of the Schedule B codes to report exports. Each commodity listing provides a 10-digit classification number; description; standard measurement unit; and duty rates. The former title of this publication was *Tariff Schedules of the U.S. Annotated* (TSUSA) which ended with the 18th edition in 1986.

U.S. Bureau of the Census. *U.S. Foreign Trade Statistics: Classifications and Cross Classifications. 1980.* Washington, D.C.: Government Printing Office. 1981. var. pg. SuDoc: C3.2:F 76/2/980
Brings together the basic commodity and geographic trade classification schedules currently used in the compilation and publication of U.S. foreign trade statistics. Updates the 1974 edition of this title and the 1978 edition of *Correlations of Selected Export and Import Classifications Used in Compiling U.S. Foreign Trade Statistics.*

The current commodity exports schedules are the Census Bureau's 1987 edition of Schedule B, a replacement of Schedule B in effect during 1977, and of Schedule E, a completely new schedule, published in the concordance listed below.

U.S. Bureau of the Census. *U.S. Foreign Trade: Schedule B: Statistical Classification of Domestic and Foreign Commodities Exported from the U.S., 1987 Edition.* Washington, D.C.: Government Printing Office. 1987. Looseleaf/Updates. SuDoc: C3.150:B/988
Provides schedules of commodity and geographic trade classification codes to be used by shippers to report exports from the U.S. The commodity classification and its seven-digit codes are based on the framework and numbering system of TSUSA. The 1988 revision of Schedule B is in accordance with the adoption of the Harmonized Commodity Descriptive Encoding System.

135054

U.S. Bureau of Census. *U.S. Foreign Trade: Concordance of Statistical Classifications of Domestic and Foreign Commodities Exported from the United States, 1978 Edition.* Washington, D.C.: Government Printing Office. 1978-SuDoc: C3.6/2:F76/2/978 ISSN: 0193–1687

Correlates in three tables the seven-digit numbers of the export commodity classifications in effect and those effective since January 1, 1978 (i.e., Schedule B and the TSUSA Schedule B and Schedule E, Standard International Trade Classification (SITC), based on the Classification of Domestic and Foreign Commodities Exported from the United States. Schedule E is based on the *Standard International Trade Classification (SITC), Revision 2* (United Nations Statistical Papers, Series M, No. 53/Rev. 3).

U.S. Bureau of the Census. *U.S. Foreign Trade: Concordance of Statistical Classifications of Commodities Imported into the United States, 1978 Edition.* Washington, D.C.: Government Printing Office. 1978. var.pg. SuDoc: C3.2:F76/4/978

Provides separate correlations between the 1978 Schedule A and TSUSA numbers, and between the 1977 and 1978 Schedule A classifications. Schedule A was constructed to provide for the summarization of data collected in the approximately 10,000 TSUSA classifications into about 3,000 commodity groups. This 1978 edition, based on the *Standard International Trade Classification (SITC), Revision 2* (United Nations Statistical Papers, Series M, No. 53/Rev. 3), is a revision that took effect with the statistics for January 1978.

Among the geographic and administrative area schedules issued by the Census Bureau are the following. They are updated at intervals and provide numeric codes for reporting and compiling the Bureau's U.S. import and export statistics.

U.S. Bureau of the Census. *Schedule C-E, Classification of Country and Territory Designations for U.S. Export Statistics.* Washington, D.C.: Bureau of the Census 1976- Irregular. SuDoc: C 3.150:C-E/

U.S. Bureau of the Census. *Schedule C-I, Classification of Country and Territory Designations for U.S. Import Statistics.* Washington, D.C.: Bureau of the Census, 1976- Irregular. SuDoc: C3.150:C-I/ ISSN: 0191–4057

U.S. Bureau of the Census. *U.S. Foreign Trade: Classification of Customs Districts and Ports: Schedule D. January 1, 1978 Edition.* Washington, D.C.: Bureau of the Census, 1979. 10p. SuDoc: C3.150:D/978

Individual Agency Publications

U.S. Department of Agriculture

Guide to USDA Statistics. (Agriculture Handbook no. 429.) Washington, D.C.: Government Printing Office. 1973. iv, 59p.
   Describes major USDA time series.

Economic Research Service. *Major Statistical Series of the U.S. Department of Agriculture—How They Are Constructed and Used.* (Agriculture Handbook no. 365.) Washington, D.C.: Government Printing Office. 1970–72. 11 vols.

U.S. Bureau of the Census

A large part of the Census Bureau's methodology appears in the footnotes and introductory texts of its statistical publications. More detailed explanations are issued in a variety of forms. Statistical program guides and manual-type information of general interest appear as separate publications. Major censuses generate manual-type publications as well as detailed, technical methodology reports. The former appear either separately or as numbered parts of a particular census. The latter are issued in a series covering sampling, data collection forms and procedures, data processing and quality control. All such reports can be located through the Bureau's catalog of publications.

Census Bureau Methodological Research. Washington, D.C.: Bureau of the Census. Annual. SuDoc: C 3.163/4: M56/968 ISSN: 0565–0828
   A bibliography of staff papers and publications dealing with Census Bureau methodological research. Arranged by subject with an author index.

Technical Paper. Washington, D.C.: Bureau of the Census. Irregular. SuDoc: C 3.212

Individual reports in this series cover all aspects of the Bureau's methodology, including the design of specific programs and surveys, results of data evaluation studies, and the development and implementation of statistical standardization tools.

Census '80: Continuing the Factfinder Tradition. Washington, D.C.: Government Printing Office. [1980.] xviii, 490p.

An overview of decennial census procedures, methodology, data collection, tabulation and analysis, 1790–1980.

U.S. Bureau of Labor Statistics

Methodology reports of the Bureau of Labor Statistics statistical series are published regularly in the *Monthly Labor Review.*

BUREAU OF THE CENSUS

The Bureau of the Census is the largest, general purpose statistical agency in the United States. It collects, tabulates, and publishes a variety of statistical data about the people and the economy of the nation. Its printed reports, computer tapes, CD-ROMS, microforms, and special tabulations are the principal source of market and business statistics in the United States.

Listed in this chapter are the Bureau's benchmark and current publications. Also included are geographical tools of general interest and those microfiche and machine-readable products which carry unpublished tables and reports that serve to extend the availability of primary data to subject or area detail.

DATA PUBLICATION

Printed Publications

Most Census Bureau data are published for general distribution in printed reports, maps, and charts. These cover all data considered to be of wide interest and applicability: the greater portion of the results of the major censuses, findings of surveys, and compilations from special statistical programs. Data too specialized or too detailed for publication are made available on microfiche or in machine-readable formats.

Microfiche

Microfiche use at the Bureau of Census has been moving from economic storage of printed reports to a medium of general distribu-

29

tion of computerized primary data. In addition, fiche are being
utilized to narrow the time lag between the availability of the data
and their publication.

In general, the Bureau provides microfiche of final data published
in printed reports that cover its censuses and surveys, including
current and special reports. These fiche are available for data issued
since January, 1968, and for selected series whose first issues may
have appeared before 1968.

Increasingly, data unavailable in print have appeared on microfiche. In some cases, such as certain foreign trade monthly statistics
and the *1990 Census of Population and Housing,* microfiche replaces
print publication. In other instances, additional data derived from
the Bureau's public use computer tapes have been added to the fiche
of the corresponding printed final reports.

Data Files and Special Tabulations

The Bureau maintains over 1,000 machine-readable data files,
most of which extend the data published on its censuses and surveys.
Among these are microdata files containing records of individual
respondents or basic survey units with names and addresses removed,
and summary statistic files which are aggregates or estimates for
geographical areas. From these files users can obtain summaries based
on individual records, totals for areas not provided separately, and
area categories unavailable in published reports.

Also available are data dictionaries in machine-readable form, a
variety of geographical area reference files, and computer programs
for use with the Bureau's files.

A single printed copy of technical documentation accompanies
each file or may be bought separately. Some data files that contain no
confidential records may be purchased. All can be used by the Bureau
to prepare special tabulations.

For users with specific requirements not met by published data,
the Bureau can prepare special tabulations from either data files or
filled-in questionnaires and retabulations of collected data, or it can
supply transcriptions of unpublished tables. All are subject to the
same review of confidentiality and conditions of use.

CD-ROM

Starting with a test product based on the *1987 Census of Agriculture* and the *1987 Census of Retail Trade,* the Bureau introduced the CD-ROM format as a distribution medium. It is the Bureau's intention to utilize this format extensively for future publication programs.

Online Information

CENDATA, the Census Bureau's online information service, is available through two information vendors, Compuserve and Dialog. This online service offers current economic and demographic data for the United States and demographic data for over 200 countries. These online files are updated regularly. For additional information about CENDATA call the U. S. Census Bureau at 301-763-2074 or write to: CENDATA Program, Data User Services, U S. Bureau of the Census, Washington, DC 20233.

Bureau of the Census data are included in the Economic Bulletin Board from the U.S. Department of Commerce, Office of Business Analysis.

Sources of Information

Information on data and their publication formats—printed reports, maps, microfiche, machine-readable files, CD-ROM, and computer programs—appears in the Bureau's catalog, guides, and other research aids. An especially useful early alert on the printed reports and microfiche of the major censuses is the order forms, which also announce upcoming reports and distinguish data available only on microfiche and on paper copy from fiche.

OBTAINING BUREAU DATA

Printed Publications

As indicated by the imprints of titles cited in this guide, Census Bureau publications are available from the Government Printing Office or from the Bureau itself:

Government Printing Office   Customer Services
Superintendent of Documents   U.S. Bureau of the Census
Washington, DC 20402-9325   Washington, DC 20233
Tel: 301-763-4100
Fax: 301-763-4794

Publications may be ordered from GPO or from Customer Services by check, MasterCard, Visa or by use of a GPO deposit account.

Microfiche

Distribution sources of Census Bureau microfiche have varied over time. Currently, fiche of printed publications of final data issued since 1968 are available from Customer Services, Bureau of the Census, Washington, DC 20233.

Computer-output microfiche of 1990 census summary tape files; technical documentation on fiche and paper copy separately priced; and paper copy of individual fiche frames and of microfiche reports may be obtained from the Customer Services Branch, Data User Services Division, U.S. Bureau of the Census, Washington, DC, 20233.

Data Files and Special Tabulation

Machine-readable files with corresponding documentation are available from the Bureau.

Special tabulations compiled to user specifications or copies of such from the Bureau's inventory are provided, subject to certain policies and conditions, at a cost-reimbursement basis. Formats of presentation may range from hand-posted tables to computer print-outs or tapes.

In addition, copies of public use tapes, printouts, data compilations, and other census data-related services may be obtained for a fee from organizations registered with the National Clearinghouse for Census Data Services or from the State Data Centers.

Orders for specific items cited in the Bureau's catalog and research aids should be directed to the sources of supply accompanying the listings. For general assistance and information on special tabulations, for data files and technical documentation, and for a list of Clearinghouse registrants and State Data Centers, researchers should contact the Customer Services Branch, Data User Services Division, Bureau of the Census, Washington, DC 20233.

Telephone Contacts

For general assistance on its data products and for locating and interpreting its statistics, the Bureau publishes a telephone directory of its Washington subject specialists and Data User Services Division staff. This roster, arranged by subject field, along with a separate listing of Information Services Specialists located in its regional and satellite offices, is also sent automatically to subscribers to *Census and You.*

Libraries

Collections of Census Bureau publications and microfiche, which vary considerably in subject and geographic scope, are available in libraries and Department of Commerce district offices. Further information on these organizations may be found in the chapter, Information Centers and Specialists.

U.S. Bureau of the Census Regional Offices

The Bureau maintains regional offices in Atlanta, GA; Boston, MA; Charlotte, NC; Chicago, IL; Dallas, TX; Denver, CO; Detroit, MI; Kansas City, KS; Los Angeles, CA; New York, NY; Philadelphia, PA; and Seattle, WA. These offices are an excellent source for answers to questions about Bureau publications and programs.

State Data Centers

The Bureau of the Census, in conjunction with a major State agency in each State, The District of Columbia, Guam, Puerto Rico and the Virgin Islands, has established State Data Centers which will make data for their States and surrounding areas available at cost or below cost. The State Data Center can provide technical services such as downloading tape files onto diskettes, customize extracts from Bureau data files, provide online information, help in developing market research statistics, and provide guides and studies based on local area census data. The State Data Centers, while they are partners of the U.S. Bureau of the Census, are not a part of the Bureau, and therefore they can provide services and data not available from the Bureau itself. The mapping capabilities of the State Data Centers is of particular interest. Contact the U.S. Bureau of the Census, State Data Program for more information.

Business and Industry Data Centers (BIDC)

The BIDC program is a new one designed to aid new or existing businesses in the use of statistical information. Using the State Data Center model these BIDCs can provide answers to specific questions or they can provide guidance to businesses on management or marketing problems. Like the State Data Centers, the BIDCs can provide answers unavailable from the Bureau of the Census itself.

National Clearinghouse for Census Data Services

The Census Bureau has established a National Clearinghouse for Census Data Service which is a roster of organizations, commercial, academic and governmental, which can provide services involving Census Bureau data. These services cover a wide range of demographic, geographic and technical processes.

RESEARCH AIDS

The research aids selected for inclusion throughout this chapter are Census Bureau publications that should help the researcher to locate, define, and interpret the data issued under its statistical programs. Those covering all subject areas are listed here; others, applicable to specific programs or publications, may be found in the subject sections that follow.

Census and You. Washington, DC: Government Printing Office. Monthly. SuDoc: C3.238:

This official newsletter covers the Bureau's activities and services; important features of statistical series, censuses and data files; and plans and developments in census and survey programs. Annual subject index.
Previously: *Data User News.* New title began April/May 1988.

Census Catalog and Guide. Washington, DC: Government Printing Office. Annual. SuDoc: C 3.163/3:
An annotated list arranged by broad subject. Contains Bureau publications, data files, computer programs, and other materials issued during the period covered. Entries include references to microfiche available, order numbers, and price. Includes a subject index. Appendices include information on subscriptions; a listing of Census Bureau contacts including GPO bookstores, Census Bureau regional and main offices, State Data Centers and affiliated organizations, field offices of the Department of Commerce, government depository libraries and private sources of Census Bureau Data.
Previously: *Bureau of the Census Catalog.*

Factfinder for the Nation. (CFF) Washington, DC: U.S. Bureau of the Census. Irregular. SuDoc: C3.252:
This ongoing series of topical leaflets, revised from time to time, describes the coverage, uses, and availability of data from a variety of census materials. Includes the following business-oriented topics: Construction Statistics; Retail Trade Statistics; Wholesale Trade Statistics; Statistics on Service Industries; Transportation Statistics; Foreign Trade Statistics; Enterprise Statistics; Census Bureau Programs and Products. The series is included as appendix D of the Census Catalog Guide.

Hidden Treasures: Census Bureau Data and Where to Find It. Washington, DC: Customer Services. 1990. 20p.
A report which describes how Census Bureau data can be obtained from government agencies and from commercial sources.

Monthly Product Announcement. Washington, DC: U.S. Bureau of the Census. Monthly. SuDoc: C3.163/7:
An annotated checklist, with order forms, of all Bureau products—publications, data files, maps, microfiche—made available during the preceding month.

Statistical Briefs. Washington, DC: Government Printing Office, 1986– . SuDoc: C3.205/8: (Nos.)
   A series of reports taken from statistics previously published in the *Current Population Survey,*, the *Survey of Income and Program Participation* and a variety of other Census Bureau Surveys.

U.S. Census Bureau Data in GPO Depository Libraries: Future Issues and Trends. Washington, DC: Government Printing Office. 1990. 142p. SuDoc: C3.2:D26/9.
   A look at how the GPO program will accommodate Census Bureau program publication in the 21st century.

GEOGRAPHIC SOURCES AND TOOLS

The Census Bureau collects and presents data not only in terms of time and subject but also in terms of geography. To carry out this function it delineates a number of statistical areas for its censuses and surveys and is concerned with the boundaries of the political, administrative, and statistical areas established by other agencies. In the course of its work it produces a variety of graphs and charts, statistical and outline maps, and computerized geographic tools, which are particularly helpful in the use and analysis of its major censuses.
   As an introduction to the compilation and application of the Bureau's geographic concepts and products, these publications may be recommended:

Factfinder for the Nation CFF no. 8. (Rev.)

1990 CPH-R-5. Geographic Identification Code Scheme.

Boundary and Annexation Survey, 1980–1989.
   Lists all changes for incorporated places.

Geographic Areas Reference Manual.
   Describes methodology for presentation in the decennial, economic and agricultural censuses. Copies of individual outline maps released on a flow basis, map sheets, reproductions of unpublished

maps, and cost estimates for reproductions may be obtained from the Customer Services Branch, Data User Services Division, U.S. Bureau of the Census, Washington, DC 20233. Questions regarding map content or boundaries should be addressed to the Chief, Geography Division, U.S. Bureau of the Census, Washington, DC 20233. Current information on Census Bureau geography is listed in *Census and You* and new products and guides are listed in *Monthly Product Announcement.* The Census Bureau's 12 regional offices have geographers and for conceptual and definitional information about geography the Geographic Assistance Staff, Geography Division, U.S. Bureau of the Census, Washington, DC 20233 is helpful.

Statistical Graphics

Graphic and cartographic presentations of data are published for some major censuses as numbered reports entitled *Graphic Summary.* In addition, geographic distribution of selected statistics are issued in separate map series.

United States Maps. (GE-50.) Washington, DC: Government Printing Office. Irregular. SuDoc: C3.62/4:
Presents for the U.S., county social and economic data from the censuses and other sources.

United States Maps. (GE-70.) Washington, DC: Government Printing Office. Irregular. SuDoc: C3.62/8: (Nos.)
A series of maps based on the *1990 Census of Population* which portray various aspects and trends relating to the population.

Outline Maps

To relate census statistics spatially to geographic units and to relate their own data to these census statistics, users must refer to definitions and boundary outlines of the areas used in published reports and summary tapes.
Political boundaries are available from many sources. Congressional districts are depicted, for example, in the following:

Congressional District Outline Maps—103rd Congress.
These maps, one for each state, appear in the 1990 Census reports (CPH-4) and the *Congressional District Atlas.* The relation of congressional districts of the 103rd Congress (1993–1995) to counties is indicated in these maps.

To identify the specifically designed statistical areas for which data are prepared requires the use of Census Bureau outline maps. Economic data, in addition to general geographic units, are shown for areas related to the subject of the statistics. Maps locating major retail centers and delineating central business districts, for example, appear in the relevant reports of the *Census of Retail Trade.* Other economic censuses, too, define their special areas in the publications reporting the statistics.

The greatest variety of geographic detail, especially in small-area data, is generated by the decennial census. Outline maps to use with theses tabulations are particularly important for blocks, census tracts, and other small statistical areas.

The geographic and statistical areas for which various Census Bureau programs tabulate data are indicated in the *Factfinder for the Nation* CFF no. 8 (Rev. March, 1991.)

State Metropolitan Area Outline Maps

Issued for each state. Each map shows boundaries for counties, MSAs, LMSAs and PMSAs and the location of larger places. These maps appear in most 1990 census reports and are available as a page-size national set.

County Subdivision Outline Maps

The series covers counties and their subdivisions, MCDs/CCDs, sub-MCDs places and AI/ANAs for which 1990 census data were tabulated. These maps are single-State maps and appear in several 1990 census report series.

American Indian/Alaska Native Area (AI/ANA) Outline Maps
This self descriptive time series of maps appears in appropriate 1990 census report series.

Census Tract/Block Numbering Area Outline Maps
The maps in this series display census tract or Block Numbering Area (BNA) boundaries and numbers, the features underlying these boundaries and the names and boundaries of counties, county subdivisions, places, and AI/ANAs for each county.

Voting District Outline Map

This series of maps displays voting district codes and boundaries, the underlying features and their names and the boundaries and names of counties, county subdivisions, places, and AI/ANAs for each county where the State participated in phase 2 of the 1990 Census Redistricting Data Program.

Urbanized Area Outline Maps
The series covers geographic units defined as urbanized areas. Each map delineates boundaries for state, county, county subdivision, place and AI/ANAs in addition to the extent of each urbanized area (UA). Boundary features are also identified in the full-size set of maps.

Geographic Reference Files

In the course of its data processing operations the Census Bureau has developed a number of computerized geographic files to define boundaries and assign codes to political and statistical areas. Conversely, users of census data files need the geographic code schemes to identify area names that are geocoded on tape records and to reference the proper maps.

The geographic reference files included here were selected for their broad scope and applications. Code schemes of a narrower scope have been produced in printed form for use with particular censuses.

1990 Census Summary Tape Files (STFs)
The STFs identify the geographic components of each State, District of Columbia, Puerto Rico and the outlying areas by code and name. Records include area measurements and geographic coordinates of internal points.

40 Data Sources

1990 CPH-R-5 Geographic Identification Code Scheme (GICS)

This report, available in a variety of formats, indexes names of geographical units and their related 1990 census and FIPS codes which correspond to the 1990 census summary tape files (STFs).

1990 TIGER/Line Files

The geographic code scheme for the 1990 census is referred to as TIGER/Line Files. In February of 1989, 55 prototype files were created in order to fulfill requests from Federal agencies for geographic information relative to the 1990 census. Eventually, prototype files were planned for all counties in the nation. These prototypes reflect 1990 census geography; they identify the codes and geographic coordinates for census tracts, block numbering areas, and census blocks: however, the political boundaries are those generally used for the 1980 census.

In October of 1989 the pre-census TIGER/Line Files were released and are comparable to the earlier prototype files with political boundaries updated to 1/1/88. Like the earlier prototypes the pre-census files have latitude and longitudinal coordinates for each line segment making up a census block boundary. The files use FIPS (Federal Information Processing Standards) codes and they contain some revisions to the prototype files. Like the prototype files, the pre-census files come on computer tape and optionally on laser disk. When all the files for the counties in a particular State are available, the file for the complete State may be purchased. Until that time only individual county files can be purchased. For information concerning cost and availability of TIGER/Line data, inquiries should be directed to the Customer Services Division of the U.S. Bureau of the Census. The TIGER/Line Files are available in CD-ROM format.

TIGER/Congressional District Equivalency File.

A tape file which correlates the districts of the 103rd Congress and the geographic areas of the 1990 census.

Boundary and Annexation Survey 1980–1989.

A tape file which identifies boundary changes for incorporated places; identifies new entities, consolidations and mergers, etc. for counties, MCDs and incorporated places; and reports both land area and change in land area for municipalities.

SPECIAL STATISTICAL REPORTS

Besides its major censuses and current reports the Bureau of the Census issues a number of general statistical publications that fall outside the scope of its subject-matter programs. Of these, the compendia are listed in an earlier chapter; listed here are those recurrent special reports considered useful in business research.

CIR Staff Papers. Washington, DC: Center for International Research, U.S. Bureau of the Census, 1984– .
An ongoing series of publications for the Center for International Research (CIR). These reports provide statistics for the Soviet Union, and a variety of other countries on demographic characteristics, vital statistics and economic statistics.

Census Bureau Research Conference Proceedings. Washington, DC: Customer Services, U.S. Bureau of the Census, 1985– (Aunual).
A report which presents the proceedings of the annual conference sponsored by the Census Bureau which examines the data collection, analysis and similar issues pertaining to Census Bureau activities.

Characteristics of Business Owners. Washington, DC: Government Printing Office. Irregular. SuDoc: C3.2:C37;
A statistical report which provides information on the characteristics of business owners and their businesses. The report is based on the *Characteristics of Business Owners Survey* and 1982 administrative records.

Consolidated Federal Funds Report. Washington, DC: Government Printing Office. Annual. SuDoc: C3.266/2: (Year/Vol.)
A summary report which details a wide variety of Federal expenditures made to States, counties, and cities. Separate volumes are issued for county areas and sub-county areas.

County Business Patterns. (CBP) Washington, DC: Government Printing Office. Annual. SuDoc: C3.204/3:
A series of 53 to 54 reports: one for each State, District of Columbia, Puerto Rico, and a U.S. summary. Presents inter-censal data on number and employment size of establishments, employment and payroll by two-, three-, and four-digit SIC industry levels for each county and State, and by four-digit SIC for the

U.S. Revised in 1974 to include most divisions of the economy, such as agricultural services, mining, manufacturing, transportation, public utilities, contract, construction, wholesale trade, retail trade, finance, insurance, real estate, and services, this is the only source for annual time-series data on detailed economic activity at the county level.

Retrospective first quarter employment and payroll data for major industry groups at the State level are available in *County Business Patterns, 1968–1977: Ten-Year History.* (CBP-77-55) Washington, DC: Government Printing Office. 1981. 428p.

Federal Expenditures by State. Washington, DC: Government Printing Office. Annual. SuDoc: C3.266: (Year)

A report which provides statistics on the widest variety of Federal expenditures by State and the District of Columbia and outlying areas. Such expenditures as grants, direct payments to individuals, procurement, contracts, and loan and insurance programs are included. A related report is the *Consolidated Federal Funds Report.*

International Research Documents. Washington, DC: U.S. Bureau of the Census. Irregular. SuDoc: C3.205/6: (Nos.)

An ongoing series of studies which provide information on demographic methodology, population studies and related topics from the developing countries of the world in particular, and foreign countries in general.

Marketers Guide to Discretionary Income. Washington, DC: U.S. Bureau of the Census/Consumers Research Center of the Conference Board, 1985. 51p.

A report which is based on information from the *Current Population Survey* and other surveys conducted by the Census Bureau, the Internal Revenue Service, and the Social Security Administration. The data contained in this study reflects information collected in 1983 and covers household discretionary income analyzed by such demographic indicators as age, education, household size, occupation, race, etc.

Quarterly Financial Report for Manufacturing, Mining, and Trade Corporations. Washington, DC: Government Printing Office. Quarterly. SuDoc: C3.267: (Yr./Nos.)

This report, formerly issued by the Federal Trade Commission, provides financial and operating statistics for manufacturing, mining, and trade corporations by industry group.

Special Demographic Analysis. Washington, DC: Government Printing Office. 1985. SuDoc: C3.261: (yr.-Nos.)
A series of reports which provide statistics on social and demographic characteristics and the relevancy of these statistics to policy-making and planning decisions. These reports also include analysis and discussions of the causes of population change.

Survey of Income and Program Participation User's Guide. Washington, DC: Customer Services Division, U.S. Bureau of the Census, 1987. 158, 20p.
A guide designed to assist persons using the Survey of Income and Program Participation (SIPP). This report presents a review of the design and methodology of SIPP.

Survey of Income and Program Participation and Related Longitudinal Surveys. Washington, DC: Customer Services, U.S. Bureau of the Census, 1985– (Annual) SuDoc: C3.2:In 2/8
A collection of reports dealing with methodology and other relevant topics related to the *Survey of Income and Program Participation (SIPP).*

Survey of Income and Program Participation. Working Paper Series. Washington, DC: U.S. Bureau of the Census. Irregular.
This series consists of a group of reports dealing with the Survey of Income and Program Participation (SIPP). The papers included in this series are directed towards the methodology and the concept of the SIPP.

Women of the World. Washington, DC: Government Printing Office, 1984– (Annual) SuDoc: C3.2:W84/ (Nos.)
A series of reports based on the Women in Development Database (WID) which provides statistics on demographic, social, and economic characteristics of women in third world countries. The reports are issued as a series of four, each of which represents a region of the world. In addition to the regional reports, a fifth report presents statistics in chart form for the regions covered.

World Population Profiles. Washington, DC: Government Printing Office. Annual. SuDoc: C3.205/3:WP (Year)

This report contains statistics formerly included in *World Population*. The first report in this new series contains statistics for 205 countries and territories with projections from 1985 through 2025 and also includes trend data from 1950. Statistics on projections of population size are included for the 85 largest world cities.
Previously: *World Population.*

MAJOR CENSUSES AND WORLD REPORTS

Statistics from the major censuses are issued in several formats. Those considered to be of widest public use are compiled in printed reports, the primary form of publication. In addition to these "published" statistics, "unpublished" data appear on microfiche, on CD-ROM, and in greatest detail on computer tape. Special tabulations are provided at user request and may be offered for distribution if the content is judged to be of general interest

The printed reports appear in one or more series designated as preliminary, advance, and final. Preliminary reports, containing statistics subject to change, are issued before final tabulation review. Advance reports containing final data supersede preliminary reports or may constitute the first published source of census results. Detailed final data, which supersede those in the advance reports, first appear in paperbound final reports, or, more recently, in microfiche. For some census series, the former are assembled and reissued in clothbound volumes which may contain additional detail, explanations and graphics. Hardbound or paper-covered, the final reports constitute the permanent edition of a census in "published" (i.e., printed) form.

Since many of the major censuses were in the process of publication at the time of compilation, the citations to the final report series and planned bound volumes may vary in bibliographic detail from the final printed set of published data. In addition to the printed reports, attention is drawn to "unpublished" data unavailable in print: data or reports announced as available only on microfiche, public use computer tapes or other formats which provide greater subject or area detail. For the economic censuses, final data only has been included for the 1987 reports.

Beginning with the 1987 economic census program, the Bureau will issue data in CD-ROM format. In addition to the release of future census data on CD-ROM, the Bureau releases further census statistics through CENDATA.

Agriculture

Census

The Census of Agriculture is taken at five-year intervals, with the censuses of irrigation and drainage added to alternate censuses. Beginning in 1982, the Census of Agriculture was taken to coincide with the economic censuses, thereby providing comparability in these benchmark statistics.

The Census of Agriculture provides detailed data on farming and farm operations, agricultural production, and farm finances. The agriculture census provides statistics for the nation as a whole, for each State and for Puerto Rico, Guam, and the Virgin Islands.

The results of the Census of Agriculture are published first as advance reports issued for each county and State, and these reports are finalized by two report series, a geographic area series and a subject series.

Guide to the 1987 Census of Agriculture and Related Statistics. Washington, DC: U.S. Bureau of the Census, Customer Services Division, 1989. iv, 33p. SuDoc: C3.6/2:Ag 8/2/987

A review of the coverage and products of the *1987 Census of Agriculture.* This guide provides information on statistics contained in the *1987 Census of Agriculture* as well as related statistics located in a variety of other census reports. Additional information is contained in "Agricultural Statistics", *Factfinder for the Nation* no.3, rev. 1989.

1987 Census of Agriculture. Advance Reports. Washington, DC: Government Printing Office, 1988– Quinquennial. SuDoc: C3.31/4:987/ac 87-A-(Nos.)

A series of reports, one for each State, the District of Columbia and a U.S. summary report, which provide advance data statistics from the *1987 Census of Agriculture* on farms, farmland and farm business operations. 1982 statistics are included for comparison. These reports are superseded by three final report series. The advanced data are also available on computer tapes and diskette with limited excerpts available through CENDATA.

1987 Census of Agriculture. Volume I. *Geographic Area Series, State and County Data.* Washington, DC: Government Printing Office, 1988– Quinquennial. SuDoc: C3.31/4:987/V.1/PT. (Nos.)

One of the three final report series from the *1987 Census of Agriculture,* these reports number 54 and cover individual States, the District of Columbia, the outlying areas and the United States (summary). The statistics which are reported by counties and subdivisions cover sales, production and inventory for specific crop or livestock type. 1982 statistics are included for comparison. This series is available as separate tape files, one for states and one for counties.

1987 Final State and County Data on CD-ROM.
This single CD-ROM is equivalent to the *1987 Census of Agriculture.* Volume I. *Geographic Area Series, State and County Data.*

1987 Census of Agriculture. Vol. II. *Subject Series.* Washington, DC: Government Printing Office, 1991– C3.31/12:987/v.2/pt.
The subject series is the second part of the final report program for the *1987 Census of Agriculture.* This series consists of separate parts:

Part 1: *Agricultural Atlas of the United States.* Washington, DC: Government Printing Office, 1991. 220p. 52p.
Part 2: *Coverage Evaluation.* Washington, DC: Government Printing Office, 1991.
Part 3: *Ranking of States and Counties.* Washington, DC: Government Printing Office, 1991. 128p.
Part 4: *History.* Washington, DC: Government Printing Office, 1992.
Part 5: *Government Payments and Market Value of Agricultural Products Sold.* Washington, DC: Government Printing Office. 1991. 500p.
Part 6: *1987 Zip Code Tabulation of Selected Items.* Washington, DC: Government Printing Office. 1991. 656p.

1987 Census of Agriculture. Vol. III. *Related Surveys.* Washington, DC: Government Printing Office. 1991– SuDoc: C3.31/12:987/v.3
A series of reports from surveys related to the Census of Agriculture:

Part 1: *Farm and Ranch Irrigation Survey.* (1988). Washington, DC: Government Printing Office. 1991. 140p.
Part 2: *Agricultural Economics and Land Ownership Survey.* (1988). Washington, DC: Government Printing Office. 1991. 336p.

Current Reports

The Bureau of the Census issues several reports dealing with cotton ginnings in the U.S.:

Cotton Ginnings by States. Washington, DC: Government Printing Office, Semimonthly during season. SuDoc: C3.20:

Cotton Ginnings by Counties. Washington, DC: Government Printing Office, Monthly during season. SuDoc: C3.20/3:

Cotton Ginnings in the U.S., Crop of (Year). Washington, DC: Bureau of the Census. Annual. SuDoc: c3.32:
   In addition, some data on agricultural services appear in its annual *County Business Patterns.*

Economic Censuses

The integrated economic census program begun in 1954 was expanded in 1977 to include the censuses of retail trade, wholesale trade, services, manufactures, construction industries, mineral industries, transportation, and outlying areas; the enterprise statistics program; and the surveys of minority-owned and women-owned businesses. The direction which the Economic Census program is taking is to publish an increasing amount of data in machine-readable format and in particular to produce CD-ROM disks which will incorporate data from all parts of the program.

Research Aids

Besides generally applicable research aids, a number of publications pertain to specific economic statistical programs.

Guide to the 1987 Economic Censuses and Related Statistics. (EC81 R-2). Washington, DC: Government Printing Office. 1990. 136p.
   Provides content and publication information on the 1987 economic censuses. Includes explanatory material and information on related economic statistical publications. A list of MSAs is included along with a list of regional offices and Census Bureau subject specialists.

1987 Industry and Product Classification Manual. (SIC Basis). (EC87-R-3). Springfield, VA. National Technical Information Service. 1989. 410p.

This report, based on the *Standard Industrial Classification Manual,* 1987, issued by the U.S. Office of Management and Budget, is an extension of that guide which provides more detail. The report lists industrial activities by their code numbers as well as alphabetically by industry activity. The report contains the classification system used for the agriculture census, the economic censuses and various related reports such as the *Annual Survey of Manufacturers.*

Additional information on the economic census program is contained in titles in the *Factfinder for the Nation* series and in video format.

1987 Economic Censuses: Geographic Reference Manual. Washington, DC: Customer Services, Data User Services Division, U.S. Bureau of the Census, 1988. ix, 320p. SuDoc: C3.253:EC 87-R-1

A listing of the geographic codes for the 1987 Censuses of Retail and Wholesale Trade, Construction, Manufactures, Transportation and Agriculture. The report is arranged by State and includes the District of Columbia and the outlying areas. The geographic sites coded are States, metropolitan areas, counties, places, and special districts. 1982 codes, State codes used by the U.S. Postal Service, the Federal Information Processing Center and the IRS are included for comparison purposes.

The following titles from the 1982 economic census program may be of help in doing comparative research.

Guide to the 1982 Economic Censuses and Related Statistics. Washington, DC: Government Printing Office, 1984. 78p. SuDoc: C3.6/2:Ec 7/2

Issued to provide users of the 1982 Economic Censuses with an introduction to the coverage and available statistics included within these censuses. Maps and an explanation of the geographic areas covered by the Economic Censuses are provided as are sample tables for each Census. Additional information is provided for the Enterprise Statistics Program, the Minority- and women-owned business surveys and for additional statistical reports.

1982 Economic Censuses: Geographic Reference Manual. Washington, DC: Government Printing Office, 1983. viii, 343p. SuDoc: C3.253:EC 82-R-1

Provides geographic codes of areas covered by the 1982 censuses of retail and wholesale trade; services, construction and mineral industries; manufactures; and transportation. Also includes 1977 codes and codes in use by the U.S. Postal Service, Federal Information Procurement System and the Internal Revenue Service.

History of the 1982 Economic Censuses. Washington, DC: Government Printing Office, 1987. 421p. SuDoc: C3.253/3:982
   A summary history of the planning, data collection, processing, and distribution and publication program for the 1982 Economic Censuses. Includes a historical overview of the Economic Censuses from 1810 to 1977 and of the legislation authorizing the Economic Censuses.

1982 Economic Censuses and Census of Governments: Evaluation Studies. Washington, DC: Government Printing Office, 1987. v, 119p. SuDoc:
   A collection of nine individual reports each examining a different aspect of the *1982 Economic Censuses and Census of Governments.* Such topics as geography, errors, reporting problems and methodology are discussed.

   1. Meaning of Enumeration.
   2. Planning Review.
   3. Stakeholders' Conference on Public Law 94-171 Program.
   4. Automation Planning Conference.
   5. Joint Meeting with Minority Groups.
   6. National Geography Areas Conference.
   7. Planning Review.
   8. Regional Geography Areas Conferences.
   9. Race and Ethnic Items.

1987 Economic Census—CD-ROM

1987 Economic Census (CD-ROM). Vol. 1.
   This CD-ROM product is the Census Bureau's initial offering in this format. The CD-ROM is being offered to depository libraries and is for sale to others.
   The publication program for this CD-ROM is structured so that as additional information becomes available a new edition of the CD-ROM will be issued. The final edition of Vol. 1 includes geographic and subject data identical to that in printed reports in the geographic area series of the *Census of Retail Trade, Census of Wholesale Trade, Census of Service Industries, Census of Transportation,* the final industry series data from the *Census of Mineral Industries* and the *Census of Manufacturers.*

Additional data from the Economic census program will be added over time. Volume 2 of the CD-ROM series is expedited to include zip code data.

Economic Censuses—Construction

Census

The Census of Construction Industries has been taken on a five-year basis since 1967. Prior to 1967, data were collected and published as part of the business censuses in 1929, 1935, and 1939.

1987 Census of Construction Industries. Washington, DC: Government Printing Office. SuDoc: C3.245/7:CC 82.
 The census is an enumeration of construction establishments that operate as general contractors and operative builders, special trade contractors and/or subdividers and developers.

Industry Series. (CC 87-I-.) 28 reports. 1990– .
 One report for each of 27 types of contractors in the industry and a U.S. summary. Individual industry reports present the following data, by State, for establishments with payrolls: number of establishments; receipts; employment; payrolls; payments to subcontractors and for materials, power, rentals, services, etc.; value added; capital expenditures; depreciable assets. The U.S. report summarizes data given in the individual reports; presents more detail at the national level for receipts; and provides limited data on establishments with no payroll.

Geographic Area Series. (CC87-A-) 10 reports. 1991– .
 One report for each census geographic division and a U.S. summary. Division reports present, by States, data similar to that in the industry reports; additional data on receipts; and limited data for establishments with no payroll. The U.S. report summarizes data given in the division reports and presents limited data for selected MSAs.

1987 Census of Construction Industries: Subject Series. (CC87-S). *Legal Form of Organization and Type of Operation.* 1991. 32p.
 This report, which is the only one in the series, presents nation-

al level statistics for each industry covered by legal form of organization and type of operation, such as corporations, individual proprietorships, partnerships and other legal forms. Includes data on employment, payroll, value of construction work done and operating costs.

Current Reports

County Business Patterns.
This series includes construction industry data.

Current Construction Reports. Washington, DC: Government Printing Office.
These reports are joint efforts of the Bureau of the Census and the Department of Housing and Urban Development.

Housing Starts. (C20.) Monthly. SuDoc: C3.215/2:C20
For U.S. and regions, data are given by location on privately owned new units started and on new privately owned units authorized and started in permit-issuing places. Also gives shipments of mobile homes; quarterly statistics on multifamily units built for sale and rent. Occasional supplements have covered historical data, condominium ownership, and townhouse construction.

New Residential Construction in Selected Metropolitan Statistical Areas. (C21.) Quarterly. SuDoc: C3.215/15: C21- .
For 40 selected MSAs, PMSAs, and CMSAs gives estimates on number annually for each of the four regions; measures change over time in the sales price with respect to ten physical characteristics of the houses sold. Limited data from this series is available on CENDATA.

Value of New Construction Put in Place. (C30.) Monthly. SuDoc: C3.215/3: C30- .
Estimates by type of construction (residential, public utility, etc.) and by type of owner (private; State, local, Federal Government). Limited data from this series available on CENDATA.

Housing Units Authorized by Building Permits (C40.) Monthly/Annual. SuDoc: 3.215/3: C40- .

Data for the U.S., regions, divisions, States, selected MSAs, places, and Puerto Rico. Monthlies report number of units awarded contracts, and total number of units and one-family structures authorized in some 5,000 permit-issuing places. Annual data are given for the individual places reported monthly and in detail for some 17,000 permit-issuing places for the U.S.

Expenditures for Residential Upkeep and Improvement. (C50.) Quarterly/Annual Summary. SuDoc: C3.215/3: C50- .
For the U.S. and regions gives estimates of expenditures for upkeep and construction improvements by number of units in a property. The summary reports annual, quarterly, and regional expenditures by type of work; and property, household and geographic characteristics of owner occupants of one-housing unit properties.

Expenditures for Nonresidential Improvements and Upkeep: Year. (Current construction reports. Special studies). Triennial.
Provides statistics on improvements and upkeep by size of building and selected building characteristics.

Economic Censuses—Manufactures

Census

The Census of Manufactures, an enumeration of establishments (i.e., plants, factories, etc.), is the second oldest of the national censuses. Since 1972, it has been taken every five years.

1987 Census of Manufactures. Washington, DC: Government Printing Office.
The 1987 Census of Manufactures is issued in the following series. As indicated earlier, some data are available on CENDATA and a major portion is available in CD-ROM format. (Reference Series. MC81-R). [1 report.]

1987 Census of Manufactures: Numerical List of Manufactured Products. (MC87-R-1.) 1988. 296p. SuDoc: C3.244:MC87

Used for coding data reported in the census. Lists the principal products and services of the manufacturing industries by seven-digit SIC codes based on the 1987 SIC manual.

Industry Series. (MC87-I.) [83 reports.] SuDoc: C3.24/4:MC 87-I- .

83 reports for 459 industries at the four-digit SIC level, this gives U.S. totals on number of establishments and companies; quantity and value of products shipped and materials consumed; assets; capital expenditures; depreciation; inventories; employment and payrolls; hours worked; value added by manufacture; and other data. Capital expenditures, employment and payrolls, value of shipments and value added by manufacture are shown by State, employment size and degree of specialization.

Geographic Area Series. [51 reports.] (MC 87-A.) SuDoc: C3.24/3:MC 87-A- .

Presents for each State and District of Columbia, MSAs, counties and selected cities, data for industries and industry groups on value of shipments, value added by manufacture, employment, payrolls, new capital expenditures, and number of establishments.

Subject Series. (MC87-S). [7 reports planned]. SuDoc: c3.24/12: MC 87-s- .

1.
2. Textile Machinery in Place.
3.
4.
5. Type of Organization.
5.
6.
7.

Analytical Reports Series. [3 reports planned]. SuDoc: C3.24/9–12:

A planned series which will present data on findings concerning individual topics. The first report is scheduled to cover exports by manufacturers.

Location of Manufacturing Plants. [1 report planned on CD-ROM or tape only.]

Current Reports

Annual Survey of Manufacturers. Washington, DC: U.S. Bureau of the Census, Customer Services Division. Annual. SuDoc: C3.24/ (Yr.-Nos.)

Based on a sample of manufacturing establishments, the survey is conducted in years not covered by the five-year Census of Manufactures. It is issued in a series of reports which are later compiled in bound volumes. Includes data of two- to four-digit SIC industry groups and industries for divisions, States, large MSAs, industrial counties and cities for employment, payrolls, value of product shipments, value added by manufacture, inventories, fuel and energy consumption, fixed assets and new capital expenditures, rental payments, origin of exports, and concentration ratios. A series of reports, *Manufacturing: Analytical Report Series,* is based on data from the *Annual Survey* and other sources.

County Business Patterns.

This report, which is described elsewhere, includes data on manufactures.

Current Industrial Reports. Washington, DC: U.S. Bureau of the Census. SuDoc. C3.158: (Series - Year.)

A series of commodity survey reports which present production and/or shipment statistics for approximately 5,000 manufactured products, generally at the seven-digit SIC level, for the U.S. Some provide data for regions, States, and other areas. May show one or more of the following: stocks or inventories, consumption, orders, materials consumed, and foreign trade.

Special Surveys

MA-200	Manufacturers' Pollution Abatement Capital Expenditures and Operating Costs Annual.
MQ-C1	Survey of Plant Capacity. Annual.

All Manufacturing Industries

M-3-1	Manufacturers' Shipments, Inventories, and Orders. Monthly.

Aerospace

MA-37D	Aerospace Orders. Annual.
MA37-G	Aircraft and Aircraft Engines. Monthly/Annual.

Apparel—Footwear

MA-23A	Apparel. Annual.
MA23-D	Gloves and Mittens. Annual.
MA31-A	Footwear. Annual/Monthly (M-31A.)
MQ-23A	Selected Apparel. Quarterly.

Chemicals—Paints

M28A.	Inorganic Chemicals. Monthly/Annual.
M28B.	Inorganic Fertilizer Materials and Related Products. Monthly/Annual.
M28C.	Industrial Gases. Monthly/Annual.
M28F.	Paint Varnish Lacquer. Monthly/Annual.

Food

M-20A	Flour Milling Products. Monthly.
M-20J	Fats and Oils: Oilseed Crushings. Monthly.
M-20K	Fats and Oils: Production, Consumption, and Stocks. Monthly.
MA-20D	Confectionery. Annual.

Glass, Clay, and Related Products

M-32D	Clay Construction Products. Monthly.
MA-32E	Consumer, Scientific, Technical and Industrial Glassware. Annual.
MA-32G	Glass Containers. Monthly.
MA-32J	Glass Fibers. Annual.
MQ-32A	Flat Glass. Quarterly.

Intermediate Metal Products

MQ-34E	Plumbing Fixtures. Quarterly.
MQ-34H	Closures for Containers. Quarterly.
MQ-34K	Steel Shipping Drums and Pails. Quarterly.

Machinery and Equipment

MA-34N	Selected Heating Equipment. Annual.
MA-35A	Farm Machinery and Lawn and Garden Equipment. Annual.
MQ-35C	Flourescent Lamp Ballasts. Quarterly.
MA-35D	Construction Machinery. Annual/Quarterly (MQ-35D.)
MA-35F	Mining Machinery and Metal Processing Equipment. Annual.
MA-35J	Selected Industrial Air Pollution Control Equipment. Annual.
MA-35L	Internal Combustion Engines. Annual.

MA-35M	Air Conditioning and Refrigeration Equipment. Annual.
MA-35N	Fluid Power Products Involving Aerospace. Annual.
MA-35P	Pumps and Compressors. Annual.
MA-35Q	Antifriction Bearings. Annual.
MA-35U	Vending Machines. (Coin-Operated.) Annual.
MA-35X	Robots. Annual.
MA-35W	Metalworking Machinery. Quarterly.
M -36D	Electric Lamps. Monthly/Annual.
MA-36E	Electric Housewares and Fans. Annual.
MA-36F	Major Household Appliances. Annual.
MA-36L	Electric Lighting Fixtures. Annual.
MA-36M	Radio and Television Receivers, Phonographs, and Related Equipment. Annual.
MA-36P	Communication Equipment. Annual.
MA-36Q	Semiconductors, Printed Circuit Boards, and Other Electronic Components. Annual.
MA-36R	Electro-Medical and Irradiation Equipment. Annual.
M-37G	Civil Aircraft and Engines. Monthly.
M-37L	Truck Trailers. Monthly.

Motors, Generators, and Electrical Distribution, Equipment

| MA-36H | Motors and Generators. Annual. |
| MA-36K | Wiring, Devices, and Supplies. Annual. |

Office Furniture and Supplies

| MA-25H | Office Furniture. Annual. |

Primary Metals

M-33A	Iron and Steel Castings. Monthly/Annual.
M-33J	Inventories of Steel Producing Mills. Monthly.
M-33-2	Aluminum Ingot and Mill Products. Monthly.
MA-33B	Steel Mill Products. Annual.
MA-33E	Nonferrous Castings. Annual/Monthly (M-33E.)
MA-33L	Insulated Wire and Cable. Annual.

Rubber and Plastic Products

MA-30A	Rubber: Production, Shipments, and Inventories. Annual.
MA-30B	Rubber and Plastic Hose and Belting. Annual.
MA-30C	Mechanical Rubber Goods. Annual.
MA-30E	Plastic Bottles. Annual.

Switchgear and Industrial Controls

MA-36E   Switchgear, Switchboard Apparatus, Relays, and Industrial Controls. Annual.

MA-36B   Selected Instruments and Related Products. Annual.

Textile Mill Products

M 22P   Consumption on the Cotton System and Stocks. Monthly/Annual.

MA-22F.1   Textured Yarn Production. Annual.

MA-22F.2   Spun Yarn Production. Annual.

MA-22G   Narrow Fabrics. Annual.

MA-22K   Knit Fabric Production. Annual.

MA-22M   Stocks of Wool and Related Products. Annual.

MA-22Q   Carpets and Rugs. Annual

MA-22S   Broadwoven Fabrics. (Finished.) Annual.

MQ-22D   Consumption on the Woolen System and Worsted Combing Quarterly/Annual.

MQ-22T   Broadwoven Fabrics. (Gray.) Quarterly.

MQ-23X   Sheets, Pillowcases and Towels. Quarterly.

Wood and Paper Products

MA-24F   Hardwood Plywood. Annual.

MA-24H   Softwood Plywood. Annual.

MA-24T   Lumber Production and Mill Stock. Annual.

MA-26A   Pulp, Paper, and Board. Annual.

Economic Censuses—Mineral Industries

Census

The Census of Mineral Industries has been taken since 1840 and is now conducted at five-year intervals.

Numerical List of Manufactured and Mineral Products. (MC87-R-1.) Washington, DC: Government Printing Office. 1990 296p.
    Using a census Bureau extension of the SIC system, lists seven-digit codes for the principal products and services for which data were collected in the Manufacturers and Mineral Industries Census. This report is the single part of the *Reference Series* for 1987.

Factfinder for the Nation, no. 16. *Statistics on Mineral Industries.* rev. 1990. Washington, DC: Customer Services Division. 4p.

The *Factfinder* number that covers the mineral industries.

1987 Census of Mineral Industries. Industry Series. Washington, DC: Government Printing Office, 1990. SuDoc: C3.216:MIC87-I-(Nos.)

One of the final report series from the *1987 Census of Mineral Industries.* This series provides statistics for 42 mineral industries classified at the SIC four-digit level. The topics included within this series are number of establishments, employment and payroll, shipments, materials and energy consumed, value added, capital expenditures and mineral rights. The industries are grouped in clusters of related industries or, if applicable, treated as a separate industry with the total number of reports equalling 12. This series is included in the 1987 Economic Censuses CD-ROM product.

1987 Census of Mineral Industries. Geographic Area Series. Washington, DC: Government Printing Office, 1990– . SuDoc: C3.216: M1C87-A-

Another of the final report series for the mineral industries census. Data similar to that in the industry series are grouped by nine Census geographic divisions and within these groupings by State. Information is provided by county and by type of operation.

1987 Census of Mineral Industries. Subject Series. Washington, DC: Government Printing Office, 1990– . SuDoc: C3.216/4:MIC 87-S-(Nos.)

One of the final series based on the *1987 Census of Mineral Industries,* the subject series is made up of two separate reports.

1. General Summary. 1991.
2. Fuels and Electrical Energy Consumed. 1991.

Current Reports

Data related to the mineral industries are included in *County Business Patterns.* On a current basis, the Bureau of Mines and the Energy Information Administration issue reports relative to the mineral industries.

Economic Censuses—Retail Trade

Census

The Census of Retail Trade was first taken in 1929 and is taken every five years.

Factfinder for the Nation, no. 10. *Retail Trade Statistics.* rev. 1989. Washington, DC: Customer Services Division. 4p.

1987 Census of Retail Trade. Geographic Area Studies. Washington, DC: Government Printing Office, 1990– . SuDoc: C3.255/:RC87-A-

One of the final report series from the 1987 retail census. The series is made up of 52 reports, one for each State, District of Columbia and a U.S. summary. The data included covers number of establishments, sales, payroll and employment. Areas covered include States, metropolitan areas (MAs), counties and places. Data from this series are included in the 1987 Economic Censuses CD-ROM product, and substantial excerpts are available on CEN-DATA.

1987 Census of Retail Trade. Nonemployer Statistic Series. Washington, DC: Government Printing Office. 1990– . SuDoc: C3.255/7: RC87-N-

A final report series, new to this census, which in four regional reports presents data for States by kind of business. Data are provided for number of establishments, sales by retail classification for each State and for MSAs, counties and places of 2,500 inhabitants or more. Both establishments with payroll and without payroll are covered.

1987 Census of Retail Trade. Special Report Series. Washington, DC: Government Printing Office. 1991. SuDoc: C3.255/:RC87-SP-1

1. Selected Statistics. 1991.

This report is the only one in this final series. *It is the only report in the 1987 economic census published output where the changes in metropolitan statistical areas between 1982 and 1987 are accounted for* and selected statistics for 1982 MSAs as now defined are presented. In addition to expected data for retail trade at State and MSA level, rankings and ratios not included in other reports are presented.

1987 Census of Retail Trade. Subject Series. Washington, DC: Government Printing Office. 1990– . SuDoc: C3.255/3:RC 87-S-

A final series of four reports.

1. *Establishment and Firm Size* (including Legal Form of Organization.) 1990.

2. *Capital Expenditures, Depreciable Assets, and Operating Expenses.* 1990

3. *Merchandise Line Sales.* 1990.

This is a summary report containing only national data. Data for States, metropolitan areas and for that area within each State outside metropolitan areas is contained on CD-ROM.

4. *Miscellaneous Subjects.* 1991.

This report covers such topics as floor space, class of customer and leased departments in retail stores.

Current Reports

County Business Patterns.

Current Business Reports. Washington, DC: Government Printing Office. SuDoc: C3.138/ :

In this series, the following reports provide data on the retail industry:

Monthly Retail Trade: Sales and Inventories. (BR.) Monthly.

Estimates for all stores by kinds of business and in lesser detail for firms operating 11 or more stores are given for the U.S., regions, divisions, selected MSAs and cities. Advance sales estimates by kind-of-business groups, with comparisons for previous months, for the U.S., selected MSAs and cities are published in:

Current Business Reports: Advance Monthly Retail Sales. (CB) Washington, DC: Government Printing Office. Monthly.

A series of unpublished statistics with more detail is planned for release.

Retail Trade: Annual Sales, Year-End Inventories, Purchases, Gross Margins and Accounts Receivable by Kind of Retail Store. (BR) Annual.

Companion publication to the monthly report listed above. For the U.S., provides estimates of sales, accounts receivable, and inventories by one or more of the following: kind of business, type of sale, legal form of organization, and type of account. Also includes sales-inventory ratios and estimated sales taxes. On an irregular basis, a report presenting revised monthly retail sales is issued.

Economic Censuses—Wholesale Trade

Census

The Census of Wholesale Trade was first conducted in 1929 and is taken every five years.

Factfinder for the Nation, no. 11 *Wholesale Trade Statistics.* rev. 1989. Washington, DC: Customer Services Division. 4p.
   The *Factfinder* number that covers wholesale trade.

1987 Census of Wholesale Trade. Geographic Area Series. Washington, DC: Government Printing Office. 1990– . SuDoc: C3.256/ :WC 87–A
   One of the final series of reports from the wholesale census. The series includes one report for each State, District of Columbia and a U.S. summary. The data are reported for each State, each MA, and for counties and places with 200 or more wholesale establishments. This series is included in the 1987 Economic Census CD-ROM product and a limited amount of information from the series is included on CENDATA.

1987 Census of Wholesale Trade. Subject Series. Washington, DC: Government Printing Office. 1990– . SuDoc: C3.256/3:WC87-S-.
   A series of final reports from the wholesale census.
   1. *Establishment and Firm Size. 1990.*
   2. *Measures of Value Produced Capital Expenditures, Depreciable Assets and Operating Expenses. 1991.*
   3. *Commodity Line Sales. 1990.*
   This is a summary report for wholesale establishments and commodity line sales for the U.S., selected States and MSAs. The CD-ROM product for the 1987 economic census contains more detailed information.
   4. *Miscellaneous Subjects. 1991.*

Contains data on a variety of subjects including business done by agent and brokers and data on petroleum bulk stations and terminals.

Current Reports

County Business Patterns.

Current Business Reports. Monthly Wholesale Trade: Sales and Inventories. (BW.) Washington, DC: Government Printing Office. Monthly. SuDoc: C3.133/.

Sales, inventories, stock-sales ratios of merchant wholesalers, by kind of business, for the U.S. and geographic divisions. Limited excerpts from this series are on CENDATA. A separate series of unpublished data is planned.

Current Business Reports. Wholesale Trade: Annual Sales and Year-End Inventories, Purchases, and Gross Margin Estimates of Merchant Wholesalers. (BW) Annual.

A companion publication to the monthly report. On an irregular basis, a report presenting revised monthly wholesale trade sales and inventories is issued.

Economic Censuses—Service Industries

Census

The Census of Service Industries was first taken in 1933 and is now taken every five years. The 1977 census was the first to be expanded beyond selected industries to services not previously covered, many of them represented by tax-exempt institutions and organizations.

Guide to Service Statistics and Related Data. Washington, DC: U.S. Bureau of the Census, 1984. 58p. SuDoc: C3.6/2:Se 6

A general guide to publications issued by the Census Bureau which deal with the service industries. Includes a description of the reports and the scope of their coverage. Statistics collected and published in reports other than those dealing directly with the service industries but which are related to these industries are also included.

Factfinder for the Nation. no. 12 *Statistics on Service Industries.* rev. 1989. Washington, DC: Customer Services Division. 4p.

The *Factfinder* number that covers the service industries.

1987 Census of Service Industries. Geographic Area Series. Washington, DC: Government Printing Office. 1990– . SuDoc: C3.257/: SC87–A–

One of the final series of the 1987 service industries census. A separate report was issued for each State, District of Columbia and the United States. The service industries are broadly defined and, except for political and religious organizations, elementary and secondary schools, colleges, junior colleges, universities, professional schools and labor unions, data are provided for most business and social service industries. Tables present data by Federal income tax status where applicable, as well as for firms exempt from Federal income tax. This series is included in the 1987 Economic Census CD-ROM product and limited excerpts appear in CENDATA.

1987 Census of Service Industries. Nonemployer Statistics Series. Washington, DC: Government Printing Office. 1990– . SuDoc: C3.257/5: SC87–N–

A final series of four reports from the 1987 service industries census. Each report covers a region of the United States—Northeast, Midwest, South and West—and presents statistics on the number of establishments without payroll and their receipts by kind of business. Data are provided for States, MAs, counties and places.

1987 Census of Service Industries. Subject Series. Washington, DC: Government Printing Office. 1990– .SuDoc: C.3.257/3: SC 87–S–

One of the final series from the 1987 service industries census, the subject series consists of four separate reports:

1. *Establishment and Firm Size* (including Legal Form of Organization.) 1990.
2. *Capital Expenditures, Depreciable Assets and Operating Expenses.* 1991.

3. *Hotels, Motels and Other Lodging Places.* 1991.
4. *Miscellaneous Subjects.* 1991.

Current Reports

County Business Patterns.

Current Business Reports: Service Annual Survey. (BS.) Washington, DC: Bureau of the Census. Annual. SuDoc: C3.
   For the U.S., presents estimated annual receipts of major kind-of-business groups and selected service categories.

Economic Censuses—Transportation

Census

The first Census of Transportation was taken in 1963 and is now taken at five-year intervals.

Factfinder for the Nation. no. 13. *Transportation Statistics.* rev. 1989. Washington, DC: Customer Services Division. 4p.
   The *Factfinder* number that covers transportation.

1987 Census of Transportation. Geographic Area Series: Selected Transportation Industries, Summary. Washington, DC: Government Printing Office. 1990. 254p. SuDoc: C3.233/ 5: TC 87–A–1
   This final report is the single report in this series. Data in the report cover establishments, revenue, employment and payroll for transportation and related industries in SIC 42, 44 and 47 by industry, State and MSA. This report is included in the 1987 Economic Censuses CD-ROM product.

1987 Census of Transportation. Selected Transportation Industries. Truck Inventory and Use Survey. Washington, DC: Government Printing Office. 1990– . SuDoc C3.233/ 5:TC 87–T–
   A final series of reports, one for each State, DC and a U.S. summary. The reports present statistics on trucks and operations and include mileage and cargo information.

1987 Census of Transportation. Subject Series. Selected Transportation Industries. Washington, DC: Government Printing Office. 1991. SuDoc: C3.233/5:TC 87–S–1.
1. *Miscellaneous.*
This is the single report in this series.

Current Reports
County Business Patterns.

Current Business Reports: Motor Freight Transportation and Warehousing Survey. (BT.) Washington, DC: Government Printing Office. SuDoc: C3.
An annual estimate of revenues and expenses for commercial motor freight transportation and warehousing services.

On a current basis statistics on transportation are issued by the Interstate Commerce Commission and by the Department of Transportation.

Economic Census Programs—Miscellaneous

Outlying Areas

1987 Economic Census of Outlying Areas. Washington, DC: Government Printing Office. 1990– . SuDoc: C3.253/: OA 87–E.
Counterpart censuses have been taken for Puerto Rico, the Virgin Islands, Guam and, starting in 1982, the Northern Mariana Islands. For each of these areas, data are collected on retail trade, wholesale trade, service industries, manufacturers and construction industries but not mineral industries or transportation. In the case of Puerto Rico, separate reports are issued for different sectors; for the other geographic areas summary reports are issued.

1. *Puerto Rico—Wholesale Trade, Retail Trade, and Service Industries.* 1991.
2. *Puerto Rico—Wholesale Trade, Retail Trade, and Service Industries. Subject Series.* 1991.
   This number includes two reports, one for establishment size

and form of organization and the other covering miscellaneous subjects.

3. *Puerto Rico—Construction Industries.* 1990.
4. *Puerto Rico—Manufacturers.* 1990.
5. *Virgin Islands of the United States—Construction Industries, Manufacturers, Wholesale Trade, Retail Trade, Service Industries.* 1989.
6. *Guam—Construction Industries, Manufacturers, Wholesale Trade, Retail Trade, Service Industries.* 1989.
7. *Northern Mariana Islands—Construction Industries, Manufacturers, Wholesale Trade, Retail Trade, Service Industries.* 1989.

Current Reports

No specific current reports are issued for these areas; however, they are included in various export and import report series from the Bureau of the Census.

Minority-Owned Business Enterprises

The survey of minority-owned business enterprises was begun in 1969 and became part of the economic census program in 1972. The program presents the extent of business ownership by specific minority groups, Blacks, persons of Spanish origin, Asian Americans, American Indians and other minorities. These data are included in the 1987 Economic Census CD-ROM product.

Factfinder for the Nation. no. 5. *We, the Asian and Pacific Islander Americans.* Washington, DC: Customer Services Division. 1990. 18p.

A statistical report which provides demographic and economic data on Asian Indian, Chinese, Filipino, Guamanian, Hawaiian, Japanese, Korean, Samoan and Vietnamese populations.

A similar report, *We, the First Americans,* no. 6, provides similar data for the American Indian population.

1987 Survey of Minority-Owned Business Enterprises. Washington, DC: Government Printing Office. 1991– . SuDoc: C3. :MB87–

1. *Survey of Minority-Owned Business Enterprises—Black.* 1990.
2. *Survey of Minority-Owned Business Enterprises—Hispanic.* 1991.

3.
4. *Survey of Minority-Owned Business Enterprises—Summary.* 1991.

Women-Owned Businesses

The economic census program also reports on the number of firms, gross receipts, number of paid and non-salaried employees and payroll for businesses owned by women. These data are included in the 1987 Economic Census CD-ROM product.

1987 Survey of Women-Owned Businesses. Washington, DC: Government Printing Office. 1991. 170p. SuDoc: C3. :WB877–1
This is the report on women-owned businesses for the 1987 economic census program. Data are shown for the U.S., States, District of Columbia and MSAs, counties and places with 100 or more women-owned businesses.

Current Reports

There are no specific reports relating to minorities and women issued on a current basis; however, special reports based on the *Current Population Survey* data are regularly issued.

Enterprise Statistics

The enterprise statistics program, a by-product of the economic censuses since 1954, retabulates the census data on establishments according to the enterprise or company that owns the establishment. The program uses an industrial classification system, which is an adaptation of the four-digit SIC, to produce consolidated company aggregates that show the various economic characteristics of the owning or controlling firm. Since they depend on the compilation of all the censuses, the enterprise statistics are, of necessity, the last to be published in the economic censuses program.

Factfinder for the Nation. no. 19. *Enterprise Statistics.* rev. 1991. Washington, DC: Government Printing Office. 4p.
This is the *Factfinder* which reports on enterprise statistics.

1987 Enterprise Statistics. Washington, DC: Government Printing Office. 1990– .SuDoc: C3. :ES87 –

A series of reports which provides combined data for establishments under common ownership or control. The data in these reports are presented in an "enterprise industry" category, which is a grouping of four-digit SIC industries adapted to combining data for separate establishments into totals for firms. These data are extensively used in Federal government planning.

1. *Large Companies.* 1990.
   Reports on companies with 500 or more employees.
2. *Auxiliary Establishments.* 1991.
3. *Company Summary.* 1991.

Current Reports

There are no specific current reports on an enterprise basis; however, enterprise data are analyzed by agencies such as the Bureau of Economic Analysis in its compilation of GDP data.

GOVERNMENTS CENSUS

The Census of Governments was first taken in 1850 and is conducted every five years for years ending in "2" and "7". It is a complete enumeration of governmental units, including school and special districts, and provides data on their functions and characteristics.

Factfinder for the Nation. no. 17. *Statistics on Governments.* rev. 1990. Washington, DC: Customer Services Division. 4p.

The Factfinder for government statistics.

1987 Census of Governments. Guide to the 1987 Census of Governments. Washington, DC: Government Printing Office, 19– . [Forthcoming]. SuDoc: C3.145/ :987/v.6.

This report is intended to be a review volume with details of tables, charts and methodology. It is issued as volume 6.

1987 Census of Governments. Washington, DC: Government Printing Office. 1988. 6 vols. SuDoc: C3.145/ :v.

Vol. I. *Government Organization.* 2 reports. (GC87–1–1).

1. *Governmental Organizations.* 344p.

National data, by States and MSAs, on number of county, municipal, and township governments by population size; on school districts and other public school systems by size of enrollment, type of area served, and other characteristics; and on special districts by function.

2. *Popularly Elected Officials.* Governments. 241p. (GC87–1–2).

Provides data nationally by State and for MSAs on the number of elected officials by type of office and type of government. Also includes the number of elected officials for each county.

Vol. II. *Taxable Property Values.* 204p. (GC87–2–1).

Data on the assessed value (gross and net), officially determined in 1986–87 for local general property taxation, are provided for countries and for each city having a 1984 population of 50,000 or more, with totals for States.

Vol. III. *Public Employment.* 3 reports.

Shows public employment, payroll, selected benefit coverage for full-time employees, and labor-management relations for the following areas (in the reports specified): States (nos. 1–3), counties (nos. 1–2), cities (no. 1), and the U.S. (nos. 2–3).

1. *Employment of Major Local Governments.* 196p.
2. *Compendium of Public Employment.* 376p.
3. *Labor-Management Relations. Governments.* 56p.

Vol IV. *Governmental Finances.* 6 reports.

Revenues, expenditures, debt, and financial assets in the governmental unit reports are shown for the U.S., States, counties (nos. 1–3, 5), and cities of varying size (nos. 1, 3–4). The census findings are summarized (no. 5) by type of government, for local governments within MSAs, and for county areas by size.

1. *Finances of Public School Systems.* 233p.
2. *Finances of Special Districts.* 136p.
3. *Finances of County Governments.* 220p.
4. *Finances of Municipalities and Township Governments.* 252p.
5. *Compendium of Government Finances.* 695p.
6. *Employee Retirement Systems of State and Local Governments.* 57p.

Vol. V. *Topical Studies.* 6 reports. [Forthcoming].
1. Employee-Retirement Systems of State and Local Governments.

Vol. VI. *Guide to 1987 Census of Governments.*

1987 Census of Governments. Directory of Governments File. Washington,
DC: Bureau of the Census. 1987. Machine-readable file.
   Provides name, address and government identification code for all
State and local governmental units in the U.S. identified in the 1987
census. A later file of the same name continues the directory.

Current Reports

   In the years between censuses, the Bureau of the Census conducts
surveys to provide statistics on government finances and employment
at the Federal, State and local level. The results of these surveys
appear in the following series of published reports. Limited excerpts
from these reports appear in CENDATA. A complete tape file is
available.

Government Employment. (GE) SuDoc: C3.140/2– : yr.
   A series of annual reports which provide statistics on public
employment, city employment, county employment and State employment. A tape file of the employment statistics is available.

Government Finances. (GF) SuDoc: C3.191/2– : yr.
   A series of annual reports which provide statistics on the finances
of States, counties, cities, employee retirement systems, public school
systems in separate annual reports. A separate summary report and
tax report are also issued. A tape file of the financial statistics is
available.

Government Retirement Systems. (GR) SuDoc: C3.242:
   A quarterly report is issued on the finances of selected public
employee retirement systems.

Government Taxation. (GT) SuDoc: C3.145/6:
   A quarterly report is issued on Federal, State and local tax revenue.
Limited excerpts from these reports are on CENDATA.

Federal Expenditures. SuDoc: C3.266: yr.

The Consolidated Federal Funds Report (CFFR) database is the source of a series of reports which provide statistics on Federal expenditures or obligations for States and local areas. These annual reports provide data on grants, salaries, wages, procurement contracts, direct payments, loans and insurance. Limited State-level data from these reports is available on CENDATA and a complete tape file for the program is available.

POPULATION AND HOUSING

Decennial Census

The Census of Population and Housing is taken every ten years in the years ending with "0." It is commonly referred to simply as the decennial census or by its censal year. Both terms, however, imply coverage of population and housing.

A complete count of population was first taken in 1790 and has been repeated every decade since. The housing census has been taken as part of the decennial census beginning with 1940.

The 1990 decennial census is the latest for which the publication of final data has been scheduled. Listed here are the final publications, including the open series, which constitute its permanent printed edition. This census includes products in CD-ROM format.

The subjects listed below were covered in the 1990 census:

100–Percent Component

Population
Household relationship
Sex
Race
Age
Marital status
Hispanic origin
Housing
Number of units in structure

Number of rooms in unit
Tenure—owned or rented
Value of home or monthly rent
Congregate housing (meals included in rent)
Vacancy characteristics

Sample Component

Population
Social characteristics:
Education—enrollment and attainment
Place of birth, citizenship, and year of entry to U.S.
Ancestry
Language spoken at home
Migration (residence in 1985)
Disability
Fertility
Veteran status
Housing
Year moved into residence
Number of bedrooms
Plumbing and kitchen facilities
Telephone in unit
Vehicles available
Heating fuel
Source of water and method of sewage disposal
Year structure built
Condominium status
Farm residence
Shelter costs, including utilities
Economic characteristics:
Labor force
Occupation, industry, and class of worker
Place of work and journey to work
Work experience in 1989
Income in 1989
Year last worked
    Note: Questions dealing with the subjects covered in the 100—
percent component were asked of all persons and housing units.

Those covered by the sample component were asked of a portion or sample of the population and housing units.

Guides

Census ABCs: Applications in Business and Community. Washington, DC: Customer Services Division. 1990. 16p.
A useful business-oriented pamphlet which includes a list of census aids and a directory of contacts.

Census '90 Basics. Washington, DC: Customer Services Division. 1990. 19p.
A review of how the census was collected and processed with a full history of data products.

1990 Census of Population and Housing Tabulation and Publication Program. Washington, DC: Customer Services Division, Government Printing Office. 1989. 51p.
A detailed review of census 1990 publications with estimated release dates and a comparison with 1980 products.

1990 Census of Population and Housing Guide. Washington, DC: Government Printing Office. [Forthcoming].
The primary guide to the 1990 census. This publication is intended to provide maximum information and direction for use of the reports in the 1990 census.

U.D.A.P.—User-Defined Areas Program. Washington, DC: Customer Services Division. 1990. 13p.
A pamphlet describing the program of customized data summaries for geographic areas not available from standard products in the 1990 tabulation and publication program.

1990 Census of Population. Strength in Numbers: Your Guide to 1990 Census Redistricting Data from the U.S. Bureau of the Census. Washington, DC: Government Printing Office. 1990. (rev. 1991). 11p. SuDoc: C3.6/2:St8.
A preliminary guide to population statistics from the 1990 census as they are used by States for redistricting.

Pre-Census 1990—Guides

Content Development Process for the 1990 Census of Population and Housing. Washington, DC: Government Printing Office. 1987. 44p.

This publication is a survey report covering meetings held with the Federal Government, private census data users, State and local government users, and concerned parties to formulate questions regarding the 1990 Census of Population and Housing. A separate series of reports, *Content Determination Reports* (CDR) explains the development of a specific topic covered in the 1990 Census. These reports are available from the Census Bureau, Customer Service Division.

1986 Test Census. General Population and Housing Statistics. Washington, DC: Government Printing Office, 1987– . SuDoc: C3.2:

These reports constitute the results of a series of tests for block numbering areas (tracts) and individual blocks in selected cities. The tests were conducted as advance trials for the *1990 Census of Population and Housing.*

The publications program for the 1990 census was in progress at the time this book was being written; as a result there may be changes and additions or deletions to the scheduled data releases. A significant amount of 1990 census data is available on CENDATA and as data are released the Census Bureau issues press releases to announce new data products.

1990 Census of Population and Housing. Official 1990 U.S. Census Form (Information Copy). Washington, DC: Customer Services Division. 1989. 8p.

This booklet reproduces the 1990 census forms.

The 1990 census data products fall into seven categories: data products for apportionment and redistricting (PL 94–171 program), general purpose data products, subject reports and summary tape files, special computer tape files, summary of differences between 1980 and 1990 census data products, map products and custom data products.

Computer tapes and printed reports will continue to be the major dissemination media for the 1990 census; however, microfiche will be used as it was in the 1980 census, CD-ROM discs will be introduced for the first time in a decennial census, and online (CENDATA) and diskette availability will also be introduced. CENDATA will be particularly important for its ability to provide up-to-date information about data products and to carry limited 1990 data.

P.L. 94–171 Program

CD-ROM Products—Guide.

1990 Census of Population and Housing;. P.L. 94–171 Data on CD-ROM Technical Documentation. Washington, DC: Government Printing Office. 1991. III, 33, 105p. SuDoc: C3.281:P81/ doc/
This publication is a guide to the use and content of the CD- ROM (PL 94–171) data files for the 1990 Census. The tape files for this information are available on a per megabyte basis and printouts from these tape files are available for detailed-level geographic area summaries (block level) sold by State or county or high-level geographic area summaries (States, counties, minor civil divisions and places) by State.

1990 Census of Population and Housing. PL 94–171 Data on CD-ROM. Washington, DC: Customer Services Division. 1990– . SuDoc: C3.281: (CT)/990/ CD
Ten CD-ROM products which include population and housing statistics by State and by State subdivisions from the 1990 census. The data are available down to the level of voting districts, blocks and block groups, and are required for redistricting purposes. The data reflect total and adult population (18+) by race and Hispanic origin, and include housing unit counts. The data are in d BASE III+ format and an IBM-compatible PC with at least 640 K random access memories is required with Microsoft CD-ROM Extension.

Summary Reports

Two reports series containing summary/preliminary data from the 1990 census have been issued:

Housing

1990 Census of Housing. Housing Highlights. (CH–5–) Washington, DC: Government Printing Office. 1991– . SuDoc: C3.224/3–8: CH–S–1–

A series of summary reports, one for each State, District of Columbia, Puerto Rico and the other outlying areas. Includes comparative data for 1980.

Population and Housing.

1990 Census of Population and Housing. 1990 Census Profile. Washington, DC: Government Printing Office. 1991– . SuDoc: C3.223/7–5:

A series of preliminary reports which profile the results of the 1990 census. Each report will cover a different topic.

Final Reports

1990 Census of Population and Housing. Summary Population Housing Characteristics. (CPH–1). Washington, DC: Government Printing Office. 1991– . SuDoc: C3.223/18: 990 CPH–1–

A series of reports, one for each State, District of Columbia, Puerto Rico, the Virgin Islands and a U.S. summary. Each report includes statistics on number of inhabitants and characteristics of housing for counties, subdivisions of counties and some unincorporated places.

1990 Census of Population and Housing. Population and Housing Unit Counts. (CPH–2). Washington, DC: Government Printing Office. [Forthcoming]. SuDoc: C3.

A series of reports, one for each State, District of Columbia, Puerto Rico and the Virgin Islands and a U.S. summary. Includes total population and housing counts for 1990 and previous censuses, geographic areas covered include States, counties, county subdivisions, places and summary geographic areas (urban and rural).

1990 Census of Population and Housing. Population and Housing Characteristics for Census Tracts and Block Numbering Areas. (CPH–3). Washington, DC: Government Printing Office. [Forthcoming]. SuDoc: C3.

These reports, one for each State, Puerto Rico, the Virgin Islands

and for each Metropolitan Area, provide 100% and sample population and housing count statistics. Provides statistics for block
numbering areas and census tracts.

*1990 Census of Population and Housing. Population and Housing Charac-
teristics for Congressional Districts of the 103rd Congress.* (CPH–4).
Washington, DC: Government Printing Office. [Forthcoming].
SuDoc: C3.

Provides population and housing statistics for congressional districts and for counties, places of 10,000+, county subdivisions of
10,000+ in selected States, and American Indian and Alaskan Native
areas.

*1990 Census of Population and Housing. Summary Social, Economic and
Housing Characteristics.* (CPH–5). Washington, DC: Government
Printing Office. [Forthcoming]. SuDoc: C3.

A series of reports, one for each State, District of Columbia, Puerto
Rico and the Virgin Islands and a U.S. summary. Includes statistics
on sample population and housing subjects.

Population (CP)

1990 Census of Population. General Population Characteristics. (CP–1).
Washington, DC: Government Printing Office. [Forthcoming].
SuDoc. C3.

Detailed statistics on age, race, sex, Hispanic origin, marital status
and household relationship characteristics. Data are presented for
States, counties, places of 1,000 or more inhabitants, MCDs of 1,000
or more inhabitants in selected States and summary geographic areas.
One report for each State and a U.S. summary, District of Columbia,
Puerto Rico and Virgin Islands.

*1990 Census of Population. General Population Characteristics for Ameri-
can Indian and Alaskan Native Areas.* (CP–1–1A). Washington, DC:
Government Printing Office. [Forthcoming]. SuDoc: C3.

Data are comparable to CP1 series for areas specified.

*1990 Census of Population. General Population Characteristics for Metro-
politan Statistical Areas.* (CP–1–1B). Washington, DC: Government
Printing Office. [Forthcoming]. SuDoc: C3.

Data are comparable to CP1 series for Metropolitan Statistical Areas and their components.

1990 Census of Population. General Population Characteristics for Urbanized Areas. (CP–1–1C). Washington, DC: Government Printing Office. [Forthcoming]. SuDoc: C3.
Data are comparable to CP1 series for Urbanized Areas and their components.

1990 Census of Population. Social and Economic Characteristics. (CP–2–). Washington, DC: Government Printing Office. [Forthcoming]. SuDoc: C3.
This series of reports provides education, ancestry, place of birth, language, migration, disability, fertility, veteran status, labor force, occupation, work-related travel and experience and income statistics. Data are provided for State, counties, places of 2,500 or more, MCDs of 2,500 or more in selected States. A separate report for each State, a U.S. summary, District of Columbia, Puerto Rico and the Virgin Islands.

1990 Census of Population. Social and Economic Characteristics for American Indian and Alaska Native Areas. (CP–2–1A). Washington, DC: Government Printing Office. [Forthcoming]. SuDoc: C3
Data are comparable to C–2– for areas specified.

1990 Census of Population. Social and Economic Characteristics for Metropolitan Statistical Areas. (CP–2–1B). Washington, DC: Government Printing Office. [Forthcoming]. SuDoc: C3.
Data are comparable to CP–2– for Metropolitan Statistical Areas.

1990 Census of Population. Social and Economic Characteristics for Urbanized Areas. (CP–2–1C). Washington, DC: Government Printing Office. [Forthcoming]. SuDoc: C3.
Data are comparable to CP–2– for Urbanized Areas.

1990 Census of Population. Population Subject Reports. (CP–3–). Washington, DC: Government Printing Office. [Forthcoming]. SuDoc: C3.
A projected series of approximately 30 reports on population census subjects such as migration, education, income, the older population and racial and ethnic groups. Geographic coverage will

generally be limited to U.S., regions and divisions. In some cases States, MAs, counties and large places.

Following is a list of population subject reports proposed for the 1990 census.

- Characteristics of the Rural and Farm Population.
- Geographical Mobility for States and the Nation.
- Recent and Lifetime Migration.
- Journey to Work: Metropolitan Commuting Flows.
- Journey to Work: Characteristics of the Workers in Metropolitan Areas.
- Place of Work.
- Detailed Social and Economic Characteristics of the Population.
- Current Language of the American People.
- Education.
- The Older Population of the United States.
- Persons in Institutions and Other Group Quarters.
- Households, Families, Marital Status, and Living Arrangements.
- Fertility.
- American Indians, Eskimos, and Aleuts in the United States.
- Characteristics of American Indians by Tribe and Language for Selected Areas.
- Characteristics of the Asian and Pacific Islander Population in the United States.
- Characteristics of the Black Population in the United States.
- Persons of Hispanic Origin in the United States.
- Ancestry of the Population in the United States.
- The Foreign-Born Population in the United States.
- Employment Status, Work Experience, and Veteran Status.
- Occupational Characteristics.
- Industrial Characteristics.
- Occupation by Industry.
- Earnings by Occupation and Education.
- Sources and Structure of Household and Family Income.
- Characteristics of Persons in Poverty.
- Poverty Areas in the United States.
- Characteristics of Adults with Work Disabilities, Mobility Limitations, or Self-Care Limitations.

Housing

1990 Census of Housing. General Housing Characteristics. (CH–1–). Washington, DC: Government Printing Office. [Forthcoming]. SuDoc: C3.

These reports, one for each State, U.S. summary, District of Columbia, Puerto Rico and the Virgin Islands provide detailed statistics on units, value, rent, size, tenure and vacancy for States, counties, places of 1,000 or more, MCDs of 1,000 or more in selected States.

1990 Census of Housing. General Housing Characteristics for American Indian and Alaska Native Areas. (CH–1–1A). Washington, DC: Government Printing Office. [Forthcoming]. SuDoc: C3.

Data comparable to CH–1 for designated areas.

1990 Census of Housing. General Housing Characteristics for Metropolitan Statistical Areas. (CH–1–1B). Washington, DC: Government Printing Office. [Forthcoming]. SuDoc: C3.

Data comparable to CH–1 for MSAs and component areas.

1990 Census of Housing. General Housing Characteristics for Urbanized Areas. (CH–1–1C). Washington, DC: Government Printing Office. [Forthcoming].

Data comparable to CH–1 for Urbanized Areas and their component parts.

1990 Census of Housing, Detailed Housing Characteristics. (CH–2–). Washington, DC: Government Printing Office. [Forthcoming]. SuDoc: C3.

This series presents data on condominium sales, plumbing and kitchen facilities, telephones, heating fuel, water, vehicles available, year of construction, year of residences, number of bedrooms, farm residence, shelter costs including utilities. A separate report is issued for each State, U.S. summary, District of Columbia, Puerto Rico, and the Virgin Islands.

1990 Census of Housing. Detailed Housing Characteristics for American Indian and Alaska Native Areas. (CH–2–1A). Washington, DC: Government Printing Office. [Forthcoming]. SuDoc: C3.

Data comparable to CH–2– for designated areas.

1990 Census of Housing. Detailed Housing Characteristics for Metropolitan Statistical Areas. (CH–2–1B). Washington, DC: Government Printing Office. [Forthcoming]. SuDoc: C3.
  Data same as CH–2– for MSAs and their component.

1990 Census of Housing. Detailed Housing Statistics for Urbanized Areas. (CH–2–1C).Washington, DC: Government Printing Office.
  Data same as CH–2– for urbanized areas.

1990 Census of Housing. Housing Subject Reports. Washington, DC: Government Printing Office. [Forthcoming].

- Metropolitan Housing Characteristics.
- Mobile Homes.
- Recent Mover Households.
- Housing of the Elderly.
- Condominium Housing.
- Structural Characteristics.
- Utilization of the Housing Stock.
- Housing Quality Indicators.
- Second Mortgage Households.
- Characteristics of New Housing Units.

In addition, the Bureau will release about 20 subject summary tape files that will be used to produce the subject reports. On the average, two reports (containing similar subject matter) will be derived from one subject summary tape file. The tapes will include the same types of data shown in the subject reports, but will include additional geographic detail. These files will be designed to meet the data needs expressed by users who have a special interest in selected subjects or subgroups of the population. They also are intended to meet the data needs previously fulfilled by the 1980 *Detailed Population Characteristics* (series PC80–1–D), *Metropolitan Housing Characteristics* (series HC80–2), and STF 5. The above listing completes the projected printed report publication from the 1990 census. Those series which are issued by State or defined area will be assigned a suffix number which will identify that unit. A listing of these suffix numbers follows.

Area Numbers for Reports

There is a numbered part for the United States, American Indian and Alaska Native areas, MSAs, UAs, States, and the District of Columbia. Listed below are the area numbers that will be used for the 1990 printed reports. (The complete list of MSA/PMSA numbers for the *Population and Housing Characteristics for Census Tracts and Block Numbering Areas* reports are not available since the list of areas is based on results from the 1990 census.)

Report number	Area	Report Number	Area
1	United States	25	Minnesota
1A	American Indian and Alaska Native Areas	26	Mississippi
		27	Missouri
1B	Metropolitan Statistical Areas	28	Montana
		29	Nebraska
1C	Urbanized Areas	30	Nevada
2	Alabama	31	New Hampshire
3	Alaska	32	New Jersey
4	Arizona	33	New Mexico
5	Arkansas	34	New York
6	California	35	North Carolina
7	Colorado	36	North Dakota
8	Connecticut	37	Ohio
9	Delaware	38	Oklahoma
10	District of Columbia	39	Oregon
11	Florida	40	Pennsylvania
12	Georgia	41	Rhode Island
13	Hawaii	42	South Carolina
14	Idaho	43	South Dakota
15	Illinois	44	Tennessee
16	Indiana	45	Texas
17	Iowa	46	Utah
18	Kansas	47	Vermont
19	Kentucky	48	Virginia
20	Louisiana	49	Washington
21	Maine	50	West Virginia
22	Maryland	51	Wisconsin
23	Massachusetts	52	Wyoming
24	Michigan		

Data Files

The principal computerized files relating to the decennial census are tapes of summary data, public-use tapes of microdata for statistical analysis, and geographic reference files.

Maps necessary to the use of tape data for enumeration districts, block groups, tracts and blocks, and other geographic reference tools issued in conjunction with the 1990 census are discussed earlier in this chapter.

The TIGER System previously described is the basis for the 1990 map products. Pre-census and post-census geographic computer tape file extracts from the TIGER database will be available, as will CD-ROM products.

1990 Census of Population and Housing: Summary Tape Files. Washington, DC: Bureau of the Census. 1990– . STF 1–4. Machine-readable files. (In process.)

The summary data presented in the Summary Tape Files (STFs) provide the major portion of the 1990 census results. Their content and that of their microfiche/CD-ROM version, where available, is comparable to the content of the printed reports but includes much greater subject and geographic detail. For example, they present statistics down to the smallest area for which census data were aggregated. Also, whereas reports show more county subdivision data in some States than in others, the STFs present not only the greatest detail for these areas but also in the same amount in each State.

The four numbered STF sets consist of lettered Files (e.g., STF 1A, STF 1B, STF 1C), each covering different geographic areas and available individually for each State, District of Columbia and Puerto Rico.

STF 1

Contains more area detail but less subject detail than STF 2. Population and housing data cells drawn from the complete count part of the census (see 100 percent items in Figure 3) for each of the following: the U.S., regions, divisions, States, standard consolidated statistical areas (SCSAs), MSAs, urbanized areas, counties, places, county subdivisions, census tracts, block numbering areas, MCDs, blocks numbering areas, and blocks in blocked areas. Also includes Congressional Districts for the 103rd Congress.

STF 2

Contains more subject detail but less area detail (down to census tract level) than STF 1. Population and Housing items drawn from the 100 percent items (Figure 3) include detailed summaries by race and Spanish origin not available in STF 1. Areas covered are the U.S., regions, divisions, States, BNAs, MSAs, urbanized areas, counties, places of 1,000 or more inhabitants, MCDs and Alaskan native areas.

STF 3

Contains more geographic detail (down to BG level) but less subject detail than STF 4. Population and Housing data from census sample items (see Figure 3) are shown for each of the following: the U.S., regions, divisions, States, MSAs, urbanized areas, counties, places, MCDs, county subdivisions, census tracts, block numbering areas, BGs. Also includes congressional districts. File STF 3B is devoted exclusively to data for 5-digit ZIP code areas for the entire U.S.

STF 4

Contains more subject detail but less area detail (down to census tract level) than STF 3. Includes detailed summaries by race, Spanish origin, and ancestry, which do not appear in STF 3. Areas covered are the U.S., regions, divisions, States, MSAs, MCDs, urbanized areas, counties, places of 2,500 or more, county subdivisions, census tracts, Indian and Alaskan native areas.

Public Use Microdata Samples (PUMS)

PUMS are computerized files containing a sample of individual long-form census records showing most population and housing characteristics. These records contain no names or addresses, and geographic identification is sufficiently broad to protect confidentiality.

Two PUMS files are planned for 1990. The first is a five-per cent sample identifying "county groups" or smaller areas that meet the minimum population-size criterion. The second is a one-per cent sample identifying MSAs used in the 1990 census.

Five Per cent (tentative size)—County Groups. Preliminary release date: 1993.

This file presents most population and housing characteristics on the sample questionnaire for a five-per cent sample of housing units. It shows data for county groups or smaller areas with 100,000 or more inhabitants. This file is similar to the 1980 PUMS-A Sample.

One Per cent (tentative size)—Metropolitan Statistical Areas Identified in 1990. Preliminary release date: 1993.

This file presents most population and housing characteristics on the sample questionnaire for a one-per cent sample of housing units. It shows data for MSAs that will be used in the 1990 census. This file is similar to the 1980 PUMS-B Sample.

Microfiche and CD-ROM

As part of the planning process for determining the dissemination media for the tabulation and publication program, the Census Bureau evaluated the feasibility of using new dissemination media representing the technological advances of the last decade. Preferences for these media as well as microfiche were discussed with data users. Based on data-user preferences and results of the research conducted by the Census Bureau, it was determined that there is a user demand for microfiche, but its use is decreasing because of the increased use of other media like CD-ROM. As a result, the number of products issued on microfiche will be limited. Products issued on CD-ROM and microfiche will be released after printed reports and computer tape files. The Bureau will reevaluate the need for microfiche later in the decade to determine if there is still a user demand for this dissemination media.

Microfiche. Microfiche will be used to disseminate data for blocks that are not available in printed form. It also provides the detailed area data from selected summary tape files for those users who do not have the computer resources to access those data. The areas for which data will be provided on microfiche in 1990 will increase substantially from previous censuses. In 1980, the smallest geographic units for which the Bureau tabulated data were blocks in the more densely populated areas and enumeration districts in the less densely populated areas. An enumeration district encompassed a much larger area than a block. In 1990, for the first time, the entire United States is block numbered. This will increase the number of blocks for which data are provided from 2.5 million in 1980 to about eight million in 1990.

The following listing describes the data and geographic content of the microfiche products:

Population and Housing Characteristics (from STF 1A). Preliminary release date: 1991–1992.

100-percent population and housing characteristics will be provided for States and their sub-areas in hierarchical sequence down to the block group level, as well as data for the State portion of American Indian and Alaska Native areas. Comparable 1980 data were provided on STF 1A microfiche.

Population and Housing Characteristics for Blocks (extract of STF 1B). Preliminary release date: 1992.

100-percent population and housing data selected from STF 1B will be shown to the block level. The comparable 1980 product was the PHC80–1, *Block Statistics* reports, prepared on microfiche.

Social, Economic, Housing Characteristics (from STF 3A). Preliminary release date: 1992.

Sample population and housing characteristics will be provided for States and their sub-areas in hierarchical sequence down to the block group level, as well as data for the State portion of American Indian and Alaska Native areas. Comparable 1980 data were provided on the STF 3A microfiche.

Laser Disks

CD-ROM laser disks are new for 1990. A CD-ROM disk will contain only files from the same series (for example, STF 3A State files). The individual CD-ROM disks will be produced as soon as enough files are available to complete a disk. They will include State files in the order of their release.

100-Percent Data to Be Released on CD-ROM

Population and Housing Characteristics (from STF 1A). Preliminary release date: 1991–1992.

100-percent population and housing counts and characteristics will be provided for States and their sub-areas in hierarchical sequence down to the block group level, as well as data for the State portion of American Indian and Alaska Native areas. Comparable 1980 data were provided on STF 1A tape and microfiche.

Population and Housing Characteristics for Blocks (extract of STF 1B). Preliminary release date: 1992.

100-percent population and housing data selected from STF 1B will be shown to the block level. The comparable 1980 product was the PHC80–1, *Block Statistics* reports, prepared on microfiche.

Population and Housing Characteristics (from STF 1C). Preliminary release date: 1992.

100-percent population and housing counts and characteristics will be shown in the following geographic structure: United States, regions, divisions, States, counties, places of 10,000 or more inhabitants, MCDs of 10,000 or more inhabitants in selected States, American Indian and Alaska Native areas, MSAs, and UAs. Similar 1980 data were shown on the STF 1C tape and microfiche.

Sample Data to Be Released on CD-ROM

Social, Economic, and Housing Characteristics (from STF 3A). Preliminary release date: 1992.

Sample population and housing characteristics will be provided for States and their sub-areas in hierarchical sequence down to the block group level, as well as data for the State portion of American Indian and Alaska Native areas. Comparable 1980 data were provided on STF 3A tape and microfiche.

Social, Economic, and Housing Characteristics (from STF 3B). Preliminary release date: 1993.

Sample population and housing data will be summarized for 5-digit ZIP Code areas within each State.

Social, Economic, and Housing Characteristics (from STF 3C). Preliminary release date: 1993.

Sample population and housing characteristics will be shown in the following geographic structure: United States, regions, divisions,

States, counties, places of 10,000 or more inhabitants, MCDs of 10,000 or more inhabitants in selected States, American Indian and Alaska Native areas, MSAs, and UAs. Similar 1980 data were shown on the STF 3C tape and microfiche.

Special Computer Tape Files and Other Data Products

The Bureau will produce and release several special computer tape files in 1993 to meet unique data needs. Others may be produced based on user demand and availability of resources.

Census/Equal Employment Opportunity (EEO) Special File
This special computer tape file will provide sample census data to support affirmative action planning for equal employment opportunity. The file will contain tabulations showing detailed occupations and educational attainment data by age. These data will also be cross-tabulated by sex, Hispanic origin, and race. Data will be provided for all counties, MSAs, and places of 50,000 or more inhabitants.

County-to-County Migration File
These files will be issued by State, providing summary records for all intrastate county-to-county migration streams and significant interstate county-to-county migration streams. Each record will include codes for the geographic area of origin, codes for the geographic area of destination, and selected characteristics of the persons who made up the migration stream.

Other Data Products

The data products listed below will be produced if there is time, adequate staffing, and availability of funds in the tabulation and publication budget.

Statistical (Thematic) Maps
The maps, which the Census Bureau issues as part of the GE–50 map series, usually depict a wide variety of statistical topics. In the past, the Census Bureau issued these maps as a single-sheet wall map. Similar maps also appeared in selected printed report series as page-size maps.

Supplementary Reports

Supplementary reports present special compilations of census data dealing with specific population and housing subjects as well as for subgroups of the population. The types of reports vary from census to census. Some examples of supplementary reports being considered for 1990 are *Advance Estimates of Social, Economic, and Housing Characteristics; Social, Economic, and Housing Characteristics for Redefined Metropolitan Statistical Areas;* graphic chartbooks; thematic maps portraying 1990 census data; and an atlas of census maps that will contain the printed publication maps.

Public-Use Microdata Sample for the Older Population

The Bureau is considering producing this product to meet the increasing demand for data on the older population. This file could be used to generate sufficient data, especially for the oldest age groups, to construct detailed cross tabulations by age, sex, race, and other characteristics.

Current Reports

The Census Bureau, in addition to the benchmark decennial census, conducts a number of surveys and other periodic programs to provide estimate data relevant to the social, economic and political characteristics of the population and to profile their housing arrangements. Substantial portions of this data are available on CENDATA.

Current Population Survey.

A significant amount of current population information available from the Census Bureau is derived from the *Current Population Survey.* The primary tasks of this survey are to produce monthly employment and unemployment statistics which are published by the Bureau of Labor Statistics in the publication *Employment and Earnings.* The Census Bureau itself collects supplemental data in this survey and publishes that data in the following current report series.

Population Characteristics (P20).

This series consists of annual reports on geographic residence and mobility, fertility, school enrollment, educational attainment, marital status, households and families, persons of Spanish origin and selected other topics. On a biennial basis reports are issued on voter registration and participation. In general, these reports present data on the national level and regional level with selected statistics at State and MSA level.

Special Studies (P23)

This series of reports includes methodology studies and special topic reports dealing with particular segments of the population or particular geographic units such as metropolitan and non-metropolitan areas. Many of the surveys included in this series are co-sponsored by other government agencies and are issued on a non-repetitive basis. The annual report listed below is a major inter-censal population survey.

Population Profile of the United States. Annual.

This report provides statistics on demographic, social, and economic characteristics of the population with some data at regional and State level.

Consumer Income (P60).

This series reports on the income-related statistics of families, individuals and households. Included in this series are reports on non-cash benefits and income as it relates to demographic and social characteristics, occupation, and work experience. The majority of reports in this series recur annually.

Population

Current Population Survey (CPS) Data Files

Topic	Years collected	Years available
January:		
Job finding	1973	1973
Job tenure and occupational mobility	1973, 1978, 1981, 1983, 1987	1973, 1978, 1981, 1983, 1987
Displaced workers	1984, 1986, 1988, 1990	1984, 1986, 1988, 1990

Job training	1983, 1984	1983, 1984
Housing, tenure/children (*also see* July)	1972, 1974–77	1972, 1974–77

February:
Unemployment compensation	1990	1990

March:
Demographic data (Annual Demographic File)	1968–90	1968–90
CPS/Social Security summary earnings extract match	1978	1978
After-tax money income estimates	1981–86	1981–86
Value of noncash benefits	1980, 1982–86	1980, 1982–86

April:
Volunteer work	1974	1974
Food stamp patricipation	1975–77	1975–77
Swine flu immunization	1977	–
Child support and alimony payments (March/April match)	1979, 1982, 1984, 1986, 1988, 1990	1979, 1982, 1984 , 1986, 1988, 1990
Immigration (*also see* June and Nov.)	1983	1983
Immigration (April/March/June match)	1983	1983
Veterans	1985	1985

May:
Multiple job holding and premium pay	1969–81, 1985, 1989	1969–81, 1985, 1989
Adult education	1969, 1972, 1975, 1978, 1981	1978, 1981, 1984
Private household workers	1971	1971
Post-secondary school enrollment	1974	1974
Job search of the unemployed	1976	1976
Job search of the employed	1977	1977

Pension/retirement plan coverage (May/March/June match)	1979, 1983, 1988	1979, 1983, 1988
Shift work/flextime	1980, 1981, 1985, 1989	1979, 1983, 1988, 1989
Employee benefits	1988	1988
Volunteer workers	1989	1989
Unemployment compensation (*see* Feb., Aug., Nov.)	1989	1989

June:

Fertility and birth expectations	1973–88, 1991	1973–77, 1979–88
Immigration (*also see* April and Nov.)	1986, 1988	1986, 1988
Fertility and birth expectations (June)	1983	1983
Marriage and birth history	1971, 1975, 1980, 1985, 1990	1975, 1980, 1985
Child care	1977, 1982	1977, 1982
Marital history	1985	1985
Emigration (*also see* July)	1988	–

July:

Survey of languages	1975	1975
Telephone availability (*also see* March [ADF] and Nov.)	1984–90	1984–90
Emigration (*also see* June)	1987	1977, 1978
Housing tenure/children (*also see* Jan.)	1977, 1978	1977, 1978

Aug.:

Food stamp participants	1977	1977
School lunch participants	1977	1977
Smoking	1967–68	1967–68
Retiree health insurance	1988	1988
Unemployment compensation (*see* Feb., May, Nov.)	1989	1989

September:

Immunization	1969, 1977–85	1969, 1977–85
Smoking	1985, 1989	1985, 1989, 1990
Veterans (*also see* Nov.)	1989	1989

October:

School enrollment	1968–90	1968–89
Recent college graduates	1971–72	–
Post-secondary school enrollment	1973	1973

November:

Voting	Every two years 1972–88 (ever since 1968)	
Ethnic background and literacy	1969, 1979, 1989	1969, 1979, 1989
Multiple job holding	1970	–
Private household workers	1974	1974
Telephone availability (*also see* March [ADF] and July)	1972, 1976, 1978, 1983–90	1972, 1976, 1978, 1983–90
Veterans (*also see* Sept.)	1987	1987
Immigration/emigration/ language (*also see* Apr.)	1989	1989
Unemployment compensation	1989	1989

December:

Farm wage workers	1971–77, 1979, 1981, 1983, 1987	1975–87 (odd years)
Food stamp participation	1975	1975
Child care	1984	1984
GED recipiency	1986	–
Receipt of pension benefits	1989	1989

Survey of Income and Program Participation. (SIPP)

This survey provides economic, serial and demographic statistics for households and persons. Housing information is also included.

Detailed data are included on participation in various cash and non-cash benefit programs. Income data are reported for labor force participation as well as for 50 other types of income. The SIPP files are available as computer files and a user's guide and technical documentation for these files are also available. Printed reports based on SIPP surveys are included in the following series.

Household Economic Studies. (P10)

This series and related data files provide statistics on the demographic, social and economic status of households and on the housing of persons within these households. Data on benefits received by persons in these households are included.

Estimates, Projections, and Special Censuses

In the years between censuses the Bureau prepares estimates of the population. The following series contain reports of these estimates.

Population Estimates and Projections. (P25)

This series of reports contains monthly estimates of the total U.S. population; annual midyear estimates of the population by age, sex, race and geographic area; and projections for the U.S. and States. Data on components of change, with deaths, and immigration are also reported on in this series. These files are available on computer tape.

Local Population Estimates. (P26)

The reports in this series provide population estimates for counties and metropolitan areas. Per capita income estimates are also included in this series. These files are available on computer tape.

International Population Reports

The Census Bureau maintains a Center for International Research which conducts demographic, social and economic population research and publishes the results of some of this research.

Factfinder for the Nation. no. 21 (rev.) *International Programs.* Washington, DC: Customer Services Division. 4p.

The Factfinder for international population statistics.

World Population Profile. Washington, DC: Government Printing Office. (WP). Biennial. SuDoc: C3.

The major publication from the Bureau which provides international population data. Included are demographic statistics for all countries and territories of the world with a population of at least 5,000. Data include population estimates, projections, growth rates, birth and death rates, life expectancy and infant mortality.

International Population Reports. (P95)

A series of current population reports providing subject coverage of international population data.

In addition to the above published reports, the Center for International Research publishes staff papers and has machine-readable data files available.

1980 Census of Population and Housing

The geographic coverage and content of the 1990 data products are similar to those produced for the 1980 census; however, there are differences as indicated below. A significant number of 1990 data products provide comparison with 1980 and in some cases with earlier census data.

Major Differences Between 1980 and 1990

Printed Reports: Advance and preliminary reports were replaced in the 1990 census by the series *Summary Population and Housing Characteristics* CPH–1. Separate reports were generated in the 1990 census for population and housing characteristics for American Indian and Alaskan Native Areas and for urbanized and metropolitan statistical areas (CH–1–) and (CP–1). A combined series containing data for census tracts and block numbering areas was issued in 1990. *Population and Housing Characteristics for Census Tracts and Block Numbering Areas,* CPH–3.

The detailed cross-tabulations produced in 1980 for population data were not produced in 1990.

Computer Tape Files: Only four STFs were produced for the 1990 census. The STFs detailed cross-tabulation tape from 1980 was not produced.

CD-ROM: This format is entirely new for 1990. An important change resulting from the use of CD-ROM is the availability of zip code data formerly only available on tape.

User-Defined Areas Program (UDAP): This is a service new in 1990 which will provide data summaries for geographic areas that are not available from the standard 1990 census products. General questions about UDAP should be directed to UDAP staff: 301–763–4282.

Useful Publications

1980 Census of Population and Housing. *1980 Census of Population and Housing: Reference Reports.* (PHC80–R.) Washington, DC: Government Printing Office. 1980– . SuDoc: C3.223/22:80/R.

A series covering the methodology and procedures used in the collection and presentation of the 1980 census data.

1. *Users' Guide.*
2. *History.* Covers work done on the 1980 census, from planning to evaluation of results, with comparisons to previous censuses.
3. *Alphabetical Index of Industries and Occupations.*
4. *Classified Index of Industries and Occupations.*
5. *Geographic Identification Code Scheme.*

1980 Census of Population and Housing. Evaluation and Research Reports. Washington, DC: Government Printing Office. 1984– . SuDoc: C3.223/16:980/E

A series of reports which comment on and evaluate the 1980 census methodology.

Census of Population and Housing 1980: Summary Tape File 1, Technical Documentation. Washington, DC: Customer Services, U.S. Bureau of the Census, 1981– .

This information, which describes the contents of Summary Tape File 1 and its organization and codes and which includes a glossary of terms relative to STF 1 and which may be applied to STF's 1–5, is issued as a main report and supplementary user notes.

Census Bureau's GBF/DIME System: A Tool for Urban Management and Planning. Washington, DC: U.S. Bureau of the Census. 1980. 58p.

A narrative description of the GBF/DIME (Geographic Base File/Dual Independent Map Encoding) system. Includes information on the development of the system; detailed availability of the files and related software; a bibliography and directory of contacts for further information. The Census Bureau's *GBF/DIME: A Tool for Urban Management and Planning* describes in detail *GBF/DIME Files* and related software packages.

Neighborhood Statistics from the 1980 Census. Washington, DC: U.S. Bureau of the Census, 1984. 15p. SuDoc: C3.2:N31/5–

A statistical report which provides data on coverage and availability of reports for individual neighborhoods from the 1980 Census of Population and Housing.

FOREIGN TRADE

The Foreign Trade data product series from the Bureau of the Census are in transition. During the 1980s changes in classification and format for trade data were of great magnitude. The data presented here were accurate at the time of writing, but changes were still being made. Questions concerning foreign trade data should be referred to the Foreign Trade Division Bureau of the Census, Washington, DC 20233 (Tel. 301–763–7754). Updated listings for foreign trade publications and products appear in *Monthly Product Announcement.* The *National Trade Data Bank* CD-ROM product, available from NTIS, provides monthly statistical and narrative information on foreign trade.

The recurring publications listed in this section represent the principal printed sources of general interest data on foreign trade. In addition, the Bureau of the Census makes available for sale and consultation a wide variety of reference tabulations of monthly data in greater detail and different arrangements on microfiche and magnetic tape. These represent the most complete and detailed sources of foreign trade statistics prepared for public reference. Foreign trade statistics are included in CENDATA.

Guide to Foreign Trade Statistics. Washington, DC: Government Printing Office, 1991. 175p. SuDoc:C3
Covers the Census Bureau's foreign trade statistical program, including descriptions and facsimile pages of published reports and a complete listing of unpublished reference tabulations available for sale or consultation. Updates and fuller explanations are included in the 1990 and 1991 *Census Catalog and Guide* chapters on foreign trade as well as in selected issues of *Monthly Product Announcements.*

U.S. Foreign Trade. Schedule B—Statistical Classification of Domestic and Foreign Commodities Exported From the United States. Washington, DC: Government Printing Office. 1989. 2v./Updates. SuDoc: C3.150:b/
The base volume of this edition (1990) represents the official schedule of commodity classifications for exports from the United States. This classification reflects the Harmonized Commodity Description and Coding System. Volume one of this set presents Schedule B, classification and descriptions; volume 2 presents Schedule C, county and territory descriptions for exports; and Schedule D, U.S. Customs Districts and Ports, along with an index to Schedule B. Updates are issued as changes are made.

U.S. Foreign Trade. Schedule K: Classification of Foreign Ports by Geographic Trade Area and Country. Washington, DC: Government Printing Office. 1991. 84p. SuDoc: C3.
A schedule listing major ports of the world grouped according to *Schedule C, Classification of Country Descriptions for the Foreign Trade Statistics, Effective January 1, 1990.* Each port is given a numeric code.

U.S. Foreign Trade. CDEX U.S. Exports of Merchandise, International Harmonized System Commodity Classification (HS—Basic Schedule B) By Country, By Customs District. Washington, DC: Government Printing Office. Monthly. SuDoc: C3.
A monthly statistical report in CD-ROM format detailing import activity.

U.S. Foreign Trade. CDIM. U.S. Imports of Merchandise, International Harmonized System Commodity Classification (HTSUSA) By Country, By

Customs District. Washington, DC: Government Printing Office. Monthly. SuDoc: C3.

A monthly statistical report in CD-ROM format detailing import activity.

Reference Materials—U.S. Exports of Merchandise on CD-ROM Technical Documentation. (CD-ROMs). Washington, DC: Customer Services Division.

Descriptive information on file. A similar guide is available for CDIM.

Combined Reports

U.S. Merchandise Trade: Selected Highlights. (FT920.) Washington, DC: Government Printing Office. Monthly. SuDoc C3.164:920/(Date)

U.S. foreign trade by commodity group, country, world area, and customs district, method of transportation, and end-use category.

U.S. Foreign Trade. U.S. Merchandise Trade: Exports, General Imports, and Imports for Consumption, Standard International Trade Classification Revision 3, Commodity By Country. (FT925). Washington, DC: Government Printing Office. Monthly. SuDoc: C3.164:925/(Month).

This report replaces both FT135 and FT410. Included are volume of exports, general imports and imports for consumption by SITC by commodity groupings. Current month and cumulative year-to-date statistics are provided.

U.S. Foreign Trade. U.S. Exports and Imports by Harmonized Commodity, 6–digit Harmonized Commodity by Country. (FT943). Washington, DC: Government Printing Office. Annual. SuDoc: C3.164:947.

A combined report on exports and imports by Harmonized commodity.

Imports

U.S. Imports for Consumption and General Imports: HTSUSA Commodity by Country of Origin. (FT247). Washington, DC: Government Printing Office. Annual. SuDoc: C3.164:247/(Year)

Detailed data for U.S. imports of commodities by HTSUSA by individual by country of origin.

Exports

U.S. Exports: Harmonized Schedule B Commodity by Country. (FT447). Washington, DC: Government Printing Office. Annual. SuDoc: C3.164:447/(Year)

Net quantity and value of commodities listed according to the harmonized Schedule B commodity number.

U.S. Possessions and Puerto Rico

U.S. Trade with Puerto Rico and U.S. Possessions. (FT895). Washington, DC: Government Printing Office. Annual. SuDoc: C3.164:895/ (Date)

Quantity and value of commodities shipped between the U.S. and Puerto Rico, Virgin Islands, American Samoa, Guam and the Northern Mariana Islands.

OTHER FEDERAL SOURCES

Complete enumeration of the multitude of publications issued by Federal agencies is beyond the scope of this guide. Consequently, greater emphasis has been placed on periodic reports of current general-use data, lesser on occasional and special purpose statistics.

Since it is a well known fact that every agency sums up its operations in annual reports only those are listed whose statistical content provides a useful summary or supplement to the periodic reports mentioned.

Similarly, only those special studies are included that provide historical or unique sources of general-purpose statistics. Statistical sources excluded here can be readily traced through the agency catalogs and bibliographies, indexes, and research aids cited throughout this work. In addition, selected non-statistical publications have been included because of their interest to the business community.

Perhaps the single greatest force affecting Federal sources of information is the recurrent reorganizations within the executive branch. To keep abreast or to research reassignments of agency responsibilities and programs as well as of Federal regulations affecting every aspect of business, the most current and comprehensive source is listed below.

Federal Register. Washington, DC: Government Printing Office. 5/week. SuDoc: GS.107

Basic source of executive branch promulgations having general applicability and legal effect. Publishes on a current basis the full texts of all Presidential proclamations and executive orders, and of regulations issued by Federal agencies under their statutory authority. Also includes among its documents and announcements of general interest notification of agency reorganizations and of new and revised agency policies and procedures. All regulations in force on the date specified are codified in the *Code of Federal Regulations,* which is completely revised annually and published with inter-edition updates. Both publications are prepared and issued by the Office of the Federal Register, National Archives and Records Service, a sub-unit of the General Services Administration. Full text available online on the Mead Data system and through Dialog. A CD-ROM version is also available.

THE CONGRESS

The primary activity of Congress is deliberation and enactment of laws, including statutes that empower executive branch agencies to originate and adjudicate administrative law. Rooted in this legislation are the rise and continuation of many Federal information resources, as well as much of business and economic activity.

Congressional publications themselves, taken as a whole, reflect the broad range of Federal legislative interests, with business, economics, marketing, foreign trade and related topics well represented. Those publications bearing on the focus of this guide may be categorized into four main groups: hearings, reports, committee prints, and selected other publications. A particularly rich source of information is the appendixes and exhibits included in congressional hearings. Access to all these publications is provided by the following:

CIS/Index. Bethesda, MD: Congressional Information Service. Monthly/Annual Cumulation.

A private-sector publication, this comprehensive and detailed abstract service covers hearings, House and Senate reports and documents, committee prints, House and Senate special publications, and Senate executive reports and documents. Its monthly index, cumulating quarterly to annual and to multiple-year compilations, provides access to the abstracts by bill number and report number; document abstracts also identify the statistical content of hearings and reports.

The publisher's corresponding database, CIS, provides online access 1970 to date and is updated monthly.

Microfiche of indexed publications, supplied singly or in groups by subscription, are available as a separate service.

In 1989, the company introduced *Congressional Master File,* a CD-ROM version of the *CIS Index* which consists of a retrospective source and a current service with quarterly updates.

Although some congressional publications—such as bibliographies of committee publications and compilations of all Federal laws on a particular topic—are issued on a recurring basis, the bulk of this output is monographic and includes a wealth of information relating to business and economics. Below is an excellent example of this type of publication.

U.S. Congress. Joint Economic Committee. *OMB's Proposed Guidelines for Federal Statistical Activities: A Survey of the Current Guidelines, Proposed Guidelines, and the Public Response to the Possible Changes.* Washington, DC: Government Printing Office, 1988. iii, 50p.

A report prepared by the Congressional Research Service which summarizes the current and proposed Office of Management and Budget (OMB) guidelines for collecting, handling, processing and reporting, of Federal statistical data.

For tracking legislation and researching statistics affecting business activity, two of the primary sources are the following:

Congressional Record. Washington, DC: Government Printing Office. Daily.

Published each day that Congress or either house sits in open session. Reports the introduction of all bills and resolutions, the debates, and floor action taken on them. Its "Daily Digest" section, in addition to indexing and summarizing the issue's proceedings, includes forthcoming House and Senate agendas and committee activity on pending legislation. A fortnightly index to this daily edition is published separately. After each congressional session ends, a revised and repaged permanent edition, spanning the session and with its own sessional index, is issued in bound form.

The *Congressional Record* is available in abstract form online through a variety of online information services, and available in full text online through Mead Data Central, Inc. as a LEXIS/NEXIS database, or from West Publishing Company as part of Westlaw Federal Database. A CD-ROM version is planned.

United States Statutes at Large. Washington, DC: Government Printing Office. Annual. SuDoc: GS 4.111:

Prepared and issued by the Office of Federal Register, National Archives and Records Service, a sub-unit of the General Services Administration. Cumulates for each session of Congress, the Acts of

Congress. A consolidation and codification of all the general and permanent laws of the U.S. that are in force on the date specified is prepared by the Committee on the Judiciary of the House of Representatives and is published approximately every six years as the *United States Code.*

The full text of the *United States Code* is available online from West Publishing company as part of the Westlaw Federal Database or from Mead Data Central, Inc. as part of the LEXIS General Federal Library.

Senate

Report of the Secretary of the Senate. Washington, DC: Senate. Semiannual. SuDoc: Y1.1/3:(S. Doc. No.)

Provides data on the salaries of officers, clerks, and employees of the Senate, Senate committees, and each Senator's office. A detailed listing of income and expenditures is also included.

House of Representatives

Report of the Clerk of the House. Washington, DC: House of Representatives. Quarterly. SuDoc: Y1.1/7:(Nos.)

A detailed report of House receipts and expenditures. Includes data on the salaries of officers and employees of the House, committees, and each representative. A description of expenditures and amount expended is also included.

U.S. Congress. House of Representatives. *Financial Disclosure Reports of Members of the U.S. House of Representatives.* Washington, DC: Government Printing Office. Annual. SuDoc: Y1.1/ 7:

An annual compilation of disclosure statements from each House member. Similar information for Senators must be requested from the Senate Select Committee on Ethics.

U.S. Congress. House of Representatives. Post Office and Civil Service Committee. *Current Salary Schedules of Federal Officers and Employees . . .* Washington, DC: Government Printing Office. Annual. SuDoc: Y4.P84/ 10–15:

Provides Federal employee salary schedules.

U.S. Congress. House of Representatives. Foreign Affairs Committee. *Country Reports on Economic Policy and Trade Practices.* Annual. SuDoc: Y4.F76/1:C83/ 3.

Provides economic statistics and U.S. trade statistics for over 100 foreign countries and the European Community.

Joint Economic Committee

Economic Indicators. Washington, DC: Government Printing Office. Monthly. SuDoc: Y4.Ec7:/(Yr.- Nos.)

A compilation of charts and tables detailing the major national economic indicators. Includes data on output, income, and spending; employment, unemployment, and wages; production and business activity; prices; money, credit, and security markets; Federal finance; and international statistics by country. Monthly, quarterly and annual data are included.

Historical tables with descriptive background and nontechnical explanations of data inputs, and incorporating major revisions adopted in 1976, were published as *1980 Supplement to Economic Indicators.* A more recent supplement was published in 1990.

Employment-Unemployment, Monthly Hearings. Washington, DC: Government Printing Office. Monthly. SuDoc: Y4.Ec7:Em 7/12/PT.

An ongoing series of hearings dealing with BLS indicators and BLS methodology.

Joint Economic Report. Washington, DC: Senate. Annual. SuDoc: Y1.1/5:(S. Rpt.)

This report contains Committee recommendations on economic policy and constitutes a critique of the *Economic Report of the President.*

General Accounting Office

The General Accounting Office, among other duties, directly assists the Congress, its committees, members, and officers, through special audits, surveys, and reviews; studies and investigations; and the issuance of numerous GAO reports.

Annual Index: Reports Issued in. . . . (Year.) Washington, DC: General Accounting Office, 1985–. Annual. SuDoc: GA 1.16/3–2:(Year.)

An index of GAO audit and evaluation reports arranged in chronological order by subject.

Homelessness: McKinney Act Programs and Funding. Washington, DC: Government Printing Office. Annual. SuDoc: GA 1.13:RCED—

Includes charts and tables with statistics on Federal programs of aid to the homeless.

Thrift Resolutions: Estimated Cost of FSLIC's Assistance Agreements Subject to Change. Washington, DC: Government Printing Office. Annual. SuDoc: GA 1.13:AFMD—

A report detailing costs of FSLIC assistance.

Obligations Immulation: Resolution Trust Corporation Compliance. Washington, DC: Government Printing Office. Quarterly.

Provides statistics from Resolution Trust Corporation's balance sheet.

Library of Congress

Access: Catalogs and Technical Publications. Washington, DC: Library of Congress. Annual.

An indexed listing of publications in hard copy and microform which function as access tools. Included are catalogs, bibliographies, classification schedules, etc. All items are available from the Library of Congress.

THE PRESIDENT AND THE EXECUTIVE OFFICE OF THE PRESIDENT

As head of the executive branch, the President relies on its departments and agencies, as well as on the several units of the Executive Office of the President, to compile the data and sometimes to produce the reports that he submits to Congress and the nation.

Because they represent presidential statements of policy and recommendations on major economic issues, the following reports are listed here rather than under the units responsible for compiling them.

Economic Report of the President, Transmitted to the Congress . . . Washington, DC: Government Printing Office. Annual. SuDoc: Pr 40.9:(Year.)
Includes the texts of the President's economic report and of the *Annual Report of the Council of Economic Advisers.* Data are provided on economic development, economic outlook, world economy, inflation, unemployment, etc.

The Executive Office of the President is composed of agencies which function to further the goals of the executive branch of the Federal government.

Office of Management and Budget (OMB)

OMB is responsible for assisting the President in the development of interagency cooperation and of efficient coordinating mechanisms. Among its many activities are some, like the assessment of Federal programs, the improvement of management practices and the preparation of the Federal budget, that give rise to publications of informational value. OMB issues notices of proposed revisions of Federal Government statistical activities in the *Federal Register.*

Budget of the United States Government. Washington, DC: Government Printing Office. Annual. SuDoc: Pr Ex 2.8
This is the official budget of the United States and detailed budget estimates. Includes actual data for the current fiscal year and projected data for the forthcoming fiscal year. The detailed estimates provided in an appendix to the document are given by agency. This report includes the previously separately issued detailed budget appendix.

Mid-Session Review of the Budget. Washington, DC: Office of Management and Budget. Annual. SuDoc: Pr Ex 2.1
Provides revised budget data which incorporate updated economic information and forecasts and include unanticipated changes in revenue and expenditures. Includes long-range projections.

Federal Statistics: A Special Report on the Statistical Programs and Activities of the U.S. Government. Washington, DC: Statistical Policy Branch, Office of Information & Regulatory Affairs. Annual. SuDoc: PrEx 2.10/2:(Year.)

A report which provides information on the funding of Federal statistical programs and activities.

Information Collection Budget of the U.S. Government. Springfield, VA: National Technical Information Service. Annual. SuDoc: PrEx 2.29:(Year.)

A report which provides statistics on the cost of implementing the *Paperwork Reduction Act.* Includes one section for each agency covered.

Managing Federal Information Resources. Washington, DC: Office of Management and Budget. Annual.

A report which reviews information management activities by agency. This report is required by the Paperwork Reduction Act of 1980.

Regulatory Programs of the U.S. Government. Washington, DC: Government Printing Office. Annual. SuDoc: PrEx 2.30:

A report detailing the regulatory activities of 24 Federal agencies.

Budget Information for States. Washington, DC: Office of Management and Budget. Annual.

A detailing of Federal grant obligations to States and local governments. The report is arranged by agency and by program.

Metropolitan Areas. Springfield, VA: National Technical Information Service. Annual.

A list of current MSAs, CMSAs, PMSAs and New England County Metro Areas with revisions and definitions.

Federal Assistance Programs

Catalog of Federal Domestic Assistance. Washington, DC: Government Printing Office. Annual/Supplements. SuDoc: PrEx 2.20:(Year.)

A detailed catalog of Federal programs of financial and nonfinancial assistance to governments, organizations, and individuals—requirements, type of assistance provided, funding, etc.

Office of U.S. Trade Representative

This Office is charged with monitoring and reporting on U.S. trade.

National Trade Estimate Report on Foreign Trade Barriers. Washington, DC: Government Printing Office. Annual.

A report which details by country, tariffs and other trade barriers imposed on U.S. exports. A significant amount of detail on the size of the country market and on U.S. investment is included. This report provides data input for the *National Trade Data Bank: The Export Connection* CD-ROM product.

Council of Economic Advisers

The Council analyzes the national economy and its various segments; advises the President on economic developments; appraises the economic programs and policies of the Federal government; recommends to the President policies for economic growth. Its *Annual Report of the Council of Economic Advisers* is appended to the *Economic Report of the President,* which it assists in preparing for presentation to Congress.

Metropolitan Statistical Area Revisions. Springfield, VA: National Technical Information Service. Irregular. SuDoc: PrEx 2.3: (Year.)

A complete listing of Metropolitan Statistical Areas and related topics, issued every two to four years and updated by supplements as needed. Latest seen 1988.

Council on Environmental Quality

The Council develops and recommends to the President national policies which further environmental quality, and assists the President in the preparation of the annual environmental quality report to the Congress.

Environmental Quality. Washington, DC: Government Printing Office. Annual. SuDoc: PrEx 14.1:(Year.)

Provides data on all facets of environmental activity. Includes trend data and projections. An irregular publication, *Environmental Trends,* provides trend data on environmental matters. The latest edition of this publication is 1989 and data for 1970–1980s are included with some earlier data.

DEPARTMENT OF AGRICULTURE

The Department of Agriculture is required by law to assemble and disseminate useful information on agricultural subjects in the most comprehensive sense. It produces an impressive amount and variety of data on all phases of agricultural economics, marketing, and distribution.

A great number of statistical reports are issued regularly or occasionally, some with periodic supplements, on a wide variety of agricultural commodities. These reports provide information on such factors as production, stocks, marketing, prices, supply and demand, and export and import trade. Many of these studies reflect national and worldwide findings.

Other areas on which the Department of Agriculture provides information include home economics and human nutrition, farm population and employment, Federal food programs, farm income and expenditures, and retail food prices. Data are provided for the consumer, industrial, and institutional markets on the nation's agricultural output, raw and processed, as well as on a wide variety of products for the farm market.

Studies of sales potentials, consumer preferences, merchandising methods, buying practices, wholesaling, store layout and related topics are specific and frequent. Detailed here are the statistical programs that result in periodic reports of the general-use type.

The crop and livestock production and demand data and forecasts that the Department of Agriculture generates are available online through private time-sharing services such as Dialog Information Services, Inc. and BRS.

General

Agricultural Statistics. Washington, DC: Government Printing Office. Annual. SuDoc: A1.47:(Year.)

Compendium of the principal statistical series on agriculture and related subjects.

Factbook of U.S. Agriculture. Washington, DC: Government Printing Office. Annual. SuDoc: A1.38/2:(Year.)
An annual report showing statistics of selected food items purchasable by the average hourly wage of factory workers.

Composition of Foods. Washington, DC: Human Nutrition Information Service, 1976–. SuDoc: A1.76:(Nos.)
A series of approximately 22 reports, each on a different food group. The reports provide data on the nutrient content of each form of each food item covered. This series is a major revision of *Agricultural Handbook, no. 8,* published in 1950 and revised in 1963. The Human Nutrition Information Service conducts research in and publishes information concerning nutrition, diet, food supplies and the value of foods. The *National Food Consumption Surveys* and the *Nutrient Data Bank* are two ongoing projects under the direction of the Human Nutrition Information Service.

Yearbook of Agriculture: Marketing U.S. Agriculture. Washington, DC: Government Printing Office. Annual. SuDoc: A1.10:(Year.)
An annual compilation of papers dealing with agricultural marketing systems.

Outlook (Year.) Proceedings. Washington, DC: World Agricultural Board. Annual.
The collected texts of papers presented at the Annual Agricultural Outlook Conference.

Agricultural Cooperative Service

The Agricultural Cooperative Service is responsible for research in the use of cooperative organizations for agricultural enterprises.

Top 100 Cooperatives, Financial Profile. Washington, DC: Agricultural Cooperative Service. Annual. SuDoc: A109.10:(No.)
An annual statistical publication based on financial report data from the 100 largest cooperatives.

Farmer Cooperatives. Washington, DC: Government Printing Office. Monthly. SuDoc: A109.11:(V. Nos. & Nos.)

A narrative publication which includes supporting statistical tables and charts on farm cooperative projects and research in the field of farm cooperatives.

Agricultural Statistics Board

The Agricultural Statistics Board is a statistical reporting arm of the National Agricultural Statistics Service.

Agricultural Statistics Board. Catalog. Washington, DC: Agricultural Statistics Board. Annual. SuDoc: A92.35/2:(Year.)

A bibliography of the most recent year's Agricultural Statistics Board publications. Includes directory information relating to State statistical offices.

Farm Labor. Washington, DC: Agricultural Statistics Board. Quarterly. SuDoc: A92.12:(Date.)

A report on employment, hours worked, salary, and method of payment arranged by State.

Farm Production Expenditures. Summary. Washington, DC: Agricultural Statistics Board. Annual.

An annual report on farm production expenditures. A related annual report is entitled *Agricultural Prices, Survey.*

Floriculture Crops: (Year.) Washington, DC: Agriculture Statistics Board. Annual. SuDoc: A92.32:(Year.)

A statistical report detailing production and sales of cut and potted flowers and foliage plants.

Agricultural Prices. Washington, DC: Agricultural Statistics Board. Annual. SuDoc: A92.16/2:(Year.)

Provides data on prices received by farmers for their products, and prices paid by farmers for items used in agricultural production and family living.

Cold Storage. Washington, DC: Washington, DC: Government Printing Office. Monthly. SuDoc: A92.21:(Date.)

Provides information on cold storage stocks of 80 commodities in ten categories. Data include commodity cold storage stock by region.

Agricultural Marketing Service

The Agricultural Marketing Service (AMS) administers standardization, grading, voluntary and mandatory inspection, market news, marketing orders, regulatory and related programs. The market news service provides current information to producers, processors, distributors, and others to assist them in the orderly marketing and distribution of farm commodities. Information is collected and disseminated on supplies, demand, prices, movement, location, quality, conditions, and other market data on farm products in specific markets and marketing areas.

Cotton

Cotton Price Statistics. Washington, DC: Agricultural Marketing Service. Monthly/Annual Summary. SuDoc: A88.11/9:(V. Nos. & Nos.)
Provides data on cotton spot prices, premiums and discounts, by grade and staple length, in designated markets.

Fruit and Vegetable Reports

A number of reports dealing with fruits and vegetables are issued by the Agricultural Marketing Service on a regular basis. Reports generally include data on price, supply, stocks, production and foreign trade.

Fresh Fruit and Vegetables. Ornamental Crops. Weekly Summary: Shipments-Arrivals. Washington, DC: Agricultural Marketing Service. Weekly/Annual Summary. SuDoc: A88.12/22:(Nos.)
Provides preliminary data on rail, truck, air, boat shipments, piggyback, arrivals of fresh fruit, vegetables, and ornamental crops.
An annual series of reports is also issued providing data on arrivals for 22 U.S. and five Canadian cities; *Fresh Fruit and Vegetable Arrivals and Shipments.* Washington, DC: Agricultural Marketing Service. Annual. SuDoc: A88.12/31:(Year.)

Feed and Grain

Grain and Feed Market News: Weekly Summary and Statistics. Washington, DC: Agricultural Marketing Service. Weekly. SuDoc: A88.18/4–2:(V. Nos. & Nos.)
   Includes statistics on production, prices, and trade of grains such as wheat, corn, rye, etc.

Livestock, Meat, and Wool Reports

Livestock, Meat, and Wool Market News. Washington, DC: Agricultural Marketing Service. Weekly. SuDoc: A88.16/4:(V. Nos. & Nos.)
   Provides data on livestock and meat marketing and prices.

National Wool Market Review, Livestock Division. Washington, DC: Agricultural Marketing Service. Weekly/Biweekly.
   Provides statistical data on trade and prices for U.S., Australian, and South African Wool.

Milk, Dairy, and Poultry Products

Dairy Market Statistics, Annual Summary. Washington, DC: Agricultural Marketing Service. Annual.
   Dairy product prices and storage holdings summarized from weekly *Dairy Market News.*

Poultry Market Statistics: Annual Summary. Washington, DC: Agricultural Marketing Service. Annual.
   Information on poultry, eggs, egg product marketing and prices.

Tobacco

Annual Report on Tobacco Statistics. Washington, DC: Agricultural Marketing Service. Annual.
   Provides data on production, prices, value, stocks, exports and imports, and tax revenue derived from sales of tobacco products. A quarterly report on tobacco stocks is also issued.

Tobacco Market Review. Washington, DC: Agricultural Marketing Service. Annual. SuDoc: A88.34/6:(Year.)

Four reports on tobacco marketing in the U.S. for three classes of tobacco. Some trend data are included.

Agricultural Research Service

The Agricultural Research Service collects and disseminates information relating to food and the agricultural sciences.

Family Economics Review. Washington, DC: Government Printing Office. Quarterly. SuDoc: A77.245:(Date.)

A compilation of articles relating to home economics and the cost of living. An annual index is included with the Fall issue. Fall 1978 contains an index af articles published 1966-Fall 1978.

Commodity Credit Corporation

The Commodity Credit Corporation is responsible for providing support and programs in areas relating to agricultural commodities. It is also authorized to exchange surplus agricultural commodities. The agency is also involved in meeting the needs of developing nations for agricultural commodities.

Commodity Credit Corporation Annual Report. Washington, DC: Commodity Credit Corporation. Annual.

A statistical and narrative report which includes financial statements for the program and investment activities of the Commodity Credit Corporation.

Economic Research Service

The ERS formulates, develops and administers a program of economic, statistical, and other social science research, analysis, and information related to food, agriculture, and rural resources and communities. The findings of its research and its statistical data collection are made available to users through research reports and economic outlook and situation reports on major commodities, the national economy, and the international economy. The 45 State-Federal offices, serving all States and the national office, prepare monthly, annual, and other periodic reports. Data on crops and livestock products appear in some 300 reports issued each year. Other reports concern prices received by farmers and prices paid by farmers, farm labor, etc.

Major Statistical Series of the U.S. Department of Agriculture. (Agriculture Handbook 671). Washington, DC: Government Printing Office. Irregular. SuDoc: A1.76.671
   A series of reports each of which examines and describes a program or methodology relating to the statistical activities of the Department of Agriculture.

Journal of Agricultural Economics Research. Washington, DC: Government Printing Office. Quarterly. SuDoc: A93.26:(V. Nos.) & (Nos.)
   Comprised of technical articles on the methods, results and findings of research in agricultural economics, statistics and marketing.

Agricultural Outlook. Washington, DC: Government Printing Office. 11/yr. SuDoc: A93.10/2:(Nos.)
   Monthly report which includes information formerly found in *Demand and Price Situation; Checklist of News Reports; Farm Real Estate Market Developments; Farm Income Situation;* and *Marketing and Transportation Situation.*
   Data covered include agricultural production, marketing, prices, supply and demand, trade, and the input industries.

Agricultural Chartbook. Washington, DC: Government Printing Office. Annual. SuDoc: A1.76/2:(Year.)
   Provides data on farm production and economics, foreign agricultural production and trade, land use, commodity trends and rural population. Data are derived to a great extent from USDA surveys and publications.

Food Cost Review. Washington, DC: Economic Research Service. Annual. SuDoc: A1.107/2:(Year.)

A statistical survey of prices and price spreads at the farm and retail level. The Report also includes marketing costs, food industry costs, profits, and productivity.

Food Marketing Review. Washington, DC: Economic Research Service, 1984 - . Annual. SuDoc: A1.107/3:(Year.)
A report in chart and tabular form which provides information on the wholesale and retail food business sector. Includes statistics on mergers and acquisitions and divestitures. Also includes statistics on value or shipments, value added, advertising expenditures, income, and other financial and marketing statistical indicators.

Outlook for U.S. Agricultural Exports. Washington, DC: Government Printing Office. Quarterly. SuDoc: A93.43:(Date.)
A statistical report which provides outlook and forecast information for U.S. agricultural exports and imports

Foreign Agricultural Trade of the U.S. Washington, DC: Government Printing Office. Bimonthly. SuDoc: A93.17/7
A review of agricultural trade by geographic area and commodity.

World Agriculture Situation and Outlook Report. Washington, DC: Government Printing Office. Quarterly. SuDoc: A93.29/2
A statistical review of the agricultural economy of the world. Lengthy narratives are included, as are articles on agriculture treaties, etc. An annual report series by region is issued, as is a monthly on livestock and crop supply and demand on a county basis.

Agricultural Finance

Economic Indicators of the Farm Sector: National Financial Summary. Washington, DC: Government Printing Office. Annual. SuDoc: A93.45/3(Year.)
A report which provides financial status statistics on farms and farming. Includes statistics on income, expenses, assets, and liabilities. Companion reports to this report include *Economic Indicators of the Farm Sector: Production and Efficiency Statistics; Economic Indicators of the Farm Sector: State Financial Summary* and *Economic Indicators of the Farm Sector: Farm Sector Review.*

Situation Reports

Situation reports analyze the supply, demand, price, and outlook for the products indicated. Tables give data on current acreage yield, production, stocks, consumption, and prices. Titles marked with an asterisk are also published as yearbooks.

Agricultural Income and Finance Situation and Outlook Report. Economic Research Service. 4/yr. SuDoc: A93.9/8:(Nos.)

Agricultural Resources Situation and Outlook Report. Economic Research Service. 4/yr. SuDoc: A93.47:(Nos.)

Agriculture Situation and Outlook Report. Washington, DC: Economic Research Service. 2/yr.

Cotton and Wool Situation and Outlook Report. Washington, DC: Government Printing Office. 4/yr. SuDoc A93.24/2:(Nos.)

Dairy Situation and Outlook Report. Washington, DC: Government Printing Office. 5/yr.* SuDoc: A93.13:(Nos.)

Fruit and Tree Nuts Situation and Outlook Report. Washington, DC: Government Printing Office. 4/yr.* SuDoc: A93.12/3:(Nos.)

Livestock and Poultry Situation and Outlook Report. Washington, DC: Government Printing Office. 6/yr. SuDoc: A93.46:(Nos.)

Oil Crops Situation and Outlook Report. Washington, DC: Government Printing Office. 4/yr.* SuDoc: A93:23/2:(Nos.)

Rice Situation and Outlook. Washington, DC: Government Printing Office. 3/yr. SuDoc: A93.11/3 :(Nos.)

Sugar and Sweetener Situation and Outlook Report. Washington, DC: Government Printing Office. 4/yr.* SuDoc: A93.31/3:(Date.)

Tobacco Situation and Outlook Report. Washington, DC: Government Printing Office. 4/yr.* SuDoc: A93.25:(Nos.)

Vegetables and Specialties Situation and Outlook Report. Washington, DC: Government Printing Office. 3/yr.* SuDoc: A93.12/2:(Nos.)

Wheat Situation and Outlook Report. Washington, DC: Government Printing Office. 4/yr.* SuDoc: A93.11:(Nos.)

Food and Nutrition Service

FNS administers the programs that make food assistance available to people who need it. These programs are operated in cooperation with State and local governments. Its reports provide data on participation in and outlays for Federal food programs.

Food Stamp Statistical Summary of Project Area Operations. Washington, DC: Food and Nutrition Service. Semiannual.

Provides data on participation in the food stamp program and the number and value of coupons issued. An annual report on the characteristics of food stamp households is also issued.

Foreign Agricultural Service

FAS is an export promotion and service agency for U.S. agriculture. It operates a global reporting and analysis network covering world agricultural production, trade, competition, marketing, prices, policy situations, and other factors affecting U.S. agriculture and its exports and imports of agricultural commodities.

Current information concerning all principal farm commodities moving in world trade is made available to U.S. farm interests and the public through its publications.

Agexporter. Washington, DC: Government Printing Office. Monthly. SuDoc: A67.712:(V. Nos. & Nos.)

Provides a review of current agricultural trade, prices, production and policies of foreign countries, by country, as they affect U.S. trade. An annual statistical compilation entitled *Foreign Agriculture* was begun in 1989 and includes statistics on agricultural production, trade, and other activities for 65 countries.

Agricultural Trade Highlights. Washington, DC: Foreign Agricultural Service, 1989–. Monthly.

A compilation of statistics with a narrative overview of agricultural export activities including trends and forecasts, prices, and economic factors affecting foreign and U.S. agricultural commerce.

U.S. Export Sales. Washington, DC: U.S. Department of Agriculture. Weekly. SuDoc: A67.40:(Date.)

A weekly report on agricultural export sales for selected commodities.

Foreign Agriculture Circulars. Washington, DC: Foreign Agricultural Service. Irregular. SuDoc: A67.18:FOP(Nos.)

An ongoing series of reports dealing with foreign and domestic trade, production and consumption of selected agricultural commodities. The circulars, each on a commodity, are generally narrative with one or more statistical tables. Most are issued on an annual basis.

Forest Service

The Forest Service has responsibility for national leadership in forestry. In this capacity it encourages the growth and development of forestry-based enterprises that readily respond to consumers' changing needs.

Production, Prices, Employment, and Trade in Northwest Forest Industries. Washington, DC: Forest Service. Quarterly. SuDoc: A13.66/13:(Date.)

Includes data on forest industry activity in Alaska, Washington, Oregon, California, Montana, Idaho, and British Columbia.

U.S. Timber Production, Trade, Consumption, and Price Statistics. Washington, DC: Forest Service. Annual. SuDoc: A13.113:(Year.)

Includes data on production, prices, trade, and consumption of timber, logs, lumber, pulpwood and veneer, and timber products. Trend data and estimates are included.

DEPARTMENT OF COMMERCE

In addition to its other duties, the Department of Commerce provides assistance and information to domestic and international business, and provides social and economic statistics and analysis for business and government planners.

The Department of Commerce has been a leader in providing information in machine-readable formats. The Economic Bulletin Board online service, the National Trade Data Bank CD-ROM product and the wide variety of CD-ROM products available from the Bureau of the Census are indicative of the Department's leadership.

Commerce Publications Update. Washington, DC: Government Printing Office. Biweekly. SuDoc: C1.24/3:(Vol.-Nos.)
Included in this listing are publications of the Commerce Department grouped by agency or office. The *U.S. Department of Commerce Publications Catalog and Index,* which was published annually until 1982, supplemented a basic volume of the same title which selectively listed Commerce Department publications published between 1790 and October, 1950.

Studies in the Economics of Production. Washington, DC: Government Printing Office, 1985–. Irregular. SuDoc: C1.81:
The reports in this series provide statistics on production, costs, and trends in particular industries. Each report includes numerous tables and charts and covers a variety of time periods beginning with the late 1950s.

Commerce Business Daily. Washington, DC: Government Printing Office. 5/week. SuDoc: C57.20
Lists U.S. government procurement invitations, contract awards, subcontracting leads, and sales of surplus property. Also includes information on foreign business opportunities.

National Trade Data Bank (NTDB): The Export Connection. Springfield, VA: National Technical Information Service. Monthly. SuDoc: C1.88
A CD-ROM product which provides narrative and statistical

information on U.S. exports, imports and related trade information. The information comes from a variety of Federal sources and the Massachusetts Institute for Social and Economic Research (MISER). A companion "Export Hotline" is available as a free (800) service from the International Trade Administration.

Bureau of Economic Analysis

The Bureau of Economic Analysis (BEA) prepares, develops and interprets the economic accounts of the U.S. Included in these accounts are the national income and product accounts, summarized by the gross national product; wealth accounts; inter-industry accounts; regional accounts; and balance of payment accounts.

In addition to its work on the economic accounts the BEA prepares and analyzes other measures of economic activity, including various tools for forecasting economic developments, such as surveys of the investment outlays and plans of U.S. business; econometric models of the U.S. economy; and a system of economic indicators. The Bureau's comprehensive compilations of business and economic indicators and time series, widely used in the analysis and forecasting of economic conditions, are classed in the chapter on compendia.

Users' Guide to BEA Information. Washington, DC: U.S. Bureau of Economic Analysis, 1988. 28p.

A listing of available publications, tapes, diskettes, etc., available from the BEA.

Index of Items Appearing in the National Income and Product Accounts Tables. Washington, DC: Government Printing Office, 1987. 18p.

A subject index to the items in the National Income and Product Accounts Tables of the U.S. Bureau of Economic Analysis. The index provides access to the most recent statistical tables, to the update in the July issue of the *Survey of Current Business,* and in shortened form to each monthly issue of the *Survey of Current Business.*

Methodology Papers: U.S. National Income and Product Accounts. Washington, DC: Government Printing Office. SuDoc: C59.19:(Nos.)

A continuing report series which examines specific areas of methodology as it applies to the National Income and Product

Accounts (NIPA). The reports contain both narrative and statistical data as well as bibliographic information.

U.S. Bureau of Economic Analysis. *Staff Papers.* Springfield, VA: National Technical Information Service. Irregular. SuDoc: C59,.14:(Nos.)
An ongoing series of reports dealing with research conducted by the U.S. Bureau of Economic Analysis.

Working Papers. Washington, DC: U.S. Bureau of Economic Analysis. Irregular.
An ongoing report series which presents the findings of research and changes or developments in methodology as applied to economic analysis and forecasting, with an emphasis on national income and product accounts and related matters.

Local Area Personal Income. Washington, DC: Government Printing Office. Annual. SuDoc: C59.18:(Years—Vols.)
A series of reports, one a U.S. summary and each of the others a separate regional report, which provide estimates of total and per capita personal income by residence, source, and for industrial units by industry division and place of work. Statistics are provided for States and substate areas, and the timespan covered is approximately five years.

BEA Regional Projections. Washington, DC: Government Printing Office. Irregular. SuDoc: c59.17:
A report which provides forecasts of employment, earnings, personal income and population for the U.S. and for individual States, BEA areas, and MSAs for 199- to 20—. Trend data are provided.

State Personal Income. Washington, DC: Government Printing Office. 1989. 311p. SuDoc: C59.2:In 2/4/989.
A statistical report which provides BEA estimates of personal income arranged by source, region and State, 1929–1987.

Fixed Reproduceable Tangible Wealth in the U.S., 1925–1985. Washington, DC: Government Printing Office, 1987. xxix, 370p. SuDoc: C59.2:W37/925–85.

A report which provides estimates for the years 1925–1985 for private and government capital stocks, and for 1820–1985 for capital investments. The estimates are made on a national income and product accounts basis.

Detailed Input-Output Structure of the U.S. Economy, 1977. Washington, DC: Government Printing Office, 1984. SuDoc: C59.2:In7/977/v.1,2

This report is the most recent in a series of reports which report on the raw materials and processed items which go into each of more than 500 industries, and the final output for each of these industries.

Foreign Direct Investment in the U.S. Benchmark Survey, 1980. Washington, DC: Government Printing Office, 1983. v, 205, 67p. SuDoc: C59.2:F76/980

An irregularly recurring report which provides benchmark statistics for foreign direct investment in the U.S. by industry and country. The benchmark data are updated by an annual report.

U.S. Direct Investment Abroad: Benchmark Survey Data. Washington, DC: Government Printing Office. Irregular. SuDoc: c59.2:In 8/4

A benchmark study which provides statistics on the operations and finances of multinational companies based in the U.S. The statistics in these reports are arranged by regions of the world, country, and industry of both the parent company and the affiliate companies. The information in these reports is based on a mandatory response survey conducted under the *International Investment Survey Act of 1976.* These benchmark statistics are updated by an annual survey.

International Trade Administration

The International Trade Administration was established to promote the international trade and investment position of the U.S. Its programs include overseas trade promotions, expansion of exports, encouragement and facilitation of American firms' entry into world trade, and analyses of U.S. commercial policies with respect to Communist countries. At the local level, assistance is provided through district offices located in over 40 cities and Puerto Rico.

Business America. Washington, DC: Government Printing Office. Biweekly. SuDoc: C61.18

Covers business outlook abroad; domestic business; executive and congressional actions affecting commerce; trade agreements and regulations; U.S. trade exhibits and missions; and information on business opportunities in selected foreign countries.

U.S. Industrial Outlook. Washington, DC: Government Printing Office. Annual. SuDoc: C61.34:(Year.)

Provides actual data and projections for over 200 manufacturing industries. Data on the number of establishments, value of shipments, receipts, value added, employment, trade, and wholesale price indexes are included for most SIC four-digit industries.

In addition to the *U.S. Industrial Outlook,* the ITA issues a number of industry-specific and region specific publications. Chief among these are the following:

Caribbean Basin Initiative Guidebook. Washington, DC: Government Printing Office. Irregular. SuDoc: C61.8/2:

A report on the Development of Business in Caribbean Countries.

Eastern Europe Business Bulletin. Washington, DC: International Trade Administration. Irregular.

A newsletter which contains information on Eastern European trade activities.

Latin American Trade Review: A U.S. Perspective. Washington, DC: U.S. International Trade Administration. Annual. SuDoc: C61.38:(Year.)

A report on the Foreign Trade of Latin American countries which includes Mexico and the Caribbean Basin.

Annual Report of the Foreign Trade Zones Board to the Congress of the U.S. Washington, DC: Government Printing Office. Annual. SuDoc: FTZ 1.1(Year.)

A report of the Free Trade Zones (referred to in the U.S. as Foreign Trade Zones) which provides statistics on the receipt and shipment of foreign and domestic goods. Includes a list of zones with directory information for the operator or grantee.

Competitive Assessment of U.S. Industries. Washington, DC: Government Printing Office. Irregular. SuDoc: C61.2:(CT)
 A series of reports which provide statistics on the trade status of specific U.S. industries from the 1970s with projections to the year 2000.

Construction Review. Washington, DC: Government Printing Office. Bimonthly. SuDoc: C61.37:(Vol. No.—Nos.)
 Provides data on residential and other construction. Includes data on new construction, housing, building permits, costs and prices, construction materials, contract construction employment, and quarterly data on vacancy rates and alteration and repair expenditures. Beginning with Mar./Apr. 1988 the report includes information on residential repairs and improvements.

Correlation: Textile and Apparel Categories with Tariff Schedules of the U.S. Annotated. Washington, DC: U.S. International Trade Administration, Office of Textiles and Apparel. Annual.
 A schedule which cross-references the Textile Agreement Category System (TACS) with the Tariff Schedule of the United States (TSUS) for categories of cotton, wool, man-made fibers, silk blends, and various other vegetable fiber textiles.

Developing Forest Product Markets. Washington, DC: U.S. International Trade Administration, 1985–. Irregular. SuDoc: C61.2:
 A series of reports which analyzes the market for pulp, paper, and solid wood industrial products in various countries from 1970 to the present.

Foreign Direct Investment in the U.S. Washington, DC: Government Printing Office. Annual. SuDoc: C61.25/2:
 A report detailing completed foreign direct and indirect ownership of U.S. business.

Foreign Economic Trends and Their Implications for the U.S.. Washington, DC: Government Printing Office. Annual/Semiannual. SuDoc: c61.11:(Country—Year.)

Each report covers an individual country and provides data on Gross National Product (GNP) or Gross Domestic Product (GDP), production, employment, money, prices, foreign trade, and balance of payments. A narrative overview of the economic impact of these factors on the U.S. is included.

Foreign Regulations Affecting U.S. Textile/Apparel Exports. Washington, DC: U.S. International Trade Administration. Biennial.
   A report which outlines the regulations which affect U.S. textile and apparel exports.

Franchise Opportunities Handbook. Washington, DC: Government Printing Office. Annual. SuDoc: C61.31:(Year.)
   Provides directory-type information for franchising business in the U.S. Includes data on capital required, assistance available, training provided, etc., as well as name, address, description of the operation, number of franchises, and date founded.

Franchising in the Economy. Washington, DC: Government Printing Office. Annual. SuDoc: C61.31/2:(Years.)
   Data on number and sales of franchising organizations, franchisers and franchisees, including location and ownership; ranking by sales and number of units; required investment; kinds of business.

Overseas Business Reports

Marketing in Individual Countries. Washington, DC: Government Printing Office. Irregular. SuDoc: C61.12:(Year—Nos.)
   Each report covers a separate country and reviews its business and economic conditions, market structure, trade practices and policies, and trade outlook.

U.S. General Imports: Customs Import Value. Washington, DC: U.S. International Trade Administration, Office of Textiles and Apparel. Monthly.
   A series of monthly reports on the value of U.S. imports of cotton, wool, man-made fiber and vegetable fiber, and silk blend textile manufactures. Statistics are provided by country of origin, TACS code and TSUSA seven-digit code.

U.S. General Imports of Cotton, Wool, Man-Made Fiber and Vegetable Fiber (Except Cotton and Silk Blend Textiles). Washington, DC: U.S. International Trade Administration, Office of Textiles and Apparel. Monthly.

A monthly report which details imports, quantity and value of the textiles indicated.

U.S. General Imports: Quantity Totals. Washington, DC: U.S. International Trade Administration, Office of Textiles and Apparel. Monthly.

A series of monthly reports, each of which covers a different fiber or textile manufacture. Included are cotton, wool, man-made fiber, vegetable fiber and other textile manufactures. Data are shown by country of origin, TACS code and TSUSA seven-digit code.

U.S. Production, Imports and Import/Production Ratios for Cotton, Wool and Man-Made Fiber Textiles and Apparel. Washington, DC: Government Printing Office. Annual. SuDoc: C61.26:(Year.)

A report on imports of the textiles indicated.

U.S. Trade Performance in the U.S. Washington, DC: Government Printing Office. Annual. SuDoc: C61.28:(Year.)

A report on trade activity, import and export, of the United States. Some trade data for major U.S. trading partners are provided.

U.S. Manufactured Exports and Export-Related Employment: Profiles of the 50 States and 35 Selected Metropolitan Areas. Washington, DC: Government Printing Office. SuDoc: C61.2:EX7/ 18(Year.)

A report which presents statistics on exports of manufactured goods and related employment and establishment subjects.

Minority Business Development Agency

The Minority Business Development Agency was established to develop and coordinate a national program for minority business enterprises.

Federal Agency Performance for Minority Business Development. Washington, DC: Minority Business Development Agency. Annual.

A statistical report which shows individual agency expenditures and funding for minority business enterprise. Includes U.S.D.A., A.I.D., D.O.D., etc.

National Institute of Standards and Technology

The National Institute of Standards and Technology (prior to 1988 the National Bureau of Standards) provides and coordinates the national system of physical, chemical, and materials measurement through the National Measurement Laboratory. In addition, the NIST performs technical work through the National Engineering Laboratory and develops and recommends Federal Information Processing Standards through the Institute for Computer Sciences and Technology.

The National Institute of Standards and Technology also aids small and medium-sized companies in adopting new technologies in order to increase competitiveness and to enhance technology development programs.

Publications of the National Institute of Standards and Technology. Washington, DC: Government Printing Office. Annual. SuDoc: C13.10.305/
An annotated bibliography of the published output of NIST.

GATT Standards Code: Activities of the National Institute of Standards and Technology. Springfield, VA: National Technical Information Service. Annual.
Provides information on activities of NIST with regard to the GATT standards. Includes narrative coverage of GATT and U.S. regulations.

Federal Information Processing Standards Publications. Springfield, VA: National Technical Information Service. Irregular. SuDoc: C13.52:
An ongoing series of individual publications each dealing with a particular Federal government information related standard.

National Oceanic and Atmospheric Administration

Among its principal functions NOAA reports the weather of the U.S. and its possessions and provides weather forecasts to the general public; conducts an integrated program of management, research, and services related to the protection and rational use of living marine resources; issues nautical and aeronautical charts; provides precise geodetic surveys; and provides Federal leadership in coastal zone management.

National Environmental Satellite, Data and Information Service

Weekly Weather and Crop Bulletin. Washington, DC: Department of Agriculture, Agricultural Weather Facility. Weekly. SuDoc: C55.209:(V. Nos. & Nos.)

A joint publication of NOAA and the USDA, this report provides data on the effect of current weather conditions on the agricultural activity for each State and Puerto Rico and summary data for selected world regions.

Monthly State, Regional and National Heating/Cooling Degree Days Weighted by Population. Washington, DC: National Climatic Data Center. Monthly. SuDoc: C55.287/60:(No. Date.)

Separate reports on heating and cooling degree days arranged by State and Census division. Biennial reports entitled *Historical Climatological Series* provide historical trend data.

Monthly Climatic Data for the World. Washington, DC: National Climatic Data Center. Monthly. SuDoc: C55.211:(V. Nos. & Nos.)

A monthly summary of climatic data collected for weather stations around the world.

Storm Data. Washington, DC: National Climatic Data Center. Monthly. SuDoc: C55.212:(V. Nos. & Nos.)

A monthly listing with maps of storms and other unusual weather activity within the U.S., Puerto Rico, the Virgin Islands, and the Pacific.

Comparative Climatic Data for the U.S. Washington, DC: National Climatic Data Center. Annual. SuDoc: C61/2:(Year.)

A compendium of monthly average weather data for weather stations in the U.S. and outlying areas.

National Marine Fisheries Service (NOAA)

Marine Fisheries Review. Washington, DC: Government Printing Office. Quarterly. SuDoc: C55.310:(V. Nos. & Nos.)
   Contains articles and statistics on U.S. and foreign fishery activities.

Current Fishery Statistics. Washington, DC: Government Printing Office. Annual. SuDoc: C55.309/2–10:(Year.)
   A report which provides statistics in summary fashion for imports and exports of fishery products and, in a separate report, for processed fishery products.

Fisheries of the U.S. Washington, DC: Government Printing Office. Annual. SuDoc: C555.309/2–2:(Year.)
   Data on U.S. fisheries. Includes information on landings, trade, prices, consumption, production, employment, etc.

Foreign Fishery Information Releases. Washington, DC: National Marine Fisheries Service. Semimonthly.
   A press release issued as a supplement to the market news report which provides statistics on Japanese fishing activities.

Fishery Publication Index, 1980–1985, Technical Memorandum Index 1972–1985. Springfield, VA: National Technical Information Service. Irregular.
   A bibliography of publications in series and technical memoranda in series from the National Marine Fisheries Service.

   In addition to the above, the National Marine Fisheries Service issues a number of reports dealing with specific fishery products. Among these reports are the following:

Frozen Fishery Products. Washington, DC: National Marine Fisheries Service. Monthly/Annual Summary. SuDoc. C555.309/2–8:(Nos.)

Fish Meal and Oil. Washington, DC: National Marine Fisheries Service. Quarterly. SuDoc: C55.309/2–7:(Nos.)

Fishery Market News Reports. Washington, DC: National Marine Fisheries Service. Weekly.

A separate report is issued for New York (N series), Boston (B series), New Orleans (O series), Terminal Island (T series), and Seattle (SW series).

National Technical Information Service (NTIS)

NTIS is a Federal publishing entity with responsibility for publishing technical reports and other information, with particular emphasis on published output done under government contract. *Government Reports Announcements and Index.* (see pps. 380–381 for annotation).

Directory of Computer Software. Springfield, VA: National Technical Information Service. Annual. SuDoc: C51.11/2:
A listing of software available from NTIS. A separate database directory is also issued.

Directory of Federal Laboratory and Technology Resources. Springfield, VA: National Technical Information Service. Biennial. SuDoc: C51.19/2–2
A listing of Federal laboratories and research facilities for private sectors use.

Patent and Trademark Office

The PTO administers the patent system and the trademark registration system for the U.S.

CASSIS (Classification and Search Support Information System). [Online Database].
A database which contains U.S. Patent Classification System (PCS) titles and also includes subject terms and patent procedures. Available at Patent Depository Libraries.

Patents

Official Gazette of the United States Patent and Trademark Office. Patents. Washington, DC: Government Printing Office. Weekly.

A weekly list of patents issued by the PTO. The index is published separately as *Index of Patents Issued from the United States Patent and Trademark Office*. Washington, DC: Government Printing Office. Annual.

Trademarks

Official Gazette of the United States Patent and Trademark Office. Trademarks. Washington, DC: Government Printing Office. Weekly.

A weekly list of trademarks registered and renewed with the PTO. The index is published separately as *Index of Trademarks Issued from the United States Patent and Trademark Office*. Washington, DC: Government Printing Office. Annual.

U.S. Travel and Tourism Administration

The Administration is responsible for advising the Secretary of Commerce on the formulation and execution of policy affecting the American tourism industry. The Administration also maintains trade development, trade policy and statistical research programs relating to the travel industry.

Summary and Analysis of International Travel to the U.S. Washington, DC: U.S. Travel and Tourism Administration. Monthly. SuDoc: C47.15·(Date.)

A report which indicates by world area and selected country of residence the number of foreign visitors to the U.S. and characteristics of their trip. An annual report is also published which provides statistics on travel and tourism to the U.S.

Outlook for International Travel to and from the U.S. Washington, DC: U.S. Travel and Tourism Administration. Annual.

A forecast of international travel between the U.S. and Canada, Mexico, and other countries.

In-Flight Survey of International Air Travelers. Washington, DC: U.S. Travel and Tourism Administration. Annual.

A brief statistical report on U.S. resident overseas air travel. Report is by State and city of origin. A similar report is done for overseas visitors traveling to the U.S.

Analysis of International Air Travel to and from the U.S. on U.S. and Foreign Flag Carriers. Washington, DC: U.S. Travel and Tourism Administration. Annual.

A statistical report on the market share for travel to and from the U.S.

Pleasure Travel Markets to North America. Washington, DC: U.S. Travel and Tourism Administration. Irregular.

A series of reports, each dealing with a separate world area and each of which is compiled by Market Facts of Canada, Ltd. The reports provide statistics and information based on surveys of adults who had taken or plan to take a vacation by air transport away from their home country.

Marketing U.S. Tourism Abroad. Washington, DC: Government Printing Office. Annual. SuDoc: C47.20:

A report with statistics on marketing programs sponsored by U.S.T.T.A.

Impact of Foreign Tourism on U.S. Industries. Washington, DC: U.S. Travel and Tourism Administration. Irregular.

A series of reports, four in number, which provide statistics on the effect of travel on the lodging industry, airline industry, inter-city bus industry, and auto rental industry. The first series of reports covered the years 1983–1986.

DEPARTMENT OF DEFENSE

The Department of Defense (DOD) has responsibility for timely and acceptable delivery of approved weapons systems, subsystems, munitions and equipment. In addition, the DOD has responsibility for defense-related procurement, production, supply, installations, construction, real property, facilities, housing, maintenance, transportation, distribution, support, real and personal property disposal, etc.

The Defense Logistics Agency provides current and potential suppliers of DOD materials and purchasers of DOD surplus with a variety of publications necessary for the efficient marketing of products to the DOD or the efficient purchase of materials from the DOD. Publications are issued with information geared to both large and small marketers.

Manpower Statistics

Selected Manpower Statistics. Washington, DC: Government Printing Office. Annual. SuDoc: D1.61/4:
  A detailed annual report on current and historical military manpower statistics. A separate quarterly report provides global manpower distribution statistics and another quarterly report details certain manpower statistics.

Defense Contracting

Prime Contract Awards. Washington, DC: Government Printing Office. Semi-annual. SuDoc: D1.57/3:(Year.)
  A statistical report which indicates the value of military contracts and other military expenditures. A similar report is issued on a semi-annual basis which lists prime contract awards by State. A separate quarterly report covering subcontractors is also published.

Guide to the Preparation of Offers for Selling to the Military. Washington, DC: Government Printing Office. Irregular. SuDoc: D1.6/2: Se4
  A how-to manual for preparing bids and proposals for Department of Defense contracts for amounts less than $25,000.

Federal Acquisition Regulations, Digest and Cross Index. 1983 with Supplements. Washington, DC: Government Printing Office. SuDoc: GS1.6/6:AC7 and D1.6/2:AC 7/2.
  A looseleaf service which includes acquisition regulators for both DOD and GSA.

DOD FAR Supplement. Washington, DC: Government Printing Office. 1986/Supplements. SuDoc: D 1.6:
  The definitive source for guidelines on all aspects of DOD contracting. Similar sources are available for NASA and the Department of the Army.

In addition to the publications above, the DOD publishes a number of regularly recurring reports, most with limited distribution, dealing with the number and variety of contracts awarded. Two such reports are the annual *100 Companies: Companies Having the Largest Dollar Volume of Military Prime Contract Awards* and *500 Contractors Receiving the Largest Dollar Volume of Prime Contract Awards for Research, Development, Testing and Evaluation.*

A number of commercially available databases are produced by DMS, a subsidiary of Janes' Information Group, which provide information on military contracts available and awarded.

Surplus Property—Real Property

How to Buy Surplus Personal Property from the Department of Defense. Irregular. Washington, DC: Government Printing Office.

Real and Personal Property. Washington, DC: Government Printing Office. Annual. SuDoc: D1.58/2:(Year.)
A listing of land and other property under the direction of the DOD.

Strategic Materials

Strategic and Critical Materials Report to the Congress . . . Washington, DC: Department of Defense. Semi-annual.
A listing of the commodities considered strategic or critical under the strategic and Critical Materials Stockpiling Act.

United States Coast Guard

The Coast Guard includes within its many functions commercial vessel safety, which includes administering vessel documentation laws, employment, and records of employment of merchant marine personnel, etc. It is also the primary maritime law enforcement agency for the United States and enforces or assists in enforcement of applicable Federal laws, treaties and other international agreements, and works with other Federal agencies in the suppression of smuggling and illicit drug trafficking.

Boating Statistics. Washington, DC: United States Coast Guard. Annual. SuDoc: TD5.11:(Year.)
Provides statistics on boat numbering registration and accidents.

Department of the Army. Corps of Engineers

The Corps of Engineers has major responsibility for federal water revenues development.

Waterborne Commerce of the United States. New Orleans, LA: U.S. Army Engineer District. Annual. SuDoc: D103.1/2:(Year./Pt.—Nos.)
Provides information on the commercial movement of freight, passengers, and vessels. The report deals primarily with domestic freight movements by detailed commodity within or between coastal and noncontiguous U.S. ports, on inland waterways, and on the Great Lakes.
The report is issued in five separately bound parts, one for each of four regions and a national summary.

Department of the Navy

The Department of the Navy produces a number of publications relating to military contracts let by the Navy.
In addition to its contracting activities, the Department of the Navy maintains databases covering time and astronomical data (U.S. Naval Observatory Automated Data Service) and engineering and technical information (Government Industry Data Exchange Program GIDEP).

Navy Contracting

Survey of Contracting Statistics. Washington, DC: Department of the Navy. Annual. SuDoc: D201.6/14:(Year.)
Provides data on Navy contracting. Includes information on major contractors and on small business participation.

Navy Small and Disadvantaged Business Personnel Directory. Washington, DC: Department of the Navy. Annual.

Provides a listing of Navy Department personnel and officers that can be contacted for assistance by small or disadvantaged business contractors seeking Navy procurement contracts.

Maritime Administration

The Administration conducts research and development activities to improve the efficiency and economy of the merchant marine.

Vessel Inventory Report. Washington, DC: Maritime Administration. Semi-annual. SuDoc: TD11.11:(Year.)
A listing of U.S. merchant ships of 1,000 tons or more and ships which are in the National Defense Rescue Fleet.

Defense Security Assistance Agency

The Defense Security Assistance Agency (DSAA) directly administers and supervises the execution of approved security assistance plans and programs, such as military assistance and foreign military sales.

Foreign Military Sales, Foreign Military Construction Sales, and Military Assistance Facts. Washington, DC: Department of Defense. Annual. SuDoc: D1.66:(Year.)
Provides data on grants and sales of military arms, equipment, and training to allied and friendly governments.

DEPARTMENT OF EDUCATION

The Department of Education establishes Federal policy and approved programs, coordinates Federal assistance to education, and supports educational research. Its activities encompass levels from elementary to postsecondary, as well as vocational, adult, and special education. Data are gathered from both the public and private sectors.

Directory of ERIC Information Service Providers. Bethesda, MD: ERIC Processing and Reference Facility. 1986. 94p.

A listing of facilities in the U.S. and abroad that offer ERIC access and maintain ERIC collections.

Center For Education Statistics

The Center for Education Statistics collects and disseminates statistics and other data related to education in the United States and in other nations. It coordinates the information-gathering activities for education programs and performs special analyses and disseminates the statistical data so gathered.

Current and Forthcoming Publications. Washington, DC: Center for Education Statistics. 3/yr.
A listing of publications, data tapes and other published formats issued by the Center.

Libraries

Public Libraries in States. Washington, DC: Center for Education Statistics. Annual.
A statistical report on the number of libraries and related staff and service for libraries in NCES Federal-State Cooperative System for Public Libraries.

Education Statistics

Condition of Education. Washington, DC: Government Printing Office. Annual. SuDoc: ED1.109:(Year./Vol.—Nos.)
Provides detailed data on enrollment, faculty, administration, finances, public and professional opinion of education, etc.

Digest of Education Statistics. Washington, DC: Government Printing Office. Annual. SuDoc: ED1.326:(Year.)
Provides a compilation of statistical data on all places of educational activity at all levels from nursery school through graduate school. Data are included for public and nonpublic schools.

Projections of Education Statistics. Washington, DC: Government Printing Office. Annual. SuDoc: ED1.120:(Year.)

Provides ten-year projections of data on enrollment, staffing, graduates, expenditures, etc., for elementary and secondary schools and institutions of higher education. Trend data are included.

Key Statistics on Public, Elementary, and Secondary Education Reported by State and Geographic Region. Washington, DC: National Center for Education Statistics. Annual.

Provides statistics on enrollment, expenditures, etc., for public elementary and secondary educational institutions. A separate annual report on dropout rates is issued.

Fall Enrollment in Institution of Higher Education. Washington, DC: National Center for Education Statistics. Annual.

Provides statistics on fall enrollment in institutions of higher education and includes information by student characteristics.

Education Directories

Directory of Post-Secondary Institutions. Washington, DC: Government Printing Office. Annual. SuDoc: ED1.111/4:

A directory of universities, and colleges at the four-year level and two-year or community or junior college levels, technical institutes, and occupationally oriented vocational schools in the United States and its outlying areas.

A national longitudinal study on post-secondary education is conducted on an ongoing basis with relevant reports issued.

Directory of Public and Elementary and Secondary Education Agencies. Washington, DC: Government Printing Office. Annual. SuDoc: ED1.111/2:(Year.)

A directory of public education agencies in the United States and outlying areas which provides location information and other relevant data.

Education Directory: Colleges and Universities. Washington, DC: Government Printing Office. Annual. SuDoc: ED1.111:

A list of accredited institutions offering at least a one-year college level program. Each listing provides full directory information including information on demographics of enrollment, religious affiliations, costs, etc.

DEPARTMENT OF ENERGY

The Department of Energy was established, effective October 1, 1977, to bring together national energy activities. The major federal energy functions consolidated into the DOE were all the responsibilities of the Energy Research and Development Administration (ERDA); the Federal Energy Administration (FEA); the Federal Power Commission (FPC); and administrative units, functions, and statistical reporting activities transferred from the Department of the Interior and other departments and agencies.

The Energy Information Administration is the unit within the DOE which is responsible for the timely and accurate collection, processing and publication of energy-related data.

Analysis Reports. Washington, DC: Government Printing Office. Irregular. SuDoc: E3.2:

A series of reports dealing with energy-related topics and the impact of energy-related issues on the economy and the environment. These reports, some of which are available from NTIS and others from GPO, are frequently issued in response to congressional or Federal agency request or public interest.

Service Reports. Washington, DC: Energy Information Administration. Irregular.

A series of reports which examine the supply and demand of energy-generating services and other impacts of these services on the economy.

Assessment of the Quality of Selected EIA Data Series. Washington, DC: Energy Information Administration. Irregular.

An ongoing series of reports which look at EIA data from the point of view of methodology, accuracy and comparability with commercially published data.

Energy

Monthly Energy Review. Washington, DC: Government Printing Office. Monthly. SuDoc: E3.9:(Date.)

Provides data on production, consumption, stocks, trade, and prices of principal energy resources. Information is also included on electric power production, sales and prices, and on oil and gas exploration.

An annual report on energy consumption and sources for individual States is also issued.

Long Range Energy Projections to 2010. Washington, DC: Government Printing Office. Biennial. SuDoc: E1.81:0082

A projection of U.S. and other countries' energy prices, supply, and demand. Includes trend data from 1960.

A quarterly short-term energy outlook report is also published.

U.S. Energy Industry Financial Developments. Washington, DC: Energy Information Administration. Quarterly.

A report which presents financial statistics for all aspects of the energy industry.

Forecast of Likely U.S. Energy Supply/Demand Balances. Springfield, VA: National Technical Information Service. Irregular.

An ongoing series of studies which present statistics and projections to the year 2000 of the supply and demand for energy. Statistics are included for sources and use.

Coal

Weekly Coal Production. Washington, DC: Government Printing Office. Weekly. SuDoc: E3.11/4:

Includes anthracite and bituminous coal and legunite.

Gas

Natural Gas Monthly. Washington, DC: Government Printing Office. Monthly. SuDoc: E3.11:

Includes natural gas and supplemental gas as well as pipeline activity.

A separate annual report is issued on interstate natural gas pipeline companies.

Electric Power

Electric Power Annual. Washington, DC: Government Printing Office. Annual. SuDoc: E3.11/17–10

Includes data on capacity of power plants, fuel use, emissions and finances. A separate annual report is issued on financial statistics of electric utilities and another report is issued on production costs and expenses.

Inventory of Power Plants in the U.S. Washington, DC: Government Printing Office. Annual. SuDoc: E3.29:
A detailed directory of electric power plants in operation and planning.

Petroleum

Gas Mileage Guide: EPA Fuel Economy Estimates. Washington, DC: Department of Energy. Annual. SuDoc: DOE/CE-0019/8
An annual report on the results of fuel economy tests on new model cars and light trucks. A separate report is issued on energy use in the transportation industry.

Petroleum Marketing Monthly. Washington, DC: Government Printing Office. Monthly. SuDoc: E3.13/14
A report on sales and prices of petroleum products. A separate monthly report is issued on petroleum supply with an annual cumulation.

International Petroleum Statistics. Washington, DC: Government Printing Office. Monthly. SuDoc: E3.11:
A report on oil production, consumption, reserves, etc. worldwide.
A separate quarterly report is issued on new discoveries of oil and gas worldwide.

Uranium

Uranium Industry Annual. Washington, DC: Government Printing Office. Annual. SuDoc: E3.46/5:
A report on reserves, mining and related activities for the uranium industry. Includes projections.

Typical Electric Bills. Washington, DC: Government Printing Office. Annual. SuDoc: E3.22:

A report on the rates charged for electric energy for residential service as well as for commercial or industrial service.

Nuclear Power

Nuclear Reactors Built, Being Built or Planned. Springfield, VA: National Technical Information Service. Annual. SuDoc: E1.28:(DOE/OSD-8200-R-51)
An inventory of all nuclear reactors built, under construction or planned for construction, shut down or dismantled.

DEPARTMENT OF HEALTH AND HUMAN SERVICES

The Department of Health and Human Services was established to administer Federal government programs in the areas of health, welfare and income security, and to advise the President in these areas.
The National Center for Health Statistics and the National Institutes of Health, also with the Centers for Disease Control, are major generators of statistical information concerning health issues.

Catalogs and Indexes

The National Library of Medicine produces MEDLINE, a database which provides access to worldwide biomedical literature, and a series of specialized databases relating to specific areas of health information.

Clearinghouse Bibliography on Health Indexes. Washington, DC: Government Printing Office. Quarterly. SuDoc: HE20.6216/2-2:
A bibliography of articles, reports and other published information on health-related subjects.

NCHS Publication Note: Publications Issued. Hyattsville, MD: National Center for Health Statistics. Quarterly. SuDoc: HE20.6216/3:
A bibliography of NCHS publication. An annual catalog is also issued and a catalog of data tapes is issued irregularly.

NIH Publications List. Bethesda, MD: National Institutes of Health. Annual. SuDoc:
A bibliography of NIH publications.

International Health Data Reference Guide. Washington, DC: National Center for Health Statistics. Biennial. SuDoc: HE20:6208/13:
A listing of the varieties of health statistics published by the U.S. and foreign countries.

Health—General

Prevention. Federal Programs and Progress. Washington, DC: Government Printing Office. Biennial. SuDoc: HE20.29:
A report on programs in health-related areas, sponsored by the Federal government.

Health, U.S. Washington, DC: Government Printing Office. Annual. SuDoc: HE20.6223:
A general compendium of statistics on health care, prevention techniques and related health issues.

HHS Data Inventory. Washington, DC: Department of Health and Human Services. Irregular.
A listing of HHS programs.

Area Resource File. Hyattsville, MD: Health Resources Administration, Bureau of Health Professions. SuDoc: HE20.9302:Ar3/(Year.)
A computerized system that provides health resources data for counties, State economic areas, MSAs, or a combination of areas.

Public Health Reports. Washington, DC: Government Printing Office. Bimonthly. SuDoc: HE20.30:
A periodical which covers all aspects of public health.

Vital Statistics

National Committee on Vital and Health Statistics. Washington, DC: Public Health Service. Annual.
A listing of members is included in this report.

Monthly Vital Statistics Report. Hyattsville, MD: National Center for Health Statistics. Monthly/Annual. SuDoc: HE20:6217:(V. Nos. and Nos.)
A report which provides provisional statistics on births, marriages,

divorces, and deaths. Estimates for the U.S. as a whole are included, as are estimated death rates by age, color, sex, and causes. Data appear approximately two months after cover date of issue. An annual summary of this report is issued approximately ten months after the year's end.

An ongoing series of supplements to the *Monthly Vital Statistics Report* which provide advance final data on marriage, divorce, natality, and mortality are also issued.

Morbidity and Mortality, Weekly Report. Washington, DC: Government Printing Office. SuDoc: HE20.7009:

Provides data on specific notifiable diseases, deaths in cities, and related data. A separate index issue is published and also an annual which provides breakdowns by various characteristics and shows geographic distribution.

Advance Data from Vital and Health Statistics of the National Center for Health Statistics. Hyattsville, MD: National Center for Health Statistics. Irregular. SuDoc: HE20.6209/3:

Provides early release data derived from NCHS surveys and collections.

Vital and Health Statistics Series. Washington, DC: Government Printing Office. Irregular. SuDoc: HE20.6209:

A collection of 18 series of reports which provide narrative and statistical data from the National Vital Statistics System and the National Health Survey. The 18 series currently published are listed below:

Programs and Collection Procedures. (Series 1).
Data Evaluation and Methods Research. (Series 2).
Analytical and Epidemiological Studies (Series 3).
Documents and Committee Reports. (Series 4).
Data from National Health Interview Survey. (Series 10).
Data from the Health and Nutrition Examination Survey. (Series 11).
Data on Health Resources Utilization. (Series 13).
Data on Health Resources: Manpower and Facilities. (Series 14).
Data from Special Surveys. (Series 15).

Data on Mortality. (Series 20).
Data on Natality, Marriage, and Divorce. (Series 21).
Data from the National Survey of Family Growth. (Series 23).
  Comparative International Vital and Health Statistics Reports.
  (Series 5).
Cognition and Survey Measurement. (Series 6).
Data from the Institutionalized Population Surveys. (Series 12).
Compilations of Advanced Data from Vital and Health Statistics.
  (Series 16).
Data from the National Mortality and Natality Surveys.
  (Series 22).
Compilations of Data on Natality, Mortality, Marriages, Divorce
  and Induced Terminations of Pregnancy. (Series 24).

Vital Statistics of the U.S. Washington, DC: Government Printing
Office. Annual. SuDoc: HE20.6210:(year. V.)
  Provides final, complete tabulation of data on natality, mortality,
marriage, and divorce. Data are published in multi-volume sets three
to four years after cover date. Trend data, explanatory material, and
technical information including sources, explanation of terminology,
etc., are included with each volume. These are issued as the
following:

Vol. I. *Natality.*
Vol. II. *Mortality.* Part A and B. Part A: final tabulation of all
  deaths registered in the U.S. Part B: geographic breakdown of
  deaths for each state, county, MSA and town of 10,000 or more,
  metropolitan-nonmetropolitan areas, Guam, Puerto Rico and
  the Virgin Islands.
Vol. III. *Marriage and Divorce.*

  Abridged life tables are included in Vol. II, Part A and are also
available separately.

Health Care Costs

Health Care Financing Review. Washington, DC: Government Printing Office. Quarterly/Annual. SuDoc: HE22.18:
  Articles and statistics on all aspects of health care financing,
especially Medicare and Medicaid.

NCHSR and HCTA Research Reports. Springfield, VA: National Technical Information Service. Irregular. SuDoc: HE20.6512:
A series of detailed reports on health services and health insurance.

National Medical Expenditure Survey. Washington, DC: U.S. Department of Health and Human Services. Irregular.
A series which reports the findings of the National Medical Expenditure survey. Includes insurance statistics.

Health Care Financing Program Statistics: Medicare and Medicaid Data Book. Washington, DC: Government Printing Office. Biennial. SuDoc: HE22.19/4
A detailed report on Medicare and Medicaid programs. Medicaid data are by State. An annual HFCA statistical report is also issued.

Annual Medicare Program Statistics. Washington, DC: U.S. Department of Health and Human Service. Annual.
A detailed report on Medicare including usage and enrollment statistics. A separate report is issued on the Federal Medical Issuance Trust Fund.

Health Care Financing Status Report. Research and Demonstration in Health Care Financing. Washington, DC: U.S. Department of Health and Human Service. Annual. SuDoc: HE22.16/2
A directory of research projects in health care financing areas.

Tobacco, Alcohol and Drug Abuse

Health Consequences of Smoking. Washington, DC: Government Printing Office. Annual. SuDoc: HE20.7614:
Provides worldwide review of the literature on the health consequences of smoking. Constitutes the report of the Surgeon General on the relationship of smoking and health. The title of this report varies.

Drug Use, Drinking and Smoking . . . Washington, DC: Government Printing Office. Annual. SuDoc: HE20.8202:
A report based on University of Michigan Institute for Social Research data on the use of illicit drugs, alcohol and cigarettes by young adults. A separate report on use of these substances based on the National Household Survey of Drug Abuse is also issued.

Mental Health

Mental Health U.S. Washington, DC: Government Printing Office.
Biennial. SuDoc: HE20.8137
   A statistical compilation on mental disorders and treatment and
care issues. An annual report is issued reporting the number of
patients in mental care facilities.

Infectious Diseases

HIV/AIDS Surveillance. Washington, DC: U.S. Department of
Health and Human Services. Monthly.
   A statistical summary of cases reported to the Centers for Disease
Control. Includes data on transmission and patient characteristics.

Tuberculosis Statistics in the U.S. Washington, DC: U.S. Department of
Health and Human Services. Annual. SuDoc: HE20.7310
   A detailed report on the incidence and death rate from tuberculosis
by State and city.

Prescription Drugs

Drug Utilization in the U.S. Springfield, VA: National Technical
Information Service. Annual.
   A statistical report on the use of prescription drugs. Includes data
on new drugs.

Population Research

Inventory and Analysis of Federal Population Research. Washington, DC:
U.S. Department of Health and Human Services. Annual. SuDoc:
HE20.3362/2
   A detailed report on Federal biological and serial population
research programs. Includes a list of projects by subject.

Social Programs

Social Security Bulletin. Washington, DC: Government Printing
Office. Monthly. SuDoc: HE3.3;(V. nos. and nos.)

A compilation of articles and statistical data providing up-to-date information on social security-related matters. Some tables are published monthly, others appear on a quarterly basis. Includes data on benefits, beneficiaries, supplemental security income, public assistance, unemployment insurance, Medicare, etc. Separate indexes to the *Bulletin* have been issued covering 1938–79 and 1980–88, and an annual statistical supplement is regularly issued with a biennial report on world social security systems.

Income of the Population 55 and Over. Washington, DC: Government Printing Office. Biennial. SuDoc: HE3.75:
A report on over-55 income, with demographic statistics. A separate report is issued on *Supplemental Security Income,* and a series of actuarial studies is issued which project costs for social security programs.

Characteristics of State Plans for Aid to Families with Dependent Children . . . Washington, DC: U.S. Department of Health and Human Services.
A detailed report for each State, District of Columbia, Puerto Rico, Guam and the Virgin Islands on receipts and payments. A separate annual report provides financial and demographic statistics for recipients of AFDC aid.

Quarterly Public Assistance Statistics. Washington, DC: U.S. Department of Health and Human Services. Annual.
A report on AFDC and State public welfare recipients. Data is provided by State and outlying area.

Financial Assistance by Geographic Area. Washington, DC: U.S. Department of Health and Human Services. Annual. SuDoc: HE1.57
A series of regional reports which detail governments and institutions receiving Federal domestic assistance.

DEPARTMENT OF HOUSING AND URBAN DEVELOPMENT

The Department of Housing and Urban Development (HUD) was created to administer the principal Federal programs for housing assistance; community development—urban, suburban, and metropolitan; promotion of interstate, regional, and metropolitan cooperation; encouragement of private homebuilding; and mortgage lending.

Mortgage Activity

Survey of Mortgage-Related Security Holdings of Major Institutions. Washington, DC: U.S. Department of Housing and Urban Development. Quarterly. SuDoc: HH1.99/4–2

A statement of residential mortgage investments held by banks, pension funds, savings and loans, insurance companies, etc.

Survey of Mortgage Lending Activity. Washington, DC: U.S. Department of Housing and Urban Development. Monthly. SuDoc: HH1.99

A press release which details loan activities of major financial groups such as pension funds, savings and loans, banks, insurance companies, etc. A separate press release is issued monthly on secondary market home loan interest rates and yields.

FHA Single Family Trends: Statistical Highlights. Washington, DC: U.S. Department of Housing and Urban Development. Monthly.

A report which provides statistics on the number and financing of new FHA mortgage applications and related activity.

Urban Issues

President's National Urban Policy Report. Washington, DC: U.S. Department of Housing and Urban Development. Biennial. SuDoc: HH1.75:988

A compendium of statistical and narrative information on urban issues and policy.

Report on Homeless Assistance Policy and Practice in the Nation's Five Largest Cities. Washington, DC: U.S. Department of Housing and Urban Development; August, 1989. SuDoc: HH1.2:H75/27

This report presents statistics on assistance programs in New York City, Philadelphia, Los Angeles, Chicago, and Houston which are directed to the homeless.

Report on the 1988 National Survey of Shelters for the Homeless. Washington, DC: U.S. Department of Housing and Urban Development, 1989. 53p. SuDoc: HH1.2:H75/24

This report presents the findings of the National Survey of Shelters for the Homeless conducted in 1988. Included are demographic and health and social characteristics of the homeless in shelters and size and service information on shelters.

DEPARTMENT OF THE INTERIOR

The Department of the Interior has responsibility for most of our nationally owned public lands and natural resources. As our principal conservation agency, the Department assesses our mineral resources and works to assure their development in the interest of all our people.

Bureau of Mines

The Bureau of Mines is primarily a research and fact-finding agency. Its goal is to stimulate private industry to produce a substantial share of the nation's mineral needs in ways that best protect the public interest.

The Bureau collects, compiles, analyzes, and publishes statistical and economic information on all phases of mineral resource development.

New Publications. Washington, DC: Government Printing Office. Monthly. SuDoc: I28.5/2:

A checklist of publications issued by the Bureau of Mines.

Mineral Commodities

Minerals and Materials: A Bimonthly Survey. Washington, DC: Government Printing Office. Bimonthly. SuDoc: I28.149/2:

Provides information on mineral commodities including iron, nickel, manganese, chromium, cobalt, aluminum, copper, tin, zinc, lead, platinum group metals, gold, and silver. Data supplied include production, consumption, foreign trade, inventories, and representative prices.

Mineral Commodity Summaries. Pittsburgh, Pa: Bureau of Mines. Annual. SuDoc: I28.148:(yr.)

Provides the earliest Federal government-published summary of industry profiles under one cover, for over 90 mineral commodities. Includes, for each commodity, data production and use, trade, demand, stocks, employment, recycling, end use, U.S. tariffs and fee schedules, government programs, price, world industry developments, production, reserves and resources, and substitute and alternate commodities.

Monthly and quarterly data on individual commodities are published in *Mineral Industry Surveys* and annual data are published in the *Minerals Yearbook.*

Mineral Industry Surveys. Pittsburgh, Pa.: Bureau of Mines. Monthly/ Quarterly/ Annual. SuDoc: I28.(no,.):

A series of reports, each on an individual commodity, provide a brief overview of the commodity and data on its production, stocks, shipments, domestic consumption, exports/imports by country, and, at times, prices.

Fuel released reports in this series have been transferred to the Energy Information Administration.

Monthly reports include the following:

Aluminum industry	Molybdenum
Cement	Nickel
Chromium	Sulfur
Cobalt	Tin Industry
Copper Industry	Tungsten
Gold and Silver	Vanadium
Iron and Steel Scrap	Zinc Industry
Iron Ore	Marketable Phosphate Rock
Lead Industry	Gypsum
Lime	Soda Ash and Sodium Sulfate
Manganese	Silicon

Quarterly reports include the following:

Antimony	Feldspar
Bauxite and Alumina	Fluorspar
Bismuth	Manganese
Cadmium	Mercury

Crushed Stone and Sand and   Platinum Group Metals
    Gravel   Titanium

Annual and biennial reports are also published for a number of commodities and more detailed data appear later in the *Minerals Yearbook, Vol. I: Metals and Minerals.*

Minerals Yearbook. Washington, DC: Government Printing Office. Annual. SuDoc: I28.37/:
Detailed narrative and statistical overview of the mineral industry, both domestic and international. The format of the yearbook is as follows:

Vol. I. *Metals and Minerals.* Data on U.S. and world production, consumption, and trade in all metals and minerals important to the U.S. economy.
Vol. II. *Area Reports: Domestic.* Data by State on metal and mineral industry production, sales, and employment by commodity.
Vol. III. *Area Reports: International.* Data by country on mineral industry policies, production, and trade by commodity.

All volumes of the *Minerals Yearbook* are preceded by preprints of individual chapters issued by the Bureau of Mines.

Mineral Position of the U.S.: (Year). A Report of Progress. Annual Report of the Secretary of the Interior Under the Mining and Minerals Policy Act of 1970. Washington, DC: U.S. Department of the Interior. Annual. SuDoc: I1.96/3:
An annual summary of the status of production of metals and nonfuel minerals, imports of minerals into the U.S., and consumption of minerals.

International Strategic Minerals Inventory Summary Reports. Washington, DC: Government Printing Office. Irregular. SuDoc: I19.4/2:
A series of reports on strategic mineral commodities throughout the world.

Federal Offshore Statistics: Leasing, Exploration, Production, and Revenues. Washington, DC: U.S. Department of the Interior. Annual. SuDoc: I72.10:

A statistical and narrative report on oil, gas, and mineral deposits administered by the Minerals Management Service. Includes statistics on revenues, leasing activities, exploration, production, and development.

Sub-agencies of the Department of the Interior have responsibility for topographic surveys, public lands use and recreational activities within public lands.

Geological Survey

New Publications of the U.S. Geological Survey. Washington, DC: U.S. Department of the Interior. Monthly. SuDoc: I19.42:(date).
A bibliography of USGS publications and articles by USGS writers in other sources. An annual catalog is also issued.

Public Lands

Public Land Statistics, (Year). Washington, DC: U.S. Department of the Interior. Annual. SuDoc: I53.1/2:
A statistical and narrative report on the use, administration, acquisition and disposition of public lands and other natural resources under the jurisdiction of the Bureau of Land Management.

Recreation

National Survey of Fishing, Hunting and Wildlife Associated Recreation. Washington, DC: U.S. Department of the Interior. Annual. SuDoc: I49.98:
An annual report on the extent of hunting and fishing and related wildlife activities such as photography, wildlife observation, and feeding.
A separate annual report on recreation fees collected by the Federal government is also available.

DEPARTMENT OF JUSTICE

Among its many responsibilities the Department of Justice is charged with enforcing the Federal antitrust laws, instituting civil and criminal proceedings in cases of unfair or deceptive consumer practices referred by other agencies to the Department, and enforcing immigration and naturalization laws.

Crime and Criminals

Sourcebook of Criminal Justice Statistics, (Year). Washington, DC: Government Printing Office, Annual. SuDoc: J29.9/6:
   A statistical compendium of information related to crime, crime prevention and criminal justice. Includes trend data.

Compendium of Federal Justice Statistics, (Year). Washington, DC: U.S. Department of Justice. Annual. SuDoc: J29.20:
   A report on the number and disposition of Federal criminal cases.

Bureau of Justice Statistics Bulletin. Washington, DC: U.S. Department of Justice. Irregular. SuDoc: J29.11
   An ongoing series of statistical reports on crime, criminals and victims.
   A separate annual report is issued which lists and describes Bureau of Justice Statistics programs and reports.

   A major source of statistical data on crime and criminals is the Federal Bureau of Investigation.

Federal Bureau of Investigation

   The FBI is the principal investigative arm of the Department of Justice.

Uniform Crime Reports. Washington, DC: Federal Bureau of Investigation. Semiannual. SuDoc: J1.14/7–2
   For cities, provides crime index trends by city; also provides travels for rural and suburban areas.
   An annual report is issued as *Uniform Crime Reports: Crime in the U.S.* Washington, DC: Government Printing Office. Annual. Includes final figures on crime trends, offenses, arrests; law enforcement employment, and demographic data on persons arrested.
   A separate annual report provides historical data on crimes against persons or property.

The Department of Justice also has responsibility for compiling prison and prisoner statistics, and statistics on specific Federal crimes such as drug use and terrorism.

Prisons and Prisoners

Correctional Populations in the U.S. (Year). Washington, DC: U.S. Department of Justice. Annual. SuDoc: J29.17:
A statistical report on the number and demographic characteristics of prisoners in Federal, State, and local correctional facilities or on parole. Includes death sentence prisoners.

Update: AIDS in Correctional Facilities. Washington, DC: U.S. Department of Justice. Annual. SuDoc: J28.23: Ac7/
A report which presents statistics on inmate AIDS and AIDS treatment and training.

Drug Usage

Drug Use Forecasting. Washington, DC: U.S. Department of Justice. Quarterly. SuDoc: J28.15/2–3:
A statistical report which presents the results of drug testing activities conducted on persons arrested for non-drug offenses.

Terrorism

Terrorism in the U.S. Washington, DC: U.S. Department of Justice. Annual. SuDoc: J1.14/22:
A narrative and statistical report on terrorist incidents in the U.S. and prevention of terrorism in the U.S. Information on terrorism outside the U.S. is also included.

Immigration and Naturalization Service

The Immigration and Naturalization Service is responsible for administering the immigration and naturalization laws relating to the admission, exclusion, deportation, and naturalization of aliens.

Statistical Yearbook of the Immigration and Naturalization Service. Washington, DC: Government Printing Office. Annual. SuDoc: J21.2/10:
  Primary source of information on number of immigrants, aliens, temporary workers, visitors, etc. Includes data by country and data on characteristics of immigrants such as sex, marital status, age, and occupation.
  A brief advance report is also issued, as is a quarterly statistical summary of non-immigrant admissions to the U.S.

DEPARTMENT OF LABOR

The Department of Labor administers the Federal labor laws and keeps track of changes in employment, prices, and other national economic measurements.

Publications of the U.S. Department of Labor. Washington, DC: U.S. Department of Labor. Irregular. SuDoc: L1.34/6:
  A listing of BLS publications.

Bureau of Labor Statistics

The BLS has responsibility for the economic and statistical research activities of the Department of Labor. It is the government's principal fact-finding agency in the field of labor economics, particularly with respect to the collection and analysis of data on manpower and labor requirements, the labor force, employment, unemployment, hours of work, wages and employee compensation, prices, living conditions, productivity and technological developments, occupational safety and health, structure and growth of the economy, urban conditions and related socio-economic issues, and international aspects of certain of these subjects.
  Information collected by BLS is issued in monthly press releases, in special publications, and in its official publication, the *Monthly Labor Review.* BLS regional offices issue additional reports and releases, usually presenting local or regional detail.
  From time to time the Bureau issues cumulative bibliographies, many of them topical, in its ongoing series of numbered bulletins.

BLS Handbook of Methods. Washington, DC: Government Printing Office. 1982. 2 Vols. SuDoc: L2.3:2134-(Vol.)
A report which describes the methods used by the Bureau of Labor Statistics in collecting, processing and presenting its statistical data. The volumes are issued as parts of the *BLS Bulletin Series.*

BLS Publications, 1886–1971. (BLS Bull. 1749.) Washington, DC: Government Printing Office. 1972. 184p.; and a supplement to it that excludes periodicals, *BLS Publications, 1972–77.* (BLS Bull. 1990.) Washington, DC: Government Printing Office. 1978. v, 42p.

Major Programs of the Bureau of Labor Statistics. Washington, DC: U.S. Bureau of Labor Statistics. Irregular. SuDoc: L2.125:
A compendium of information on BLS programs and publications.

General

Monthly Labor Review. Washington, DC: Government Printing Office. Monthly. SuDoc: L2.6:
The official publication of the BLS, the *Monthly Labor Review* provides data and statistics on labor, prices, and productivity, along with data on other areas covered by BLS. Included are quarterly articles analyzing changes in the Consumer Price Index and Producer Price Index; summaries of special labor force reports; significant decisions in labor cases; major agreements expiring next month; matters relating to industrial relations; and book reviews and notes.

Handbook of Labor Statistics. (BLS Bull.) Washington, DC: Bureau of Labor Statistics. Irregular. SuDoc: L2.3/5:
Makes available in one volume the major series produced by BLS. In general, each table is complete historically, beginning with the earliest reliable and consistent data. Related series from other governmental agencies and foreign countries are included.

Time Series Data for Input-Output Industries. (BLS Bull. 2018). Washington, DC: Government Printing Office. 1979. v, 114p.
Provides output, employment and prices data for 95 manufacturing sectors and 60 non-manufacturing sectors. Data cover 1958–76. An annual article in the *Survey of Current Business* provides current input-output data.

Historical and Projected Input-Output Tables of the Economic Growth Project. (BLS Bull. 2056.) Washington, DC: Government Printing Office. 1980. 2 vols.
   Provides data on the interaction of demand and supply among 160 industry sectors, 1963–90.

Capital Stock Estimates for Input-Output Industries: Methods and Data. (BLS Bull. 2034.) Washington, DC: Government Printing Office. 1979. vi, 125p.
   Provides estimates of fixed capital assets for 72 private sector industries included in BLS input-output tables, 1947–74. Detailed methodology and documentation for BLS capital stock data base are also provided.

Employment and Labor Force Including Wages

How the Government Measures Unemployment. Washington, DC: U.S. Department of Labor. Irregular. SuDoc: L2.71:742
   An updated report on the methodology employed by the Bureau of Labor Statistics in measuring unemployment.

Mass Layoffs. Washington, DC: Government Printing Office. Annual. SuDoc: L2.3:
   A BLS Bulletin which documents the number of business plant closings and the resulting number of layoffs.

Employment Situation. Washington, DC: Bureau of Labor Statistics. Monthly. SuDoc: L2.53/2:
   A press release which provides up-to-date statistics on the size of the U.S. labor force and its characteristics. Information on total employed and unemployed, and an industry breakdown of employment, hours and earnings are included.

Employment and Earnings. Washington, DC: Government Printing Office. Monthly. SuDoc: L2.41/2:
   Provides current information on U.S. employment, unemployment, hours, earnings, turnover, and unemployment insurance. Trend data for this series are published as *Employment and Earnings, U.S., 1909-.* Washington, DC: Government Printing Office. Annual. Also a companion publication, *Employment and Earnings, States*

and Areas, 1939-. Washington, DC: Government Printing Office. Biennial. The latter provides data for all States and over 200 areas.

Occupational Outlook Handbook. (BLS Bull.) Washington, DC: Government Printing Office. Biennial. SuDoc: L2.3/4:
Provides data on employment situations and outlook for occupations and major industries. Kept up to date by *Occupational Outlook Quarterly.* Washington, DC: Government Printing Office. Quarterly.
A biennial report on projections of employment by occupation is also issued.

State and Metropolitan Area Employment and Unemployment. Washington, DC: Bureau of Labor Statistics. Monthly. SuDoc: L2.111/5
A press release which provides up-to-date estimates for unemployment by State and large MSAs. A more detailed monthly report is also issued.

Area Wage Surveys. Washington, DC: Bureau of Labor Statistics. Annual. SuDoc: L2.122
An ongoing series, consisting of one report per area issued annually, which provides data on hourly earnings and supplementary benefits for selected plant and office occupations in labor market areas. Only establishments with 50 or more employees are surveyed and the number of establishments and workers covered varies from place to place.
More detailed surveys covering more occupations and establishments are covered in *Area Wage Surveys.* (BLS Bull.) SuDoc: L2.121: Washington, DC: Government Printing Office. This series is an ongoing one, covering selected MSAs. Each MSA in the series is covered every three years.

Industry Wage Surveys. (BLS Bull.) Washington, DC: Government Printing Office. Irregular. SuDoc: L2.3/3
An ongoing series of reports which provide information for the total U.S., selected regions, States, and MSAs on employment, earnings and supplementary benefits of non-supervisory workers in selected large manufacturing and nonmanufacturing industries. The reports are updated periodically.

Special Labor Force Reports. Washington, DC: Bureau of Labor Statistics. Irregular. SuDoc: L2.3:

An ongoing series of reports, most of which appear without detailed tables and notes in the *Monthly Labor Review*. The reports are based on surveys and studies.

National Survey of Professional, Administrative, Technical, and Clerical Pay. (BLS Bull.) Washington, DC: Government Printing Office. Annual. SuDoc: L2.3/13–2
  Provides information on wages of private industry white collar workers.

Employment in Perspective: Minority Workers. Washington, DC: U.S. Department of Labor. Quarterly. SuDoc: L2.71: (Nos.)
  Employment statistics for blacks and Hispanic Americans.

Collective Bargaining—Labor Unions

Bargaining Calendar. (BLS Bull.) Washington, DC: Government Printing Office. Annual. SuDoc: L2.3/8
  Provides data on the number of collective bargaining agreements expiring during the year of publication and number of workers covered. Information is provided by industry, individual company, and union for agreements covering 1,000 or more workers.

Current Wage Developments. Washington, DC: Government Printing Office. Monthly. SuDoc: L2.44:
  Presents information and statistical data on changes in wages and employee benefits resulting from collective bargaining agreements and unilateral employer decisions. Includes data for manufacturing and non-manufacturing industries for changes affecting 1,000 or more workers.

State Workers' Compensation Laws. Washington, DC: U.S. Department of Labor. Semiannual. SuDoc: L36.2:
  A narrative report with supporting statistics on workers' compensation laws for each of the 50 States and outlying areas.

Prices and Productivity

CPI Detailed Report. Washington, DC: Government Printing Office. Monthly. SuDoc: L2.38/3:

Provides changes in CPI for individual commodities and services and for category of expenditures. Areas covered are the U.S., four regions, and 28 MSAs. Publications are issued two to three months after month of coverage. A major revision of this series was introduced with the January, 1978, issue.

A monthly press release on changes in the CPI is issued two or three weeks after the end of the month of coverage as *Consumer Price Index.* Washington, DC: Bureau of Labor Statistics. Monthly.

Consumer Price Index Revision, 1978. Washington, DC: Government Printing Office. 1977–78. 4 reports.

A series of reports providing explanatory data for the 1978 major revision of the CPI Data series. Reports in this series include the following:

> *Consumer Price Index: Concepts and Content Over the Years.* (BLS Rpt. 517.) Washington, DC: Bureau of Labor Statistics. 1977. ii, 18p.
>
> *Facts About the Revised Consumer Price Index.* Washington, DC: Bureau of Labor Statistics. 1978. 7p.
>
> *Escalation and the CPI: Information for Users.* Rev. Washington, DC: Bureau of Labor Statistics. 1978. 18p.
>
> *Announcement to Users of the Consumer Price Index.* Washington, DC: Bureau of Labor Statistics. 1978. 5p.

Relative Importance of Components in the Consumer Price Indexes. (BLS Rpt.) Washington, DC: Government Printing Office. Annual. SuDoc: L2.3/9:

Provides weights assigned to commodities and services and to selected metropolitan areas in the CPI for urban consumers (CPI-U) and the revised CPI for urban wage earners and clerical workers (CPI-W). Information is presented for the U.S. and selected metropolitan areas with cross-classifications by region and population-size classes.

Consumer Expenditure Survey. Washington, DC: Government Printing Office. Annual. SuDoc: L2.3:

A report on consumer spending for food, housing, utilities, and fuels, furnishings, etc., and on consumer income. A quarterly report is also issued.

Retail Food Prices Historical Data. Washington, DC: Bureau of Labor Statistics. 1978. 278p.

A collection of historical statistics through October 1977 on U.S. retail prices for selected food items included in the CPI market basket sample. Prior to July 1978, a monthly report, *Estimated Retail Food Prices by City,* was issued.

Producer Price Indexes. Washington, DC: Government Printing Office. Monthly. SuDoc: L2.61:

Provides detailed information on changes in producer prices and price indexes. Producer price indexes were formerly referred to as wholesale price indexes. Publication is approximately two months after month of coverage.

A monthly press release is issued approximately one to two weeks after the end of the month of coverage: *Producer Price Indexes.* Washington, DC: Bureau of Labor Statistics. Monthly.

An annual supplement, providing annual averages and monthly indexes at all levels for the Producer Price Index (PPI) and the Industry Sector Price Index (ISPI), is also issued.

U.S. Import and Export Price Indexes. Washington, DC: Bureau of Labor Statistics. Quarterly. SuDoc: L3.60/3

Provides export and import price indexes for selected categories of manufactured products and food commodities. Report is published approximately six weeks after quarter of coverage.

U.S. Department of State Indexes of Living Costs Abroad and Living Quarters Allowances. Washington, DC: Government Printing Office. Quarterly. SuDoc: L2.101

Provides revised information for State Department indexes for U.S. government civilian employees stationed abroad. Revisions for selected posts are published quarterly, the entire list is revised every 12 to 15 months.

Technology and Productivity Reports Series. Washington, DC: Government Printing Office. Irregular. SuDoc: L2.3

A series of narrative and statistical reports on the impact of technology on productivity in specific industries.

Employment and Training Administration

The Employment and Training Administration (ETA) includes a group of offices and services that have been established to implement the responsibilities of the Department of Labor for certain work training and work experience programs; and for conducting a continuing program of research, development, and evaluation.

Area Trends in Employment and Unemployment. Washington, DC: Employment and Training Administration. Monthly. SuDoc: L37.13:
Provides information, by State, on local areas eligible for preferential treatment in award of Federal procurement contracts because of a labor surplus. Also includes a listing of major labor market areas showing labor force, employment, and unemployment.

Unemployment Insurance Weekly Claims Report. Washington, DC: Employment and Training Administration. Weekly. SuDoc: L37.12/2–2
Provides information on unemployment insurance claims, with comparisons to previous week and past year. An annual financial report is also issued.

Comparison of State Unemployment Insurance Laws. Washington, DC: Government Printing Office. Semiannual. SuDoc: L37.212:
A comparison of provisions of unemployment insurance laws in the 50 States, District of Columbia, Puerto Rico, and the Virgin Islands. Report is issued in looseleaf format. A separate tabular report is also issued.

Occupational Safety and Health Administration

The Occupational Safety and Health Administration has been established within the Department of Labor to report on health and safety related matters.

Report of the President to the Congress on Occupational Safety and Health. Washington, DC: Government Printing Office. Annual. SuDoc: L35.1

Includes statistics on occupational injuries, illnesses, and fatalities by industry.

Bureau of International Labor Affairs

The Bureau of International Labor Affairs, among other functions, assists in formulating international economic and trade policies affecting American workers; administers the trade adjustment assistance program under the Trade Act of 1974, which provides special benefits for workers adversely affected by import competition; helps to represent the U.S. in bilateral and multilateral trade negotiations and on various international bodies; and helps provide direction to U.S. labor attachés at embassies abroad.

Foreign Labor Trends. Washington, DC: Government Printing Office. Annual. SuDoc: L29.16
A country by country series of reports on labor related issues. A series of reports on the impact of immigration on the U.S. economy is also issued.

Women's Bureau

The Women's Bureau is responsible for formulating standards and policies relating to the welfare of wage-earning women and for investigating and reporting on all matters pertaining to the welfare of women in industry.

The Women's Bureau has regional offices in ten areas throughout the U.S.

Facts on U.S. Working Women. Washington, DC: U.S. Women's Bureau. Annual. SuDoc: L36.114/3
A statistical and narrative report on working women with demographic, economic and social data.

DEPARTMENT OF STATE

The primary duty of the Department of State is to provide the President with advice in the formulation and execution of foreign policy. The Department of State publishes various reports that are of business or economic interest.

General

Background Notes on the Countries of the World. Washington, DC: Government Printing Office. Irregular. SuDoc: S1.123:(Country).

An ongoing series of reports, each dealing with a specific country. These brief surveys include a statistical overview of the country and data on geography, population, government, recent history, political conditions, foreign trade, and foreign relations. The reports are updated periodically and a separate index is published for the series. A separate irregularly published series details geographic changes worldwide.

U.S. Department of State Dispatch. Washington, DC: Government Printing Office. Weekly. SuDoc: S1.3/5

The successor to the *Department of State Bulletin* which serves as the official record of U.S. foreign policy through its articles, listings of policy actions, etc.

Treaties

Treaties in Force. Washington, DC: Government Printing Office. Annual. SuDoc: S9.14:

An annotated listing of all U.S. bilateral and multilateral treaties and other international agreements in force on January 1st of the year of publication.

Bureau of Consular Affairs

The Bureau of Consular Affairs, in its capacity for the administration and enforcement of the provisions of the immigration and naturalization laws insofar as they concern the Department of State and the Foreign Service, and as a result of its responsibility for the issuance of passports and visas, produces several reports of interest to business. Chief among these are the following:

Summary of Passport Statistics. Washington, DC: Bureau of Consular Affairs. Quarterly/Annual Supplement. SuDoc: S1.27/2:

Provides statistics on passports issued, country destination, age of passport recipients, object of travel, proposed length of stay, time of next trip, traveler's State of residence, and traveler's occupation. Some trend data and projections are included. In addition to the quarterly report, an annual supplement is also issued.

Forecast of Citizen Departures to Europe. Washington, DC: Passport Office. Monthly. SuDoc: S1.121:
A brief tabulation of passport applications and departures of U.S. citizens for Europe. Includes data for previous 12 months, month of publication, and next month.

Report of the Visa Office (Year). Washington, DC: U.S. Department of State. Annual. SuDoc: S1.1/4:988
A report on the number of immigrant and non-immigrant visas issued and denied by class of applicant and by nationality or country.

Proposed Refugee Admissions for FY(Year). Report to the Congress. Washington, DC: U.S. Department of State. Annual.
A forecast report on admissions and allocations for refugees by country of origin.
A separate monthly report on worldwide refugee admissions is also issued, along with a more detailed annual report on refugee programs worldwide.

DEPARTMENT OF TRANSPORTATION

The Department of Transportation (DOT) administers the transportation programs of the Federal government and develops national transportation programs and policies. The central management concept of DOT is that operating programs, organized generally by mode (air, rail, etc.), are carried out by the operating administrators.

DOT produces a number of reports dealing with the market(s) for transportation modes and other economic aspects of the transportation sector.

National Transportation Statistics. Washington, DC: Government Printing Office. Annual. SuDoc: TD 10.9:(year)
Provides statistical data on various aspects of the transportation

sector. Includes data on air carriers, general aviation, rail, water, oil and natural gas pipelines, automobile, truck, bus, and local transit modes. Financial, inventory, and performance data are provided.

This report was formerly called *Summary of National Transportation Statistics* and now includes summary energy consumption data for the transportation sector and some of the energy supply information formerly published as *Energy Statistics: Supplement to the Summary of National Transportation Statistics.*

U.S. Department of Transportation Awards to Academic Institutions. Springfield, Va.: National Technical Information Service. Annual.

Provides information on DOT grants and contracts awarded to academic institutions. Includes listing by sub-agency, university, and contract's grant title, subject area, university, and State.

Air Transportation

U.S. International Air Travel Statistics. Cambridge, Mass.: Department of Transportation, Transportation Systems Center. Monthly.

Provides information on passenger travel, commercial and military, between the U.S. and foreign countries. Information is derived from data collected by the U.S. Immigration and Naturalization Service. Includes data on arrivals and departures of citizens and aliens, by U.S. and foreign flag carriers, and by scheduled and chartered flights. Commercial travel data are shown by port for selected U.S. ports.

Air Carrier Traffic Statistics Monthly. Washington, DC: Transportation Systems Center. Monthly. SuDoc: TD10.9/3:

A statistical report on air traffic and on air carrier performance.

Air Travel Consumer Report: Flight Delays, Mishandled Baggage, Oversales, and Consumer Complaints. Washington, DC: U.S. Department of Transportation. Monthly. SuDoc: TD1.54:

A statistical report on flight delays, mishandled baggage, and other passenger complaints against airlines, travel agents, cargo handlers, etc.

Air Carrier Financial Statistics Quarterly. Washington, DC: Transportation Systems Center. Quarterly.

A statistical report on the financial characteristics of individual certified route air carriers.

FAA Air Traffic Activity. Washington, DC: Government Printing Office. Annual. SuDoc: TD4.19:
   Provides data on air traffic activity at FAA-operated air traffic control facilities.

Air Carriers and Civil Airmen

Census of U.S. Civil Aircraft. Washington, DC: Government Printing Office. Annual. SuDoc: TD4.18
   Provides information, by type, manufacturer, and model, State, county, etc., for all FAA-registered civil aircraft in the U.S. Selected earlier data are included.

U.S. Civil Airmen Statistics. Washington, DC: Federal Aviation Administration. Annual. SuDoc: TD4.2:
   Reports the number of U.S. civil airmen, both pilots and nonpilots. Information is provided by type of certificate held, sex, age, FAA region, and State. Selected trend data are included.

Ground Transportation

Highway Statistics. Washington, DC: Government Printing Office. Annual. SuDoc: TD2.23
   A compendium of highway-related statistics including motor fuel consumption, vehicles, driver licensing, highway user taxation, State highway finance, highway mileage, and Federal aid for highway finance. Highway finance data are included for various levels of government.

Public Roads. Washington, DC: Government Printing Office. Quarterly. SuDoc: TD2.19
   A publication that includes technical articles dealing with highway design and construction. Also provides data on new Federal research contracts and a publications list.

Traffic Volume Trends. Washington, DC: Federal Highway Administration. Monthly. SuDoc: TD2.50

Provides traffic volume data for city and rural roads and streets. Comparison data are included for prior month and year.

Drivers and Vehicles

Drivers Licenses. Washington, DC: Federal Highway Administration. Annual. SuDoc: TD2.2:D83/2/
Provides information on the number, age, and sex distribution of drivers in the 50 States and District of Columbia.

Waterborne Transportation

Merchant Vessels of the U.S. Washington, DC: Government Printing Office. Annual.
Provides a listing of all American merchant vessels and yachts registered as of January 1st of the year indicated. Vessels are listed alphabetically by name. Other listings are included, such as an index of managing owners.
The listing is kept up-to-date by a monthly publication, *Supplement to Merchant Vessels of the U.S.* Washington, DC: Commandant, United States Coast Guard. Monthly.

Merchant Fleets of the World: Oceangoing Steam and Motor Ships of 1,000 Gross Tons and Over. Washington, DC: Merchant Marine. Annual. SuDoc: TD11.14: (Year)
A statistical report which provides the number of ships and the tonnage of the ships in the U.S. fleet and the 15 largest fleets of foreign vessels.

Foreign Flag Merchant Ships Owned by U.S. Parent Companies. Washington, DC: Merchant Marine Semi-annual. SuDoc: TD11.16: (Year)
A listing of registered ships arranged by parent company.

Bulk Carriers in the World Fleet: Oceangoing Merchant Type Ships of 1,000 Gross Tons and Over. Washington, DC: Merchant Marine. Annual. SuDoc: TD11.20:(Year)
A report which lists oceangoing bulk carriers by country of registration and type. A similar report provides information for tanker ships.

U.S. Oceanborne Foreign Trade Routes. Washington, DC: Maritime Administration. Annual. SuDoc: TD11.13:(Year)

A report which lists the 33 essential and 21 non-essential U.S. foreign trade routes. The report provides statistics on the tonnage and value of exports and imports for the top ten groups of commodities by liner, tanker, and non-liner.

Containerized Cargo Statistics. Washington, DC: Maritime Administration. Annual. SuDoc: TD11.21:(Year)

Statistical report which provides data on containerized cargo for U.S. and foreign ship operators.

An annual report detailing domestic waterborne trade is also issued.

Boating Statistics. Washington, DC: United States Coast Guard. Annual. SuDoc: TD5.11:

Provides statistics on boat numbering registration and accidents.

U.S. Merchant Marine Data Sheet. Washington, DC: Maritime Administration. Monthly. SuDoc: TD11.10:(Date)

A report which provides statistics on shipbuilding and shipbuilding employment.

Report to Congress on the Status of the Public Ports of the U.S. Washington, DC: Maritime Administration. Annual. SuDoc: TD11.30:(Year)

A report which lists major seaports by coastal region and inland waterway ports by State.

Urban Transportation

Directory of Urban Public Transportation Service. Springfield, VA: National Technical Information Service. Annual.

A directory with statistical tables on public transportation systems in urban areas with populations of 50,000 or more.

Status of the Nation's Local Mass Transportation: Performance and Conditions. Washington, DC: U.S. Department of Transportation. Biennial. SuDoc: TD7.18:

A narrative report with statistical data on the national public transit systems. Contains trend data. An annual report on the financial and operating statistics of public transit systems is also issued.

DEPARTMENT OF THE TREASURY

The Department of the Treasury performs four basic types of functions: formulating and recommending financial, tax and fiscal policies; serving as financial agent for the U.S. government; law enforcement; and manufacturing coins and currency.

General

Annual Report of the Secretary of the Treasury on the State of the Finances. Washington, DC: Government Printing Office. Annual.

Provides an overview of major economic developments, both domestic and international, as well as a review of financial operations of the Treasury. Also includes administrative reports on the activities of various Treasury units.

A statistical appendix to this report is issued as a separate volume and provides statistical data on fiscal operations, receipts and outlays, savings bonds and notes, public debt securities, assets and liabilities of the U.S. Treasury, currency and coin in circulation, stock, trust and other funds, customs operations, engraving and printing operations, international financial transactions, international claims, indebtedness of foreign governments, Federal corporations and other business questions.

Treasury Bulletin. Washington, DC: Government Printing Office. Monthly. SuDoc: T63.103/2:

Includes information on Federal fiscal operations, Federal obligations, account of the U.S. Treasury, monetary statistics, Federal debt, public debt operations, U.S. savings bonds and notes, ownership of Federal securities, market quotations on Treasury securities and average yield of long-term bonds, national bank reports, international financial statistics, capital movements, foreign currency positions, financial operations of government agencies and funds, and related data.

Foreign Debt Owed to the U.S.

Status of Active Foreign Credits of the U.S. Government Foreign Credits by U.S. Government Agencies. Washington, DC: Department of the Treasury. Quarterly.

A report on accounts receivable and long- and short-term loans extended since 1941 to foreign official and private sources.

Domestic International Sales Corporations

Operation and Effect of the Domestic International Sales Corporation Legislation, Annual Report. Washington, DC: Government Printing Office. Annual.

Provides data on the number and financial operations of DISCs and of their effect on U.S. exports, tax revenues, etc.

Fiscal Activities of the Government

Monthly Treasury Statement of Receipts and Outlays of the U.S. Government. Monthly. Washington, DC: Government Printing Office. SuDoc: T63.113/2:

A monthly statement of the receipts and expenditures of the Federal government. The September 30th issue is the cumulative issue for the year.

A daily cash flow statement is also issued as is a final annual statement with which all other reports must agree (*U.S. Government Annual Report*).

A separate annual report prepared according to accounting standards is issued as *Consolidated Financial Statements of the U.S. Government.*

Currency and Coin in Circulation

Monthly Statement of U.S. Currency and Coin. Washington, DC: Department of the Treasury. Monthly.

Provides a statement of currency and coin in circulation held by the Treasury or Federal Reserve Banks, and total outstanding, as of the end of each month. Includes data on total and per capita money in circulation for selected months from 1910 to current month.

Bureau of Alcohol, Tobacco and Firearms

The Bureau is responsible for enforcing and administering laws related to firearms and explosives, and criminal violations and forfeiture aspects of Federal wagering laws, as well as those covering alcoholic beverages and tobacco products.

Alcohol, Tobacco and Firearms Summary Statistics: Distilled Spirits, Wine, Beer, Tobacco, Firearms, Enforcement, Taxes. Washington, DC: Government Printing Office. Annual.

Includes data on production, manufactures, stocks, withdrawals, losses, ingredients, permits, tax revenues, etc. Trend data are included from 1880 or first year of series. A transition quarterly issue of this report is also issued. A series of statistical releases on beer, wine, distilled spirits, cigarettes and cigars, issued on a quarterly basis, provides the data for these reports.

Internal Revenue Service

The Internal Revenue Service is responsible for administering and enforcing the internal revenue laws, except those relating to alcohol, tobacco, firearms, explosives, and criminal violations of wagering tax laws. In addition to administration and enforcement of tax laws, basic IRS activities include providing taxpayer service and education; determination of pension plan qualifications; determination of exempt organization status; and the issuance of rulings and regulations to interpret provisions of the Internal Revenue Code.

Statistics of Income

The IRS publishes several reports based on data collected from samples selected from income tax returns in each category.

Statistics of Income Bulletin. Washington, DC: Government Printing Office. Quarterly. SuDoc: T2.35/4:

Preliminary data from the *Statistics of Income* reports prepared by the Internal Revenue Service.

Statistics of Income, Individual Income Tax Returns. Washington, DC: Government Printing Office. Annual. SuDoc: T22.35/8:

Includes information on number of returns, sources of income, deductions and exemptions, tax rates, etc. Includes State and regional data.

Statistics of Income, Corporation Income Tax Returns. Washington,DC: Government Printing Office. Annual. SuDoc: T22.35/5:
Provides information on income, assets, dividends, deductions, credits, income tax, and tax payments. Data are arranged by major industry divisions or groups similar to the SIC two- and three-digit classes and by selected financial items.

Source Book. Statistics of Income: . . . Washington, DC: Government Printing Office. Annual. SuDoc: T22.35/:
An annual compilation of income statistics data.

Projections: Information and Withholding Documents, U.S. and Service Center Areas. Washington, DC: Government Printing Office. Annual. SuDoc: T22.2:P
A report which projects the number of IRS documents by type to be filed in future years. A separate report projects the number of returns to be filed.

Banks and Thrift Institutions

Quarterly Journal: Comptroller of the Currency Administration of National Banks. Washington, DC: Comptroller of the Currency. Quarterly. SuDoc: T12.18:
A detailed report of bank activities including statistics on mergers and finances. Also includes information on enforcement actions of the Comptroller of the Currency.

Office of Thrift Supervision

In 1989, the Office of Thrift Supervision was established as one of the administrative units which would replace the Federal Home Loan Bank Board and the FSLIC. Some of the publications issued by this unit are:

Thrift Institution Activity. Washington, DC: Office of Thrift Supervision. Monthly.
A press release with asset statistics on financial activities of institutions insured by the Savings Association Insurance Fund. A quarterly release is also issued.

Office of Thrift Supervision Journal. Washington, DC: Office of Thrift Supervision. Monthly. SuDoc: T71.15:

This publication replaces the *Federal Home Loan Bank Board Journal.* In 1989, a special issue was devoted to the effects of the 1989 Financial Institution Reform, Recovery and Enforcement Act. This publication contains narrative and statistical information on OTS regulatory activities with information on specific institutions.

Combined Financial Statements: . . . Washington, DC: Office of Thrift Supervisor Annual.

An annual balance sheet and income statement report on institutions covered by the Savings Association Insurance Fund and the Federal Deposit Insurance Corporation.

SPECIALIZED OR INDEPENDENT AGENCIES

Agency for International Development

The Agency for International Development (AID) has responsibility for the U.S. foreign economic assistance programs. Publications from AID are, for the most part, printed in small editions or for other reasons are not generally available. Some of these are distributed by commercial organizations in microfiche or other formats.

Some AID publications having business and economic interest are listed here:

Status of Loan Agreements. Washington, DC: Agency for International Development. Quarterly.

U.S. Overseas Loans and Grants and Assistance from International Organizations. Washington, DC: Agency for International Development. Annual.

The reports above provide varying amounts of information on the status of AID loans by country, type of program, etc.

Country Financial Report: Economic Assistance. Washington, DC: Agency for International Development. Quarterly.

A country by country report on AID assistance.

Board of Governors of the Federal Reserve System

The Board's principal duties consist of influencing monetary policy and credit conditions and supervising Federal Reserve Banks and member banks.

The Board issues many types of statistical data in an ongoing series of statistical releases issued weekly, monthly, quarterly, semiannually, and annually. These releases provide trend data useful in analyzing current business conditions and forecasting economic trends. In some cases, the data in these releases are republished in their entirety in the *Federal Reserve Bulletin*. A complete schedule of all releases is published in the June and December issues of the *Federal Reserve Bulletin*.

In addition to these releases, the Board regularly issues many publications containing the principal series used in economic and market analysis. Chief among these are the following:

General

Federal Reserve Bulletin. Washington, DC: Board of Governors of the Federal Reserve System. Monthly.

Principal source for current data on money and banking; credit; and related financial statistics. Consists of a narrative section and a comprehensive series of statistical tables, domestic and international.

A concordance of statistics in the *Bulletin* with statistics in the *Annual Statistical Digest* is published annually.

Annual Statistical Digest. Washington, DC: Board of Governors of the Federal Reserve System. Annual.

A source of historical data of tables in the *Federal Reserve Bulletin* and to continue series omitted from it since its revision in January 1977. Generally covers data for a five-year time span. Long historical time series are contained in *Banking and Monetary Statistics, 1914–41* and *Banking and Monetary Statistics, 1941–70*.

Banking and Monetary Statistics, 1914–41. Washington, DC: Board of Governors of the Federal Reserve System. 1943 (reprinted 1976). 682p.

A compendium of banking and monetary statistics first printed in 1943. Included are most of the financial series published in the *Federal Reserve Bulletin*. Data sources are indicated.

This report is carried forward by *Banking and Monetary Statistics, 1941–70.* Washington, DC: Board of Governors of the Federal Reserve System. 1976. vii, 1168p. Some of the data are also contained in *Annual Statistical Digest.*

Consumer Credit

Consumer Installment Credit. Washington, DC: Board of Governors of the Federal Reserve System. Monthly. SuDoc: FR1.36:(date)

A Federal Reserve statistical release consisting of three tables. One table presents the amount of consumer credit extended for automobile, mobile home, home improvement, bank credit card and other loans. Also provides data on the amount liquidated and amount outstanding.

Another table provides data on consumer installment credit extended, liquidated and outstanding by holder, including commercial banks, finance companies, credit unions, retailers, etc., and by type of credit.

A third table presents terms of credit. A separate release covers credit held by finance companies.

Indexes of Industrial Production

Industrial Production. Washington, DC: Board of Governors of the Federal Reserve System. Monthly. SuDoc: FR1.19/3:

A Federal Reserve statistical release that presents indexes of industrial production and industrial electric power use.

Interest Rates

Selected Interest Rates. Washington, DC: Board of Governors of the Federal Reserve System. Monthly. SuDoc: FR1.32/6:

A listing of interest rates for commercial debt, Federal funds, U.S. Treasury bills and bonds, corporate bonds, conventional mortgages, etc.

Federal Reserve District Banks

Each of the district banks issues publications of regional and national importance. The following is a listing of selected publications from the district banks.

Federal Reserve Bank of Atlanta. 6th Federal Reserve District: Alabama, Florida, Georgia, and portions of Louisiana, Mississippi, and Tennessee.
Economic Review. Monthly.

Federal Reserve Bank of Boston, 1st Federal Reserve District: Maine, Vermont, New Hampshire, Massachusetts, Rhode Island, and portions of Connecticut.
New England Economic Review. Bimonthly.
New England Economic Indicators. Monthly.

Federal Reserve Bank of Chicago. 7th Federal Reserve District: Iowa and portions of Illinois, Indiana, Michigan, and Wisconsin.
Economic Perspectives. Bimonthly.

Federal Reserve Bank of Cleveland. 4th Federal Reserve District: Ohio, and portions of Kentucky, Pennsylvania, and West Virginia.
Economic Review. Quarterly.
Economic Trends. Monthly.

Federal Reserve Bank of Dallas. 11th Federal Reserve District: Texas, and portions of Louisiana, New Mexico, and Oklahoma.
Economic Review. Monthly.

Federal Reserve Bank of Kansas City. 10th Federal Reserve District: Colorado, Kansas, Nebraska, Wyoming, and portions of Missouri, New Mexico, and Oklahoma.
Economic Review. Bimonthly.

Federal Reserve Bank of Minneapolis. 9th Federal Reserve District: Minnesota, Montana, North Dakota, South Dakota, and portions of Michigan and Wisconsin.
Federal Reserve Bank of Minneapolis Quarterly Review. Quarterly.
Fedgazette. Quarterly.

Federal Reserve Bank of New York. 2nd Federal Reserve District: New York, Puerto Rico, Virgin Islands, and portions of Connecticut and New Jersey.
Quarterly Review, Federal Reserve Bank of New York. Quarterly.

Federal Reserve Bank of Philadelphia. 3rd Federal Reserve District: Delaware, and portions of New Jersey and Pennsylvania.
 Business Review, Federal Reserve Bank of Philadelphia. Bimonthly.

Federal Reserve Bank of Richmond. 5th Federal Reserve District: District of Columbia, Maryland, North Carolina, South Carolina, Virginia, and portions of West Virginia.
 Economic Review, Federal Reserve Bank of Richmond. Bimonthly.

Federal Reserve Bank of St. Louis. 8th Federal Reserve District: Arkansas, and portions of Illinois, Indiana, Kentucky, Mississippi, Missouri, and Tennessee.
 Review, Federal Reserve Bank of St. Louis. Bimonthly.
 Monetary Trends. Monthly.
 National Economic Trends. Monthly.
 U.S. Financial Data. Weekly.
 International Economic Conditions. Quarterly.
 Annual U.S. Economic Data. Annual.
 Prices of Eight. Quarterly

Federal Reserve Bank of San Francisco. 12th Federal District: Alaska, Arizona, California, Guam, Idaho, Nevada, Oregon, Utah, Washington.
 Economic Review, Federal Reserve Bank of San Francisco. Quarterly.

Central Intelligence Agency

The CIA produces and disseminates foreign intelligence relating to national security, including foreign political, economic, scientific, technical, military, geographic, and sociological intelligence.

General

World Factbook. Washington, DC: Government Printing Office. Annual. SuDoc: PrEx 3.15:
 A compilation of current data on demographics, economics, politics, and sociology of more than 200 countries.

Handbook of Economic Statistics. Springfield, VA.: National Technical Information Service. Annual. SuDoc: PrEx3.10/7–5
    Annual compilation of economic statistics for selected countries.

Energy

Economic and Energy Indicators. Springfield, VA: National Technical Information Services. Biweekly.
    Provides data on production, consumption, reserves, and trade of oil and natural gas by country. Also provides major economic indicators by country. A monthly energy review is also issued.

Consumer Product Safety Commission

The Consumer Product Safety Commission has primary responsibility for establishing mandatory product safety standards. In addition, the Commission has the authority to ban hazardous consumer products and to conduct extensive research on consumer product standards. The Commission also engages in broad consumer and industry information and education programs and operates a comprehensive inquiry information clearinghouse.

Consumer Product Safety Commission Annual Report. Washington, DC: Government Printing Office. Annual. SuDoc: Y3.C76/3:
    Appendixes include data on deaths and injuries associated with consumer products.

Environmental Protection Agency

EPA is charged with controlling and abating pollution in the areas of air, water, solid waste, noise, radiation, and toxic substances. In addition, EPA coordinates and supports research and antipollution activities by state and local governments, private and public groups, individuals, and educational institutions.

EPA Publications Bibliography Quarterly Abstract Bulletin. Springfield, VA.: National Technical Information Service. Quarterly. SuDoc: EP1.21/7:

A bibliography of reports prepared by or for EPA and added to the NTIS collection. A cumulative index is included with the last issue of the year.

EPA Research Program Guide. Washington, DC. Environmental Protection Agency. Annual. SuDoc: EP1.23/6–2:
   An annual listing of grant programs and funding available from EPA. EPA publishes annual and more frequent statistical reports on air pollution, radiation levels, ozone levels, toxic emissions, water quality, and solid waste disposal.

Equal Employment Opportunity Commission

The EEOC is a major publisher of data on the employment status of minorities and women. On a continuing basis the EEOC conducts surveys and tabulates the data from these surveys to document employment by ethnic origin, race and sex

Job Patterns for Minorities and Women in Private Industry. Washington, DC: Equal Employment Opportunity Commission. Annual. SuDoc: Y3.Eq2:12–7/
   A report based on survey data which provides statistics on employment of women and minorities by industry.
   Similar reports are prepared for employment in State and local government and in the Federal government.

Federal Communications Commission

The Federal Communications Commission (FCC) regulates interstate and foreign communications by radio, television, wire, and cable.

Statistics of Communications Common Carriers. Washington, DC: Government Printing Office. Annual. SuDoc: CC1.35:
   Provides detailed information on assets, liabilities, income, earnings, dividends, revenues, facilities, services, employment, and wages. Data are provided for telephone companies, telegraph companies and communication satellite companies.

Trends in the International Communications Industry. Washington, DC: Federal Communication Commission. Annual.

A financial report on international telephone, telegraph and telex traffic and income.

Federal Deposit Insurance Corporation

The FDIC insures deposits in national banks, in State banks that are members of the Federal Reserve System, and in State banks that meet certain prescribed qualifications of the Federal Deposit Insurance Corporation.

Quarterly Banking Profile. Washington, DC: Federal Deposit Insurance Corporation. Quarterly.

A statement of assets, deposits and net income of FDIC-insured banks.

FDIC Banking Review. Washington, DC: Federal Deposit Insurance Corporation. Quarterly.

Detailed articles in this journal provide statistics on specific banking situations on a current basis.

Statistics on Banking. Washington, DC: Federal Deposit Insurance Corporation. Annual.

A compendium of banking statistics which includes financial statistics on FDIC-insured banks. Topics covered include number of banks and branches, finances of banks and financial rates.

Data Book, Operating Banks and Branches: Summary Deposits in all FDIC-Insured Commercial and Savings Bank and U.S. Branches of Foreign Banks. Washington, DC: Federal Deposit Insurance Corporation. Annual. SuDoc: Y3.F31/8:22/

A series of regional volumes and a U.S. summary volume which provides statistics and directory information for individual banks.

Federal Housing Finance Board

The Federal Housing Finance Board was established in 1989 to succeed, in part, the Federal Home Loan Bank Board.

Federal Home Loan Banks: Statement of Condition. Washington, DC: Federal Housing Finance Board. Monthly.
A summary statistical release which provides data on the Federal Home Loan Banks.

Mortgages

Conventional Home Mortgage Rates. Washington, DC: Federal Housing Finance Board. Monthly.
A monthly statement of loans, interest rates and other mortgage related statistics for the U.S. and large MSAs.

Federal Trade Commission

Prevention of unfair competition and deceptive practices in commerce is the major function of the Federal Trade Commission. Summaries of FTC investigations are sometimes published for general distribution, either as Senate or House documents or as Commission publications Occasional economic studies of individual industries are made from the monopoly aspect. Periodic statistical publications report financial statement data.

FTC Report to Congress: Pursuant to the Federal Cigarette Labeling and Advertising Act. Washington, DC: Federal Trade Commission. Annual. SuDoc: FT1.2:C48/2:
A narrative report and statistical supplement issued as separate parts. Includes data on cigarette labeling and advertising; domestic cigarette sales and consumption; advertising and promotional expenditures by type of media; domestic market share of and expenditures for advertising and promotion of filter, longer, and low-tar cigarettes. Trend data are included.

General Services Administration

GSA is charged with managing property and records, including construction and operation of buildings, procurement and distribution of supplies, utilization and disposal of property, transportation, traffic and communications management, stockpiling of strategic materials, and the management of government-wide automatic data processing resources program.

Summary Report of Real Property Owned by the U.S. Throughout the World. Washington, DC: Government Printing Office. Annual. SuDoc: GS1.15:

Includes real property owned or held in trust by the general government in States, outlying areas, and foreign countries. Land, buildings and other permanent facilities of civil defense agencies are covered.

A companion publication, *Summary Report of Real Property Leased to the U.S. Throughout the World* (Washington, DC: Government Printing Office. Annual), is also available. GSA also publishes detailed inventories of properties owned by the Federal government and used by the Department of Defense and by civil agencies throughout the world.

Automatic Data Processing Equipment in the U.S. Government. Washington, DC: Government Printing Office. Semiannual. SuDoc: GS 12.10:

This report constitutes an inventory of all digital computers in use throughout the Federal government except computers built or modified to special Federal government design.

Annual Report of the President on Federal Advisory Committees. Washington, DC: General Services Administration. Annual. SuDoc: Pr40.10:

A detailed listing of Federal Advisory Committees which includes members, functions and costs. Newly established and terminated committees are identified.

Interstate Commerce Commission

The Interstate Commerce Commission (ICC) regulates interstate surface transportation, including trains, trucks, buses, inland waterways and coastal shipping, freight forwarders, and express companies.

Transport Statistics in the U.S. Washington, DC: Government Printing Office. Annual. SuDoc: IC1.25:

A source of statistical data on railroads and motor carriers. Data provided include information on traffic operations, equipment, finances, and employment. This report is issued in the following two parts.

Part 1. *Railroads.*
Part 2. *Motor Carriers.*

National Aeronautics and Space Administration

NASA's principal statutory functions include research dealing with the solution of flight problems within and outside the earth's atmosphere; the development and construction of space vehicles and aeronautical vehicles; and other activities required for the exploration of space.

Earth Resources: A Continuing Bibliography with Indexes. Springfield, VA: National Technical Information Service. Quarterly. SuDoc: NAS1.21:
    An index/bibliography of studies and reports based on data collected from aerial or space surveys.

Scientific and Technical Aerospace Reports. Washington, DC: Government Printing Office. Semimonthly. SuDoc: NAS1.9/4:
    This major bibliographic resource includes reports that deal with technical and economic aspects of the aerospace industry. Annual and semiannual indexes are issued.

National Credit Union Administration

The National Credit Union Administration (NCUA) is responsible for the chartering, insuring, supervising, and examining of Federal credit unions.

NCUA Midyear Statistics for Federally Insured Credit Unions. Washington, DC: National Credit Union Administration. Semiannual. SuDoc: NCU1.9/3:
    Financial statistics on Federal Credit Unions and Federally insured State credit unions.

A separate report is issued on the National Credit Union Shore Insurance Fund.

Credit Union Directory. Washington, DC: National Credit Union Administration. Annual. SuDoc: NCU1.16:
  A directory of NCUA credit unions.

National Endowment For the Arts

National Endowment For the Humanities

Both NEA and NEH issue annual reports which list grants awarded and include officials and advisory personnel directories.

National Science Foundation

The National Science Foundation (NSF) initiates and supports fundamental and applied research in all scientific disciplines. This support is made through grants, contracts, and cooperative agreements awarded to universities, nonprofit, and other research organizations. In addition to its other functions, the NSF develops and disseminates information relating to scientific resources including manpower.

Research

Science and Engineering Indicators. Washington, DC: Government Printing Office. Biennial. SuDoc: NS1.28/2:
  A detailed examination of relevant indicators relating to scientific and engineering research. Includes data on expenditures, education, employment, publishing, technology and social attitudes. Comparisons between the U.S. and other countries are included. A separate biennial report examines similar data for women and minorities.

Science and Technology Data Book. Washington, DC: National Science Foundation. Annual. SuDoc: NS1.2:Sci2/47/
  A graphic presentation of science indicators.

Science Education

Academic Science/Engineering: Graduate Enrollment and Support. Washington, DC: National Science Foundation. Annual. SuDoc: NS1.22/4:
A statistical report on graduate science and engineering education. Includes data on students, programs and funding.

Science Employment

U.S. Scientists and Engineers. Washington, DC: National Science Foundation. Biennial. SuDoc: NS1.22/7:
A statistical profile of the employment status and employment characteristics of scientists and engineers. A separate report is issued irregularly which provides statistics on immigrant scientists and engineers.

National Transportation Safety Board

The National Transportation Board is responsible for investigating and reporting on transportation related accidents.

Aircraft Accident Reports . . . Springfield, VA.: National Technical Information Service. Irregular. SuDoc: TD1.109/13:
These reports provide detailed information on air carrier and general aviation accidents involving U.S. aircraft. Press releases providing more current information are also issued.

Nuclear Regulatory Commission

The Nuclear Regulatory Commission licenses and regulates the use of nuclear energy to protect the public health and safety and the environment.

Licensed Operation Reactors, Status Summary Report. Washington, DC: Government Printing Office. Monthly. SuDoc: Y3.N88:
Provides operating and inspection data on all currently licensed and operating commercial nuclear power plant units in the U.S.

Office of Personnel Management

The agency's basic function is to provide qualified people for government agencies. It is the central personnel agency of the executive branch.

Federal Civilian Workforce Statistics. Washington, DC: Government Printing Office. Monthly. SuDoc: PM1.75:
Provides statistical data on Federal civilian employees. Includes information on employment by branch, agency, and area; turnover, with comparison to U.S. manufacturing industries; demographic data; salary statistics; etc.
A separate report on Federal Civil Service Pay is issued annually.

Resolution Trust Corporation

The Resolution Trust Corporation was established in 1989 to manage and resolve failed savings associations.

Resolution Trust Corporation Real Estate Asset Inventory. Grand Prairie, TX. Resolution Trust Corporation. Semiannual.
A three-volume listing of real properties available under the jurisdiction of the RTC. The volumes cover commercial projects, residential properties and multiple dwelling properties.

RTC Review. Grand Prairie, TX: Resolution Trust Corporation. Monthly.
A report on RTC operations. A quarterly report is also issued.

RTC Inventory of High Yield Securities. Grand Prairie, TX: Quarterly.
A report issued as a press release which provides a list of securities held by the RTC. These securities fall into the "junk bond" category.

Securities and Exchange Commission

The Securities and Exchange Commission (SEC) provides the fullest possible disclosure to the investing public and protects the interests of the public and investors against malpractice in the securities and financial markets.

Stock Market Statistics

Official Summary of Security Transactions and Holdings. Washington, DC: Government Printing Office. Monthly. SuDoc: SE1.9:(v. nos. and nos.)
A monthly summary of securities transactions and holdings of officers, directors, and principal stockholders.

Directories

Directory of Companies Required to File Annual Reports with the Securities and Exchange Commission Under the Securities Exchange Act of 1934. Washington, DC: Government Printing Office. Annual. SuDoc: SE1.27:
Companies required to file annual reports with the SEC are listed alphabetically and by industry.

Small Business Administration

The Small Business Administration (SBA) aids, counsels, assists, and protects the interests of small business. The agency conducts economic and statistical research into matters affecting small business.

Handbook of Small Business Data. Washington, DC: Government Printing Office. Irregular. SuDoc: SBA 1.19:D26
A statistical abstract of data relating to small business activities.

States and Small Business: A Directory of Programs and Activities. Washington, DC: Government Printing Office. Irregular. SuDoc: SBA1.34:
A detailed directory of State small business programs.

State of Small Business. Washington, DC: Government Printing Office. Annual. SuDoc: SBA1.1/2:
A report which contains a narrative statement of the state of small

business and includes the President's report on small business. A statistical appendix provides data on the number, failure rate, employment, productivity, financing etc. of small businesses.

Government Contracts

U.S. Government Purchasing and Sales Directory. Washington, DC: Government Printing Office. Irregular. SuDoc: SBA1.13/3:(Year)

A major guide for the small business person interested in selling to or buying from the Federal government. Included are separate listings of the products and services bought by the military departments and civilian agencies. Information is provided on obtaining government prime and subcontracts, the sales of government surplus property, and the government market for R and D.

Small Business Investment Companies

SBIC Digest. Washington, DC: Small Business Administration. Semiannual. SuDoc: SBA1.30:

Provides data on financing, licensing, and regulation of Small Business Investment Companies (SBIC) and SBIC financing of small business.

Directory of Operating Small Business Investment Companies. Washington, DC: Small Business Administration. Semiannual. SuDoc: SBA1.13/4:

A listing of SBICs and their branch offices.

United States Arms Control and Disarmament Agency

In addition to its other functions with regard to arms control and disarmament policies, the Agency conducts research and studies or makes arrangements for their conduct (through contracts and agreements) by private or public institutions or persons. It also coordinates such efforts by or for other government agencies.

World Military Expenditures and Arms Transfers. Washington, DC: Government Printing Office. Annual. SuDoc: AC1.16:(Year)

Provides information on outlays for and imports and exports of conventional arms by country. Trend data for ten years are provided.

United States International Trade Commission

The United States International Trade Commission furnishes studies, reports, and recommendations involving international trade and tariffs to the President, the Congress, and other government agencies. In this capacity, the Commission conducts a variety of investigations, public hearings, and research projects pertaining to the international policies of the United States.

Among the functions carried out by the USITC are investigations related to U.S. and foreign customs laws; competition of foreign industries with those of the U.S.; preferential removal of customs duties (advice to the President); import relief for domestic industries; East-West trade monitoring system; trade with Communist countries; anti-dumping investigations; establishment of uniform statistical reporting system for imports and exports; and issuance of *Harmonized Tariff Schedules of the U.S.*

General

Selected Publications of the U.S. International Trade Commission. Washington, D.C.: United States International Trade Commission. Annual. SuDoc: ITC1.9/3:(Year)

An index of general reports on trade programs and commodity classifications; reports on commodities imported from specific countries or geographic areas; reports on individual commodities; and reports on individual domestic firms, as published by the USITC.

International Economic Review. Washington, DC: U.S. International Trade Commission. Monthly.

A narrative and statistical review of international trade and its U.S. impact.

Tariff

Harmonized Tariff Schedule of the U.S. Annotated . . . Washington, DC: Government Printing Office. Irregular/supplements. SuDoc: ITC1.10:

The 1991 edition was the third edition of this official tariff schedule for the United States. Supplements are regularly issued between editions.

Reports

The USITC issues a number of reports of its investigative findings under a variety of legislative mandates. These reports focus on various topics including import relief for domestic producers of specified products on domestic industries producing like or competitive products; effect of imports on USDA price-support programs for like or competitive products; effect of duty-free import sales of specified products from specified countries on domestic industries producing like or competitive products; and effect of increased imports from Communist countries on domestic industries producing like or competitive products.

In addition to these reports, a group of regularly recurring reports is also issued. These reports deal with the effect of various trade agreements and with specific industries.

BOARDS, COMMITTEES AND COMMISSIONS

A great number of boards, centers, commissions, councils, panels, study groups, and task forces are established by congressional or presidential action. The functions of these bodies often include the publication of reports, studies, and so forth. Many of these publications are of major interest to the business community. A listing of these bodies may be found in the *United States Government Manual*, the *Federal Yellow Book* and the *Congressional Yellow Book*.

Another group of bodies of interest to the business community are Federal Advisory Committees, as defined by the Federal Advisory Committee Act (86 Stat. 770). A complete listing of these can be found in *Federal Advisory Committees' Annual Report to the President*.

Samples of the output of these bodies of particular interest from a business or economic viewpoint are listed below.

Advisory Commission on Intergovernmental Relations

The Advisory Commission on Intergovernmental Relations, as part of its mission to review relations among Federal, State and local governments, produces several statistical reports on government finances.

Significant Features of Fiscal Federalism. Washington, DC: Advisory Commission on Fiscal Federalism. Annual. SuDoc: Y3.Ad9/8:
A major review of income and expenditure accounts for Federal, State and local governments.

Commission on Civil Rights

Catalog of Publications, U.S. Commission on Civil Rights. Washington, DC: Commission on Civil Rights. 1989. 19p.
A listing of publications of the Commission on Civil Rights. Includes hearings, studies, working papers, etc. This report is issued at frequent intervals.

Commodity Futures Trading Commission

Commitments of Traders in Commodity Futures. Washington, DC: Commodity Futures Trading Commission. Semimonthly. SuDoc: Y3. C73/5:
A report on futures contracts of markets supervised by the Commodity Futures Trading Commission. Includes financial futures.

Federal Council on Aging

Aging America, Trends and Projections. Washington, DC: Federal Council on Aging. Biennial. SuDoc: Y3.F31/15:
A detailed statistical compendia on all aspects of aging.

Federal Financial Institutions Examination Council

Country Exposure Lending Survey. Chicago, IL: Federal Financial Institutions Examination Council. Quarterly.
A statistical report on lending by U.S. banks to foreign borrowers.

Trust Assets of Financial Institutions. Chicago, IL: Federal Financial Institutions Examination Council. Annual.
A statistical report on trust assets and investment fund activity at

commercial banks savings and loans, trust companies and savings banks regulated by the FFIEC.

Uniform Bank Performance Report State Averages. Chicago, IL: Federal Financial Institutions Examination Council. Quarterly.
   A statistical report on income profitability, liability rates and other financial data for Federally insured or regulated commercial banks.

Interagency Council on the Homeless

Nation Concerned . . . Washington, DC: Interagency Council on the Homeless. Annual.
   An annual report on the Federal programs directed to the homeless and on the demographic and social statistics related to homelessness.

National Advisory Council on International Monetary and Financial Policies

International Finance. Washington, DC: National Advisory Council on International Monetary and Financial Policies. Annual. SuDoc: Y3.N21/16:
   A narrative and statistical report on the U.S. position in the international banking and financial institutions arena.

National Commission on Libraries and Information Science

Information 2000: Library and Information Services in the 21st Century. Washington, DC: Government Printing Office. 1991. IV, 78p. SuDoc: Y3.W58/20:21N3/summ.
   A listing of recommendations from the 1991 White House Conference delegates.

Prospective Payment Assessment Commission

   The Prospective Payment Assessment Commission was established to oversee the Medicare prospective payment system.

Medicare Prospective Payment and the American Health Care System.
Washington, DC: Prospective Payment Assessment Commission.
Annual. SuDoc: Y3.P29:
    A narrative and statistical report on Medicare expenditures.

FEDERAL GOVERNMENT DATA BASES

The Federal government has developed numerous databases to store
data relating to Federal programs. A number of these are available
online through the individual agencies and a few such as CENDATA
are available through commercial online services such as DIALOG
Two examples of such databases are:

Social Security

    A database produced by the Social Security Administration and
available on CompuServe which provides data on Social Security
benefits.

Morbidity and Mortality Weekly Report

    A database in fulltext equivalent to the print product of the same
name which provides current morbidity and mortality statistics. This
database is available on NewsNet.

    A good listing of commercially available and agency-available
databases of the Federal government is contained in the *Directory of
Online Databases.*

REGIONAL AND LOCAL SOURCES—
OFFICIAL AND QUASI-OFFICIAL

Historically, the amount and nature of the statistical supply available from States and localities have varied from area to area. Even within the same area, diversity in data collection, reporting, and analysis, and an overlap in agencies' statistical projects are to be expected.

GOVERNMENTS

In recent years, the growth of State and local programs has generated a trend toward an improved data base for official decision-making. Consequently, attention is being directed toward a better statistical output, standardization in coverage and quality, coordination of statistical activities, and exchanging information on all matters of statistical interest.

Serious efforts have been made toward coordinating Federal, State, and local statistics. Since 1967 the Bureau of the Census has conducted a program involving a Federal-State effort in the development, preparation, and publication of population estimates for small areas. Population estimates from this program are published annually by the Bureau of the Census under the auspices of the Federal-State Cooperative Program for Population Estimates. The State Data Center program has been discussed earlier.

A number of other Federal-State cooperative programs are in effect, particularly in the areas of employment and income. Vital statistics and certain industry data are collected locally in cooperation with or for transmittal to Federal agencies for publication and dissemination.

In general, data compiled by State and local governments, like those by the Federal government, are strongly characterized by the administrative, regulatory, and planning functions of the respective agencies. Permits, fees, licenses, registrations, and taxes immediately suggest the existence of quantitative facts on the local level in published or unpublished form. Officials charged with the activities of planning departments, development commissions, departments of commerce and their equivalents are also in a position to supply information and advice out of their knowledge and experience.

State

Each State issues a number of periodic publications of value in local market and economic analysis. Unpublished data are often available upon application to the proper authorities. Such information may be loosely grouped into several types common to most of the States.

Directories of manufacturers, products, and new plant locations have been issued consistently by many States, some with basic industrial data added. These are treated in greater detail in a subsequent chapter and, in many cases, their publication has been privatized.

A number of States publish statistical compendia of varying frequencies but on a regular basis. These abstracts are a good source of current and historical facts. Moreover, they constitute useful guides to the research data collected regularly. A current list of these is provided in the Appendix.

Periodicals containing reviews of State economic activity are issued by some States—a few by State agencies, others by university bureaus of business research.

Among the many periodic statistical reports, those on labor and agriculture stand out in terms of quantity and detail. Most States have issued series on employment and unemployment, hours and wages, cost of living, labor supply and turnover, on a continuing basis for a number of years. Similarly, State agriculture departments collect and disseminate production statistics; demand, supply, and price information; movement and storage data on agricultural products of importance to their economies. State agricultural experiment stations, many of which are located at colleges and universities, supplement and augment this output with studies on the markets for and the marketing of specific agricultural commodities.

Tax collections by source reflect income, sales of certain products, number and location of licensed retail and service establishments, and other economic activity subject to State assessment. These and similar data on such subjects as housing, vital statistics, vehicle registrations, banks, utilities, transport, and manufacturing industries, are either published or made available for consultation by the agency concerned.

Area market studies (consumer and industrial), market analyses, industrial censuses, resources and growth reports prompted by State economic and industrial planning activity are issued from time to time. A trend which began in the 1980s was toward privatization of statistical and directory publication.

Local

Like States, many local governments collect statistics in the course of their regulatory and administrative activities but seldom publish them for wide distribution.

Although a certain amount of unpublished data is available from local agencies, the basic statistical supply for these areas emanates primarily from Federal and State governments, chambers of commerce, and other sources.

Where close State-local economic relationships exist (as in population, income, local business activity), State interests usually activate research and development and State publications provide city, county, and regional breakdowns.

The publishing programs of both State and local governments have been impacted by the economic problems of the late 1980s and 1990s.

CHAMBERS OF COMMERCE

The Chamber of Commerce of the United States was organized as a privately supported national organization by President Taft and his Secretary of Commerce to provide a viewpoint on matters of Federal policy of concern to the business community.

A large staff produces for its membership numerous bulletins and studies on economic business and governmental developments affecting American enterprise on national and international levels. It also issues a monthly magazine, *Nation's Business,* and informational reports of interest to business management.

State and local chambers of commerce, because of their aggressive and competitive interest in promoting and developing the commercial, industrial and other economic activity of their areas, provide a number of useful publications.

The two most prevalent types, directories and monthly bulletins, closely parallel and complement those issued by State and local governments and university bureaus of business research. Industrial directories often carry descriptive information on the State and its resources. Some include similar detail for their municipalities. Further discussion of this source appears in the chapter on directories. Monthly bulletins that review general business conditions and statistical data affecting the local economic climate are issued by a number of State and city chambers. Also available is information on building projects and plant expansions, and occasional projections of population, housing, and employment.

City chambers of commerce also compile and distribute occasional studies dealing with their areas as a whole or with particular factors of current local interest.

Both State and local organizations can assist in supplying unpublished information and pertinent advice relating to their areas. The larger organizations maintain collections of directories, trade journals, government publications, and other reference materials for serving the business interest of their community.

In pursuing questions of overseas business one may contact the national chamber, American chambers of commerce in foreign countries, and/or the foreign chamber of commerce offices which some countries have established in the United States. The latter issue membership lists, directories, and other publications which are of use to foreigners wishing to do business in the country represented.

OTHER LOCAL GROUPS

A number of other local groups issue a limited number of publications that provide useful regional, State, and local information.

Included in this category are statistical coordinating agencies established by local chapters of professional associations; regional plan organizations; interstate agencies active in environmental programs, and land/water resources development and transportation planning.

Commerce and industry associations, local merchant and similar groups, organized on a city level or on smaller district levels, exist in large metropolitan areas. Concerned with the business activity in their immediate community, they constitute a relatively obscure but often unique source of information and assistance.

The self-supporting, quasi-governmental port authorities are a source of information not only for the facilities under their jurisdiction, but also for the geographical areas where they are concerned with the maintenance and development of their activities.

RESEARCH AIDS

Regional, State, and local data are generated by many kinds of organizations and are scattered throughout all types of sources. Local newspapers, university bureaus of business research, field units of Federal agencies and other suppliers of area statistics are treated in their respective chapters. Particularly rich in area data are Federal publications, especially those of the Bureau of the Census.

Gathered here are a number of comprehensive research aids oriented generally or topically toward area data published, from a range of government and commercial sources.

Regional

Recent Publications on Governmental Problems. Chicago, Ill.: Merriam Center Library. Monthly/Annual Cumulation. ISSN 0034–1185.

Up-to-date listings of interest to planners and others concerned with State, local and regional matters such as energy, finance, environment, housing, etc. Includes articles, books, reports from regional, State, local, Federal and private publishers. A cumulative index is available.

CPL Bibliographies. Chicago, Ill.: Council of Planning Libraries. Irregular.

Ongoing series of bibliographies on all aspects of planning and related regional and local activities. A three-volume index to the series, formerly titled *Exchange Bibliographies,* was issued in 1979 as *CPL Bibliography no. 1–3.*

Statistical Reference Index: A Selective Guide to American Statistical Publications from Sources Other Than the U.S. Government. American *Statistics Index: A Comprehensive Guide and Index to the Statistical Publications of the U.S. Government.*

Regional Differences in America: A Statistical Sourcebook. Boulder, Co.: Numbers and Concepts. 1988. xiv, 590p.

A regional statistical abstract which includes sections on demographics, social statistics, economic statistics and political statistics.

Data Base

Regional Economic Information System. Washington, DC: U.S. Department of Commerce, Bureau of Economic Analysis. Economic Projections.

State

Omnibus Aids

The Book of the States. Lexington, KY: Council of State Governments. Biennial with supplements.

Provides information on the structure and functions of State governments. Its administrative officials supplement lists these officials by function and serves as an excellent key to State statistical data sources. A second supplement is a roster of State elected officials.

Sources of State Information and State Industrial Directories. Washington, DC: Chamber of Commerce of the United States. Irregular.

A directory of public and private agencies which provide information about their States. Also lists manufacturers' directories issued by State and private agencies.

World Chamber of Commerce Directory. Loveland, Co.: World Chamber of Commerce Directory.

Domestic and foreign chambers of commerce are arranged geographically with name of acting executive, address, and telephone number given for each.

U.S. Library of Congress. *Monthly Checklist of State Publications.* Washington, DC: Government Printing Office. Monthly.

Lists publications of State agencies, arranged by State, and of State associations, councils, etc., received by the Library of Congress. Includes an annual subject index and list of periodicals.

State and Local Statistics Sources: A Subject Guide to Statistical Data on States, Cities, and Localities . . . Detroit, MI: Gale Research. 1990. xx, 1124p.

A State-by-State, subject-arranged list of statistics sources. Includes a source list and a list of State Data Centers.

City and State Directories in Print. Detroit, MI: Gale Research. 1990–91. xvii, 966p.

A State-by-State directory of directories. Includes a subject index and a title and keyword index.

State Yellow Book. New York, NY: Monitor Publishing. Quarterly.

One of the Monitor series of "yellow books," this lists State agencies and officials.

Databases

ADRG Master Database. Arlington Heights, IL: Applied Demographic Research Group.

Demographic, economic and social statistics.

Allstate Census Use System. Middlefield, N.J.: Allstate Insurance Company Economic and Demographic Research Division.

Market statistics and site locator data.

America Profile. Stamford, CT.: Donnelly Marketing Information Services.

Demographic and economic statistics.

Census Information Data Center. New York, NY: Market Statistics.

Economic and demographic statistics to zip code level.

CENDATA. U.S. Bureau of the Census. Data User Service. Washington, DC.

Demographic and Economic Data Online.

Datamap Database. Eden Prairie, MN.
   Computerized mapping services.

Dun's Electronic Yellow Pages. Parsippany, N.J.
   Directory services online and customized.

Econobase: Timeseries and Forecasts. Bala Cynwyd, PA.: WEFA
Group.
   Business and economic forecasts.

EEO/Census Occupational Profiles Database. Ithaca, NY: National
Planning Data Corporation.
   Demographic data for small areas.

Federal Market Analysis Division. Fairfax, VA: CACI, Inc.
   Demographic and economic projections.

Geofiles. Andover, MA: GSI/Tactics.
   Computer mapping.

Local Marketing Data Center. Encinitas, CA: National Decision
Systems.
   Demographic and local market data.

Marketing Economic Institute Database. Jamaica, NY: Marketing
Economic Institute.
   Economic, demographic and environmental data.

NPA Economic Database. Washington, DC: NPA Data Services.
   Demographic and economic forecasts.

Onsite Reports. Los Angeles, CA: Urban Decision Systems.
   Demographic and economic statistics.

Randata. Skokie, IL: Rand McNally.
   Demographic and economic data to zip code level.

Sitenet. Norcross, GA: Conway Data.
   Demographic and economic data online.

Zip Code Database. Culver City, CA: Demographic Research.
Demographic and economic data at zip code level.

Single-State Aids

The last decade has seen a reduction in the number of bibliographic aids published by individual States; however, the output of
the individual State Data Centers and the development of statistical
databases of the State universities or by individual State departments
have made access to State statistical data easier. The State Data
centers are listed in a variety of publications including the *Bureau of
the Census Catalog.* The following list of databases represents those
available at time of publication.

Alabama
Alabama University Center for Business and Economic Research
Database. Tuscaloosa, AL.
Demographic and economic data for the State and localities.

Arizona
Arizona University Division of Economic and Business Research.
Database.
Demographic and economic data for the State and localities.

California
California Center Database. Center for Continuing Study of Califor-
nia Economy. Palo Alto, CA.
Demographic and economic data for counties and cities. UCLA
Business Forecasting Project, Los Angeles, CA.

Colorado
Colorado Business/Economic Data Bank. Colorado: University Busi-
ness Research Division. Boulder, CO.
Business statistics for State and local areas.

Florida
Florida University Bureau of Economic and Business Research
Database. Gainesville, FL.
Demographic and economic statistics for the State and local areas.

Indiana
Economic Development Information Network. Indiana University Business Research Center. Bloomington, IN.
Demographic and economic statistics for the State and local areas.

Kansas
Kansas University Institute for Public Policy and Business Research Database. Lawrence, KS.
Economic information for the State.

Cellar Database. Wichita State University. Wichita, KS.

Kentucky
Kentucky Economic Information System. Kentucky University Center for Business and Economic Research. Lexington, KY.
Provides demographic and economic data for the State online.

Michigan
Michigan Metropolitan Information Center. Wayne State University Center for Urban Studies. Detroit, MI.
Demographic and economic data for the State and Southeastern Michigan including Detroit.

Minnesota
Minnesota State Planning Agency Database. Minnesota State Planning Agency. St. Paul, MN.
Demographic and economic data for the State and local areas.

Missouri
Missouri University Business and Public Administration Research Center Database. Columbia, MO.
Demographic and economic data for the State and local areas.

Montana
Montana Department of Commerce Census and Economic Database. Montana Department of Commerce Census and Economic Information Center. Helena, MT.
Demographic, environmental and economic data.

New Hampshire
New Hampshire University State and Regional Indicators Archive
Database. Durham, NH.
   Demographic and economic data.

New Mexico
Bureau of Business and Economic Research Data Bank. New Mexico
University. Institute for Applied Research Services. Albuquerque,
NM.
   Demographic and economic data.

Oklahoma
Oklahoma University Center for Economic and Management Re-
search Database. Norman, OK.
   Demographic and economic data for Southwestern Oklahoma.

South Dakota
South Dakota University Business Research Bureau Database. Ver-
million, SD.
   Demographic and economic data.

Tennessee
Tennessee University Center for Business and Economic Research
Database. Knoxville, TN.
   Demographic and economic data.

Texas
Texas University Bureau of Business Research Database. Austin, TX.
   Demographic and economic data.

Utah
Utah University Bureau of Business and Economic Research Data-
base. Salt Lake City, UT.
   Demographic and economic data.

Virginia
Virginia University Center for Public Service Database. Charlottes-
ville, VA.
   Demographic and economic data.

Local

Omnibus Aids

The Municipal Yearbook. Washington, DC: International City Management Association. Annual.

Provides information on subjects affecting urban government and directories of officials for cities of 5,000 population and over. Includes an extensive bibliography for major areas of local government.

World Chamber of Commerce Directory.

Index to Current Urban Documents. Westport, Conn.: Greenwood Press. Quarterly/Annual Cumulation. ISSN 0046–8908.

For cities and counties, arranged by State, cites the local government publications and those State publications that deal specifically with the cities and counties listed. A companion program offers microfiche of listed items.

Urban Affairs Abstracts. Washington, DC: National League of Cities/ U.S. Conference of Mayors. Weekly/Semiannual and Annual Cumulations.

Up-to-date abstracts of urban literature include business, industry, and related topics.

Recent Publications on Governmental Problems.

CPL Bibliographies.

State and Local Statistics Sources . . .

City and State Directories in Print.

Municipal Yellow Book. New York, NY: Monitor Publishing. Semiannual.

One of the Monitor series of "yellow books" which lists in telephone directory fashion municipal offices and officials.

Single-Area Aids

Research guides to local-area data sources for individual localities are not well developed. Even identifying and locating local
government publications is very difficult. Although a few cities
publish a checklist of one kind or another, these tend to be the
exception rather than the rule. For publications of such areas the
comprehensive listings in the *Index to Current Urban Documents* must
be consulted.

Topical Aids

The omnibus sources already listed have subject indexes which
will provide a guide to topical information at regional, State and
local level. A selection of topical statistical sources covering multiple
regional, State and local areas follows.

General

Baseline Data Reports. Washington, DC: International City Management Association. Bimonthly.
    An ongoing series of reports with statistics on municipal issues.

Council of State Governments Database. Lexington, KY: Council of
State Governments. [Database.]
    A database of fiscal and legislative data for States.

Research Reports on America's Cities. Washington, DC: National League
of Cities. Irregular.
    A series of reports with statistics on urban issues.

Financial Data Center. Austin, TX. Municipal Analysis Services.
[Database.]
    A database of economic information for State and local areas.

State of the States. Washington, DC: Review America. Annual.
    A series of reports with emphasis on environmental issues at State
level.

Crime

National Crime Information Center. Washington, DC: U.S. Federal Bureau of Investigation.
Online information on crime.

Education

State Education Indicators. Washington, DC: Council of Chief State School Officers. Annual.
State education system cost data.

Health

State Report: State Progress on Health Objectives for the Nation. Washington, DC. Public Health Foundation. Annual.
State-by-State report on progress toward Surgeon General's goals.

Population–Economics

NPA Economic Database. Washington, DC: NPA Data Services. [Database.]
Forecasts of economic and demographic data.

Onsite Reports. Los Angeles, CA.: Urban Decisions Systems. [Database.]
Economic and demographic trend data.

Randata. Skokie, IL. Rand McNally. [Database.]
Economic projections.

Sitenet. Norcross, GA. Conway Data. [Database.]
Demographic and economic data for site selection.

Zip Code Database. Culver City, CA. Demographic Research. [Database.]
Demographic and economic data at ZipCode level.

Marketing

Local Marketing Data Center. Encinitas, CA. National Decision Systems. [Database.]
　Customized local market data.

Marketing Economic Institute Database. Jamaica, NY. Marketing Economic Institute. [Database.]
　Demographic, economic and environmental data.

Company Data

How to Find Company Intelligence in State Documents. Washington, DC: Washington Researchers. Annual.
　A State-by-State list which describes documents that each State must collect on companies operating within that State, and tells where such documents can be found.

FOREIGN SOURCES—NATIONAL AND INTERGOVERNMENTAL

On a current basis, domestic sources (governmental and commercial) can provide quick and timely access to economic, business, and marketing data on foreign countries. Some of these data are generated internally; other data are reported or derived from the announcements and publications of official foreign sources, both national and intergovernmental.

Internationally oriented domestic newspapers, business and trade magazines, newsletters, abstracts, databases, services, and other sources are cited throughout this guide. Similarly represented are many Federal publications which result from the international responsibilities and programs of United States departments and agencies.

Researchers seeking current, comprehensive local coverage may attempt to locate comparable sources originating in a particular country by using relevant research guides. For those concerned with basic national data and cross-national analyses, this chapter covers the principal, easily accessible publications that present official statistics of foreign countries.

Statistical data, in greater or lesser quantity and with greater or lesser accuracy, are available from virtually every region and country in the world. National governments of most developed and many developing countries publish statistical compendia, censuses, statistical abstracts, and special studies. Many of the countries that publish statistical abstracts on a regular basis also issue interim statistical bulletins on a regular basis. Some also issue recurrent statistical publications devoted to data on vital statistics, labor, finance, foreign trade, and other topics. In many instances the data are compiled and distributed by national statistical offices. In addition, central banks frequently publish economic and financial data for the country and, on occasion, analyses of regional or world conditions that impact their national economies.

213

The most common statistical publication worldwide is the statistical abstract, or compendium of basic national data. A limited number of countries have also complemented these with compilations of historical statistics. In Western Europe, Canada, Japan, and in other areas where business and marketing activities are well developed, there are backup publications and information services similar to those in the United States. Foremost among the services are the trade offices or representatives of foreign governments overseas. Many such in the United States can supply from a local office information, data, and publications of interest to business researchers. Chambers of Commerce in foreign cities offer services similar to those offered by domestic chambers.

In addition to compiling and publishing their own statistics, national governments report data to international organizations, including intergovernmental bodies such as those listed below. Those like the Organization for Economic Cooperation and Development, the United Nations, and its regional and specialized affiliates primarily assemble, compile, and publish statistics reported by their member countries. In the process they promote standardization at the national level to achieve uniformity and comparability of the data collected. To a lesser degree these organizations also compile and publish data resulting from their own research and statistics obtained from nonmember countries, mainly those that apply to the needs of the organization and its members.

Publications issued by intergovernmental organizations fall into categories recognizable to the statistical researchers:

Compendia, issued annually but usually covering several years, contain statistics for each of the member countries. In many cases a historical volume provides lengthy time series data for the tables in the annual.

Statistical bulletins, issued more frequently, report data on a more current basis.

Recurrent topical compilations, published at regular intervals, cover such areas as national accounts, foreign trade, production, etc.

Ad hoc statistical reports are issued as a result of specific situations.

The publications of international and multinational intergovernmental organizations selected for listing are basic sources of foreign country and regional data. Their value to the researcher is that they are more universally available than those of individual countries; they present otherwise unpublished or difficult to obtain official statistics for countries and topics; text and tables are in English; they frequently include notes explaining the data and their limitations; they facilitate national summarizations and cross-national comparisons. On the other hand, there is often considerable time lag between the period covered by the data and their appearance in these publications. However, extensive footnotes in many instances lead to more timely publications of member and nonmember countries.

INTERNATIONAL ORGANIZATIONS

United Nations (UN)

Membership consists of 159 countries. Information centers and depository libraries for U.N. publications exist worldwide.

United Nations Publications Catalog. New York: United Nations. Annual.
Lists sales publications and periodicals available on annual subscription.

UNDOC: Current Index. New York: United Nations. 10/yr. ISSN 0250-5584.

United Nations Documents and Publications. [Microform]. New Canaan, CT: Readex.
A microfiche service which includes both sales publications and documents. The United Nations also produces microfiche which are available through UNIPUB. A CD-ROM index to United Nations publications is available from Readex.

Compendia

Monthly Bulletin of Statistics. New York: United Nations. Monthly. ISSN 0041-7432.

Statistical Yearbook. New York: United Nations. Annual. ISSN 0082-8459.

World Statistics in Brief. New York: United Nations. Annual.

Social Statistics

Population and Vital Statistics Report. New York: United Nations. Quarterly.

Population Bulletin . . . New York, NY: United Nations. Bi-annual.

Compendium of Social Statistics. New York: United Nations. Irregular.

Demographic Yearbook. New York: United Nations. Annual. ISSN 0082-8041.

————. *Historical Supplement.* (Statistical Papers, Series A.) New York: United Nations. 1980. vii, 1171p.

Handbook on Social Indicators—Studies in Methods. New York, NY: United Nations. 1989. E.89. xvii, 6p.
  A guide to regional national and international social indicators.

Economic Statistics

In addition to the following, the United Nations publishes a number of regularly recurrent publications dealing with the world economy and economics of individual regions. A selection follows:

United Nations. National Accounts Statistics. New York: United Nations. Annual.

Industrial Statistics Yearbook. New York: United Nations. Annual.

Construction Statistics Yearbook. New York: United Nations. Annual.

Energy Statistics Yearbook. New York: United Nations. Annual.

International Trade Statistics Yearbook. New York: United Nations. Annual.

UNCTAD Commodity Yearbook. New York: United Nations. Annual.

Food and Agricultural Organization (FAO)

A specialized agency of the United Nations. Membership consists of 159 countries. In addition to the general works listed, FAO issues statistics on individual food crops, horticultural crops, forests and forest products and livestock and fisheries.

Food Outlook. Rome: Food and Agriculture Organization. Monthly.

FAO Quarterly Bulletin of Statistics. Rome: Food and Agriculture Organization. Quarterly.

Production Yearbook. Rome: Food and Agriculture Organization. Annual. ISSN 0071-7118.

Trade Yearbook. Rome: Food and Agriculture Organization. Annual. ISSN 0071-7126.

General Agreement on Tariffs and Trade (GATT)

Membership consists of 92 contracting parties.

International Trade. Geneva: Contracting Parties to the General Agreement on Tariffs and Trade. Annual. ISSN 0072-064x.

International Bank For Reconstruction and Development

A specialized agency of the United Nations, also referred to as the World Bank. Membership consists of 151 countries.

World Bank Catalog of Publications. Washington, DC: International Bank for Reconstruction and Development. Annual. ISSN 0253-7389.

Living Standards Measurement Studies. Washington, DC: International Bank for Reconstruction and Development. Irregular. ISSN 0253-4517.

World Bank Atlas. Washington, DC: International Bank for Reconstruction and Development. Annual. ISSN 0085-8293.

World Tables. Baltimore: Johns Hopkins University Press. Biennial. (A separate debt tables annual is issued.) ISSN 1043-5573.

Social Indicators of Development. New York: Oxford University Press. Annual. ISSN 1012-8026.

Emerging Stock Markets Fact Book. Washington, DC: International Bank for Reconstruction and Development. ISSN 1012-8115.

International Labour Organization

A specialized agency of the United Nations. Membership consists of 150 countries.

Bulletin of Labour Statistics. Geneva: International Labour Organization. Quarterly/Supplement. ISSN 0378-5505.

Yearbook of Labour Statistics. Geneva: International Labour Organization. Annual. ISSN 0084-3857.

Statistical Sources and Methods. Geneva: International Labour Organization. Irregular. ISSN 0255-3465.

Cost of Social Security. Geneva: International Labour Organization. Triennial. ISSN 0538-8295.

International Monetary Fund (IMF)

A specialized agency of the United Nations. Membership consists of 151 countries.

International Financial Statistics. Washington, DC: International Monetary Fund. Monthly/Supplement. ISSN 0020-6725.

Direction of Trade Statistics. Washington, DC: International Monetary Fund. Monthly/Annual. ISSN 0252-306x.

Balance of Payments Statistics. Washington, DC: International Monetary Fund. Monthly/Annual. ISSN 0252-3035.

Government Finance Statistics Yearbook. Washington, DC: International Monetary Fund. Annual. ISSN 0250-7374.

IMF Survey. Washington, DC: International Monetary Fund. Biweekly. ISSN 0047-083x.

United Nations Educational, Scientific and Cultural Organization (UNESCO)

A specialized agency of the United Nations. Membership consists of 160 countries.

UNESCO Statistical Yearbook. Paris: United Nations Educational, Scientific and Cultural Organization. Annual. ISSN 0028-7541.

World Health Organization (WHO)

A specialized agency of the United Nations. Membership consists of 159 countries.

World Health Statistics Quarterly. Geneva: World Health Organization. Quarterly. ISSN 0379-8510.

World Health Statistics. Geneva: World Health Organization. Annual. ISSN 0250-3794.

MULTINATIONAL ORGANIZATIONS

Organization for Economic Cooperation and Development

Membership consists of Australia, Austria, Belgium, Canada, Denmark, Finland, France, Germany, Greece, Iceland, Ireland, Italy,

Japan, Luxembourg, Netherlands, New Zealand, Norway, Portugal, Spain, United States of America and Yugoslavia.

Main Economic Indicators. Paris: Organization for Economic Cooperation and Development. Monthly. ISSN 0474-5523.

OECD Economic Outlook. Paris: Organization for Economic Cooperation and Development. Semiannual. ISSN 0474-5574.

OECD Economic Survey. Paris: Organization for Economic Cooperation and Development. Annual. ISSN 0376-6438.
    An ongoing series of annuals, one for each member country plus Yugoslavia.

OECD Financial Statistics. Paris: Organization for Economic Cooperation and Development. Monthly/Annual. ISSN 0304-3371.
    A three-part series which includes financial statistics, financial accounts and non-financial enterprise statistics.
    Methodology supplement is also issued.

Quarterly Labour Force Statistics. Paris: Organization for Economic Cooperation and Development. Quarterly/Annual. ISSN 0255-3627.

Financial Market Trends. Paris: Organization for Economic Cooperation and Development. 3/year. ISSN 0378-651x.

Monthly Statistics of Foreign Trade. Paris: Organization for Economic Cooperation and Development. Monthly. ISSN 0474-5388.

European Communities Organization

The European Communities Organization has regulatory as well as advisory powers. Membership consists of Belgium, Denmark, France, Germany, Greece, Ireland, Italy, Luxembourg, Netherlands, Portugal, Spain and the United Kingdom.
    The major publications for the EC are available through UNIPUB and its databases are selectively available on NEXIS. Eurostat, the statistical publishing arm of the EC, is a key source of European statistical information.

Statistical Databases

The EC produces three major statistical databases: CRONOS, a time series database; COMTEXT, a database of external trade statistics; and REGIO, a regional statistics database. Information concerning these databases is available from the Statistical Office of the European Communities in Luxembourg.

A selection of statistical publications of the EC follows.

General

Bulletin of the European Communities. Luxembourg: Statistical Office of the European Communities. Monthly. ISSN 0007-5116.

Eurostat News. Luxembourg: Statistical Office of the European Communities. Quarterly. ISSN 0378-4207.

Basic Statistics of the Community. Luxembourg: Statistical Office of the European Communities. Quarterly. ISSN 0081-4873.

Eurostatistics. Luxembourg: Statistical Office of the European Communities. Monthly. ISSN 0252-8266.

Eurobarometer: Public Opinion . . . Luxembourg: Statistical Office of the European Communities. Semiannual.

Social Statistics

Demographic Statistics. Luxembourg: Statistical Office of the European Communities. Irregular.

Social Europe. Luxembourg: Statistical Office of the European Communities. 3/year/supplements. ISSN 0255-0776.

Economic Statistics

Consumer Price Index. Luxembourg: Statistical Office of the European Communities. Monthly.

Graphs and Notes on the Economic Situation in the Community. Luxembourg: Statistical Office of the European Communities. Monthly.

European Economy. Luxembourg: Statistical Office of the European Communities. Quarterly. ISSN 0379-0991.

National Accounts. Luxembourg: Statistical Office of the European Communities. Annual.

Results of the Business Surveys Carried Out Among Managements in the Community. Luxembourg: Statistical Office of the European Communities. Monthly. ISSN 0378-4474.

Transport Statistics. Luxembourg: Statistical Office of the European Communities. Annual.

External Trade. Luxembourg: Statistical Office of the European Communities. Monthly.

Balance of Payments. Luxembourg: Statistical Office of the European Communities. Annual.

Panorama of EC Industry. Luxembourg: Statistical Office of the European Communities. Annual.

Industry: Statistical Yearbook. Luxembourg: Statistical Office of the European Communities. Annual.
A monthly on industrial publication is also issued.

Nordic Council

Membership consists of Denmark, Finland, Iceland, Norway, and Sweden.

Yearbook of Nordic Statistics. Stockholm: Nordic Council. Irregular. ISSN 0078-1088.

Organization of American States (OAS)

Membership consists of 32 countries of North, Central, and South America, with observers.

Statistical Bulletin of the OAS. Washington, DC: Organization of American States. Semiannual. ISSN 0250-6092.

CECON Trade News. Washington, DC: Organization of American States. Monthly. ISSN 0250-6203.

Statistical Compendium of the Americas. Washington, DC: Organization of American States/Inter-American Statistical Institute. Irregular.

International Commodity Quarterly. Washington, DC: Organization of American States. Quarterly. ISSN 0250-6084.

Arab Monetary Fund

Membership consists of 21 countries and the PLO.

Arab Countries Economic Indicators. Abu Dhabi: Arab Monetary Fund. Annual.

Arab Fund for Economic and Social Development

Membership consists of 21 countries and the PLO.

National Accounts for Arab Countries. Kuwait: Arab Fund. Annual.

Organization of the Petroleum Exporting Countries

Membership consists of Algeria, Ecuador, Gabon, Indonesia, Iran, Iraq, Kuwait, Libya, Nigeria, Qatar, Saudi Arabia, United Arab Emirates, and Venezuela.

OPEC Bulletin. Vienna: Organization of the Petroleum Exporting Countries. Monthly. ISSN 0474-6279.

OPEC Annual Statistical Bulletin. Vienna: Organization of the Petroleum Exporting Countries. Annual. ISSN 0475-0608.

Facts and Figures . . . Vienna: Organization of the Petroleum Exporting Countries. Annual.

OPEC Review. Vienna: Organization of the Petroleum Exporting Countries. Quarterly. ISSN 0277-0180.

NATIONAL STATISTICAL ABSTRACTS

Most developed countries and many developing countries issue a statistical abstract. However, frequency and regularity vary widely from country to country. Generally these publications contain national and some lower area-level demographic, economic, social, industrial, and political data. Text and tables are commonly in the language of the country, with a very limited number being issued in English as well. Those in languages using non-roman alphabets may include English-language equivalents of table and column headings.

In using these publications, it should be kept in mind that they may appear much later than the edition year indicated, and that in many cases footnotes will lead to more current and more frequently issued statistical publications.

Included here are statistical abstracts of countries receiving a major share of United States exports. These and other statistical publications of foreign countries may be located by checking the relevant research aids listed in the last chapter. Hungary and China have been included because of increasing demand for data on these areas. The changes that have occurred in Eastern and Central Europe since 1989 make it imperative that current bibliographic sources be checked for statistical publications from these areas.

North America

Canada

Canada Yearbook. Ottawa. Statistics Canada. Annual.

Mexico

Anuario Estadistico de los Estados Unidos Mexicanos. Mexico City: Direccion General de Estadistica. Annual. ISSN 0068-8142.

South America

Brazil-Venezuela

Anuario Estatistico do Brasil. Rio de Janeiro: Fundacao Instituto Brasileiro de Geografia e Estatistica. Annual. ISSN 0100-1299.

Anuario Estadistico de Venezuela. Caracas: Oficiana Central de Estadistica e Informatica. Annual.

Europe

Belgium-Luxembourg

Annuaire Statistique de la Belgique. Brussels: Institut National de Statistique. Annual. ISSN 0066-3646.

Annuaire Statistique de Luxembourg. Luxembourg: Service Central de la Statistique et des Etudes Economiques. Annual.

France

Annuaire Statistique de la France. Paris: Institut National de la Statistique et des Etudes Economiques. Annual. ISSN 0060-3654.

Federal Republic of Germany

Statistisches Jahrbuch fur die Bundesrepublik Deutschland. Wiesbaden: Statistisches Bundesamt. Annual. ISSN 0081-5351.
The new Germany is expected to have a new statistical yearbook.

Hungary

Statistical Yearbook. Budapest: Central Statistical Office. Annual. ISSN 0073-4039.

Italy

Anuario Statistico Italiano. Rome: Istituto Centrale de Statistica. Annual.

Netherlands

Statistical Yearbook of the Netherlands. Hague, Netherlands: Centraal Bureau voor de Statistiek. Annual. ISSN 0303-6448.

Portugal

Anuario Estatistico: Continente, Acores e Madeira. Lisbon: Instituto Nacional de Estatistica. Annual. ISSN 0079-4112.

Spain

Anuario Estadistico de Espana. Madrid: Instituto Nacional de Estadistica. Annual. ISSN 0066-5177.

Sweden

Statistical Abstract of Sweden. Stockholm: Statistics Sweden. ISSN 0081-5381.
In Swedish and English.

Switzerland

Statistisches Jahrbuch der Schweiz. Bern: Bundesamt für Statistik. Annual. ISSN 0081-5330.
In German and French.

United Kingdom

Annual Abstract of Statistics. London: Central Statistical Office. Annual.

Middle East

Israel

Statistical Abstract. Jerusalem: Central Bureau of Statistics. Annual. ISSN 0081-4679.

Saudi Arabia

Statistical Yearbook. Riyadh: Central Department of Statistics. Annual

Africa

Egypt

Statistical Yearbook. Cairo: Central Agency for Public Mobilisation and Statistics. Annual.

South Africa

South African Statistics. Pretoria: Central Statistical Sources. Biennial.

Asia

China (Taiwan)

Statistical Yearbook of the Republic of China. Taipei: Directorate-General of Budget, Accounting and Statistics. Annual. ISSN 1011-2154.

China (People's Republic)

Statistical Yearbook of China. Hong Kong: State Statistical Bureau. Annual. ISSN 0255-6766.

Hong Kong

Hong Kong Annual Digest of Statistics. Hong Kong: Census and Statistics Department. Annual/Semiannual Supplement.

Japan

Japan Statistical Yearbook. Tokyo: Statistics Bureau. Annual. ISSN 0389-9004.

Korea (South)

Korea Statistical Yearbook. Seoul: Economic Planning Board. Annual.

Philippines

Philippine Statistical Yearbook. Manila: National Economic and Development Authority. Annual.

Singapore

Yearbook of Statistics. Singapore: Department of Statistics. Annual. ISSN 0583-3655.

Oceania

Australia

Yearbook Australia. Canberra, Australia: Australian Bureau of Statistics. Annual. ISSN 0312-4746.

RESEARCH AIDS

The following directories list and describe international and multinational organizations, intergovernmental and private. English-language publications of these bodies and of foreign governments, if relevant to economic and business topics, are covered by a number of titles cited in the chapter on abstracts and indexes. Further detail on national statistical sources, published and institutional, is available in the guides listed in the chapter on research aids.

Europa Yearbook. London: Europa Publishers Ltd. 2 vols. Annual. ISSN 0071-2302.
Volume I includes directory information on international organizations. Regional editions are published for the Middle East, Africa, the Far East and Australia, and South America, Central America and the Caribbean, and Eastern Europe.

Yearbook of International Organizations. Brussels: Union of International Associations. Annual.

Statesman's Year Book. New York: St. Martin's Press. Annual. ISSN 0081-4601.

Directory of Government Documents Collections and Librarians. Bethesda, MD: Congressional Information Service. Irregular.
This directory is compiled by the Government Documents Round Table of the American Library Association and includes directory information for libraries and other agencies having Federal, State, local, foreign and international documents collections.

Guide to Official Publications of Foreign Countries. Chicago, IL: American Library Association. 1990. xx,359p.
This directory is compiled by the Government Documents Round Table of the American Library Association and on a country by country basis describes the published output of the government and lists guides and other access tools useful for locating this output.

NON-OFFICIAL STATISTICS

European Directory of Non-official Statistical Sources. London: Euromonitor/Detroit, MI: Gale. Irregular. ISSN 0953-0258.
A directory of key non-official statistical sources for Europe. Includes published sources and contact sources.

International Directory of Non-official Statistical Sources. London: Euromonitor/Detroit, MI.: Gale. Irregular.

A companion volume to the *European Directory . . .* which covers the rest of the world.

Databases

The intergovernmental organizations such as the U.N., the O.E.C.D., and the E.C. have developed large-scale databases of statistical information which are available through online sources such as Data-Star, DIALOG, Reuters and NEXIS, or directly from the producer. Individual countries have likewise developed statistical databases and these are available in a similar manner. As is the case with statistical information, the quality and quantity of the data will vary greatly from country to country. The *Directory of Online Databases* is an excellent source for locating these databases.

Eastern Europe

At this time, Central and Eastern Europe are emerging as participants in the international market. The following publishers are producing current and useful statistical data for this area. Database production for this area is just beginning.

Business International/Economist Intelligence Unit. New York/ London.
A series of current country reports and special studies.

Frost & Sullivan. New York.
A series of industry studies.

Financial Times. London.
Several periodicals dealing with East European business.

UNIVERSITY PROGRAMS

The significant increase in the number of MBA degrees conferred during the 1980s is reflected in an increasingly sophisticated cadre of middle- and top-level management personnel. This academic orientation, coupled with major advances in computer technology and the ability to store, retrieve, and process data, has given new impetus to the trend toward academic-business cooperation that began in the post-World War II years. Substantial databases containing economic and demographic data have been developed by the university sector, and the information generated from these data bases and from university-based business and economic research is a regular part of the input data utilized in business management and research. A number of these databases are listed in the regional, state, local section.

Moreover, as in other areas, institutions of higher learning are assuming an increasingly prominent and diversified role in business and marketing. Faculty and students in recent years have undertaken both basic and applied research projects of interest to the business community. Staff members continue to contribute widely as consultants to industry and government. Pure research, on the institutional level, continues to produce new methods and refinements of value to economic and market analysis. Academic work is also finding wider dissemination in various forms, including working papers that appear sometimes long before the final reports are issued and offer certain data not contained in those publications.

PRIVATE GRANT PROJECTS

A great deal of research is conducted by universities and university-affiliated units under grants from trade and professional associations, foundations, government agencies (Federal, State, and local), and business firms. These projects are usually undertaken by university research centers in addition to their own staff studies and continuing programs. Reports resulting from this research, depending upon governmental or commercial restrictions, are available in a variety of ways. Those produced under contract are often available only from the sponsoring body; some are commercially published; some are restricted to intramural use. Federally sponsored studies may be available through the National Technical Information Service. Those sponsored by the university under its own projects or continuing programs are usually distributed by the institution itself.

The 1990s have seen a trend in graduate business education toward global business and this should be reflected in their publication programs.

CONTINUING PROGRAMS AND PUBLICATIONS

Although much university research stems from individual effort, continuing projects reflect cooperative work on a departmental or institutional level. Such, for example, have been the operating results studies issued regularly.

Operating Results of Self-Service Discount Stores and the Mass Retailers Merchandising Report. Ithaca, NY: Cornell University. Annual.

Among the continuing research projects of interest to business the following may be cited:

University of Michigan Econometric Model of the U.S. Economy.
    Used to forecast the economic outlook.

UCLA Business Forecasting Project, complex econometric models for California and the U.S., maintained by the Graduate School of Management, University of California at Los Angeles.
    Online databases, covering key economic and financial indicators, provide historical time series, 1950 to date, short-term forecasts quarterly, and long-term forecasts annually.

University of Chicago. National Opinion Research Center.
    The National Opinion Research Center is an affiliate of the University of Chicago which publishes the results of its public opinion surveys.

University of Pennsylvania. Wharton Center for Applied Research, Inc.

The Center was formed in 1985 to conduct ongoing, for profit, research on business, finance and marketing.

In addition to this unit the University of Pennsylvania, Wharton School maintains the Real Estate Center, the Rodney L. White Center for financial research and the Sol C. Snider Entrepreneurial Center.

Purdue University. Credit Research Center.

This center publishes an annual, *Household Credit Data Book,* based on its continuing research on household credit market conditions.

Washington University. Center for the Study of American Business.

This center conducts ongoing research on the relationship of government regulation and policies to business activity.

Georgia State University. Economic Forecasting Center.

Conducts ongoing economic forecasting for the nation, the South East and Georgia.

INSTITUTES

Another source of information is the research centers and institutes supported by universities and colleges. Although these institutes exert their greatest influence in the areas of science, engineering, agriculture, and government, many are engaged in research related to management, mass communications and marketing.

Among the institutes of interest to businessmen is the following:

Institute for Social Research, University of Michigan, Ann Arbor, Mich.

The economic behavior program of the Institute focuses on individual households. Its *Economic Outlook U.S.A.* provides data and commentary from the program. The *Survey of Consumer Financials,* issued annually, presents measurements of consumer attitudes and expectations in areas of personal finances, and general business and economic conditions.

BUREAUS OF BUSINESS RESEARCH

University bureaus of business research provide researchers, faced with specific geographic area problems, with a variety of applicable facts. Quantitatively, the largest body of information concerns local and regional business and economic conditions and presents analyses of previously published and original data.

Graduate business schools and other university units, too, issue a number of useful publications on economics and marketing topics of more universal scope.

Available data from both these sources, therefore, fall into two general categories: regional and "national." Regional data are issued in periodicals, statistical compendia, state statistical abstracts like those listed in the Appendix, industrial directories, area studies, and industry reports. Although the majority of "national" studies are critical analyses or evaluative treatments of various industries and phases of business, a certain amount of primary data not available elsewhere is presented either on a continuing basis or in single reports.

Periodical publications of business schools, research bureaus, and other university divisions consist of journals, bulletins, newsletters, etc. These carry summaries of the regions' business and economic conditions, timely articles on economic developments, and analyses of principal industries—all documented with local statistics. From time to time faculty and research bureau studies are reported in these publications.

The following college and university periodicals reflect State and regional interests. Others, more management or single-industry oriented, have been omitted since they more closely resemble business periodicals and are treated as such in periodical indexes and directories. The frequency of publication for many university journals has been reduced in recent years.

Alabama

Alabama Business. University, AL: University of Alabama, Center for Business and Economic Research. Monthly. ISSN 0002-4163.

Troy State University Business and Economic Review. Troy, AL: Troy State University, Center for Business and Economic Services. Quarterly.

Arizona

Arizona Business. Tempe, AZ: Arizona State University, Center for Business Research. Monthly. ISSN 0093-0717.

Arizona Review. Tucson, AZ: University of Arizona, Division of Economics and Business Research. Annual. ISSN 0004-1629.

Arkansas

Arkansas Business and Economic Review. Fayetteville, AR: University of Arkansas, College of Business Administration, Bureau of Business and Economic Research. Quarterly. ISSN 0001-1742.

California

Global Finance Journal. Fresno, CA: California State University, School of Business and Administration Services. Quarterly. ISSN 1044-0283.

Business Forum. Los Angeles, CA: California State University, Los Angeles, Bureau of Business and Economic Research. Quarterly.

Colorado

Journal of Macromarketing. Boulder, CO: University of Colorado, Business Research Division. Semiannual. ISSN 0276-1467.

Journal of Marketing Education. Boulder, CO: University of Colorado. Business Research Division. 3/year. ISSN 0273-4753.

Florida

Florida Long-Term Economic Forecast. Gainesville, FL: University of Florida, Bureau of Economic and Business Research. Annual.

Economic Leaflets. Gainesville, FL: University of Florida, Bureau of Economic and Business Research. 10/year.

Georgia

Business: The Magazine of Managerial Thought and Action. Atlanta, GA: Georgia State University, College of Business Administration. Quarterly. ISSN 0163-531X.

Georgia Business and Economic Conditions. Athens, GA: University of Georgia, College of Business and Administration, Division of Research. Bimonthly. ISSN 0297-3857.

GSU Economic Forecasting Center Projections. Atlanta, GA: Georgia State University Economic Forecasting Center. Monthly.

Illinois

Illinois Business Review. Urbana, IL: University of Illinois Bureau of Economic and Business Research. Bimonthly. ISSN 0019-1922.

Quarterly Review of Economics and Business. Urbana, IL: University of Illinois, Bureau of Economic and Business Research. Quarterly. ISSN 0033-5797.

Indiana

Indiana Business Review. Bloomington, IN: Indiana University. Graduate School of Business. Divisional Research. Bimonthly. ISSN 0019-6541.

Business Horizons. Bloomington, IN: Indiana University. Graduate School of Business. Division of Research. Bimonthly. ISSN 0895-1772.

Mid-American Journal of Business. Muncie, IN: Ball State University. Bureau of Business Research. Semiannual.

Kansas

Kansas Business Review. Lawrence, KA: University of Kansas, Institute for Public Policy and Business Research. Quarterly. ISSN 0164-8632.

Kentucky

Growth and Change. Lexington, KY: University of Kentucky, College of Business and Economics. Quarterly.

Business and Public Affairs. Murray, KY: Murray State University, College of Business and Public Affairs. Semiannual.

Louisiana

Louisiana Business Survey. New Orleans, LA: University of New Orleans, College of Business Administration. Semiannual. ISSN 0193-5712.

Delta Business Review. Monroe, LA: Northeast Louisiana University, Center for Business and Economic Research. Biannual.

Massachusetts

Massachusetts Business and Economic Report. Amherst, MA: University of Massachusetts, School of Management, Management Research Center. Quarterly.

Mississippi

Mississippi's Business. University, MS: University of Mississippi, Bureau of Business and Economic Research. Quarterly.

Montana

Montana Business Quarterly. Missoula, MT: University of Montana, Bureau of Business and Economic Research. Quarterly. ISSN 0026-9921.

Nebraska

Business in Nebraska. Lincoln, NE: University of Nebraska, Bureau of Business Research. Monthly. ISSN 0149-4163.

Nevada

Nevada Review of Business and Economics. Reno, NV: University of Nevada, Bureau of Business and Economic Research. Quarterly. ISSN 0148-5881.

New Mexico

New Mexico Business Current Economic Report. Albuquerque, NM: University of New Mexico, Bureau of Business and Economic Research. Monthly. ISSN 0889-5937.

North Carolina

Carolina Coast Business Review. Wilmington, NC: University of North Carolina and Wilmington. Center for Business and Economic Research. Semiannual.

Ohio

Ohio Economic Trends Review. Cleveland, OH.: Cleveland State University. College of Urban Affairs. 3/year.

Oklahoma

Oklahoma Business Bulletin. Norman, OK: University of Oklahoma, Center for Economic and Management Research. Monthly. ISSN 0030-1671.

Pennsylvania

Journal of Economics and Business. Philadelphia, PA: Temple University, School of Business Administration (New York: Elsevier). 4/yr. ISSN 0148-6195.

Pennsylvania Business Survey. University Park, PA: Pennsylvania State University, College of Business Administration. Quarterly. ISSN 0031-4382.

Rhode Island

Northeast Journal of Business and Economics. Kingston, RI: University of Rhode Island, Research Center for Business and Economics. Semiannual. ISSN 8755-5123.

South Carolina

Business and Economic Review. Columbia, SC: University of South Carolina, College of Business Administration, Division of Research. Quarterly. ISSN 0007-6465.

South Carolina Economic Indicators. Columbia, SC: University of South Carolina, College of Business Administration. Monthly. ISSN 0038-304x.

South Dakota

South Dakota Business Review. Vermillion, SD: University of South Dakota, Business Research Bureau. Quarterly. ISSN 0038-3260.

Tennessee

Survey of Business. Knoxville, TN: University of Tennessee, Center of Business and Economic Research. Quarterly. ISSN 0099-0973.

Tennessee Business and Economic Review. Murfreesboro, TN: Middle Tennessee State University, Business and Economic Research Center. Quarterly.

Business Perspectives. Memphis, TN: Memphis State University, Bureau of Business and Economic Research Center. Quarterly. ISSN 0896-3703.

Mid-South Business Journal. Memphis, TN: Memphis State University, Bureau of Business and Economic Research. Quarterly. ISSN 0279-8174.

Texas

Texas Business Review. Austin, TX: University of Texas, Bureau of Business Research. Bimonthly. ISSN 0040-4209.

Texas Industrial Expansion. Austin, TX: University of Texas, Bureau of Business Research. Monthly. ISSN 0040-4365.

Utah

Utah Economic and Business Review. Salt Lake City, UT: University of Utah, Bureau of Economic and Business Research. Quarterly. ISSN 0042-1405.

Virginia

Virginia Business Report. Williamsburg, VA: College of William and Mary, Bureau of Business Research. Monthly. ISSN 0363-3551.

Washington

Pacific Northwest Executive. Seattle, WA: University of Washington, Graduate School of Business Administration. Quarterly. ISSN 1043-5212.

Wisconsin

Update. Madison, WI: University of Wisconsin, Bureau of Business Research. 3/year.

Wyoming

Wyoming Quarterly. Laramie, WY: University of Wyoming, Institute for Policy Research. Quarterly.

Statistical compendia for the home State are issued by a number of university research bureaus. Although varying in frequency and scope, they are, however, useful sources of population, industry, services, trade, financial, and other economic data for the State, its counties, and metropolitan areas. A current list of these appears in the Appendix.

Industrial directories, compiled by bureaus of business research, represent a unique marketing tool, and as such are treated in greater detail in a subsequent chapter on directories. Many of these are now published privately.

Area studies cover economic analyses and projections of State resources and potentials; studies of personal income; retail sales; price trends; marketing analysis of consumers goods sold within the State or the State's commodities produced for distribution elsewhere.

Industry reports highlight the status and development of those industries important to the area's economic growth. Information ranges from agricultural outlook reports to statistical analyses of local business and surveys of such factors as tourist trade.

Many topics relating to various aspects of the national economy, business management, and marketing are treated in university periodicals and studies. Some periodicals, such as the *Harvard Business Review,* Indiana University's *Business Horizons,* and Chicago University's *Journal of Business,* offer a mixture of academic and executive thinking and are more specialized in their approach.

DISSERTATIONS

Graduate dissertations in business, economics, and marketing, and in the allied sciences offer a growing volume of information. Yet they are often neglected because their content and availability are probably the least publicized of any source among practitioners.

RESEARCH AIDS

University Research and Publications

Research Centers Directory. Detroit: Gale Research. Irregular/ Supplements. ISSN 0080-1518.

Lists university-related and other nonprofit research organizations established on a permanent basis and conducting research in a wide variety of areas including business. Includes information on activities, publications, library facilities, directors' names, and structure. Supplements are called *New Research Centers.* Also available online.

Government Reports Announcements and Index.

Statistical Reference Index: A Selective Guide to American Statistical Publications from Sources Other Than the U.S. Government.

Economics Working Papers: A Bibliography. Dobbs Ferry, NY: Trans-Media Publishing. Semiannual. ISSN 0094-6451.

A listing, with accompanying microfiche service, of working papers received at the University of Warwick Library. Arranged by subject with author and series indexes. Covers all social sciences and includes such topics as demography, urban studies, management and business.

University Research in Business and Economics. Morgantown, WV: West Virginia University, Bureau of Business Research. Annual. ISSN 0738-3215.

Lists publications of member institutions by classified subjects and by name of institution. Author index.

Dissertations

American Doctoral Dissertations. Compiled for the Association of Research Libraries. Ann Arbor, MI: University Microfilms. Annual. ISSN 0065-809x.

All doctoral dissertations accepted by American and Canadian institutions are arranged by subject and indexed by author. Also available online.

Dissertation Abstracts International, Section A: The Humanities and Social Studies. Ann Arbor, MI: University Microfilms. Monthly. ISSN 0419-4209.

Not a complete listing like the one above, but a compilation of abstracts of North American dissertations submitted to the publisher. Arranged by broad subject classification with an annual cumulative keyword title index. Retrospective subject and author indexes have been issued. Section B covers the sciences and engineering. Also available online and in CD-ROM format.

In addition, separately published topical lists of dissertations are issued on a recurring basis. Besides those cited below, others may be located by referring to *Public Affairs Information Service Bulletin* under the subject heading "Dissertations—Bibliography".

"Doctoral Dissertations Accepted." *Journal of Business.* Chicago: University of Chicago Press. Annual in January issue.

Marketing Doctoral Dissertation Abstracts. (A.M.A. Bibliography) Chicago: American Marketing Association. Annual. ISSN 0193-9351.

Data Bases

In the chapter on regional, State and local sources, databases produced by universities reflecting regional interests were listed. Here are listed databases produced by university business schools which have more general business interest or which are subject-oriented.

Columbia University, Columbia Business School. Center for International Business Cycle Research. New York, N.Y.
The Center produces databases which contain statistics on inflation and business cycles. Available as a Haver Analytics database.

University of North Carolina. Carolina Population Center. Chapel Hill, N.C.
The Center produces Popline, a database available through the National Library of Medicine and also available in CD-ROM format. The database contains information on vital statistics, demography, AIDS, and other health-related population issues.

RESEARCH INSTITUTIONS

Nonprofit research organizations, whose main purpose is to explore and disseminate basic knowledge, function in many subject and industry areas. A number of these institutions operate in the field of marketing and a great number are associated with educational institutes.

Advertising Research Foundation (ARF). New York, N.Y.

A foundation whose membership is comprised of advertisers, advertising agencies, commercial research concerns, advertising associations and colleges and universities. The stated aim of the foundation is to further scientific practices and promote greater effectiveness of advertising and marketing by means of objective and impartial research; develop new research methods and techniques; analyze and evaluate existing methods and techniques; establish research standards, criteria, and reporting methods. Its published research studies have covered many phases of industrial advertising and marketing. In addition, ARF publishes *Journal of Advertising Research,* bimonthly. In 1977, it absorbed the Center for Marketing Communications. ARF has a library of more than 2,500 volumes.

Marketing Science Institute (MSI). Cambridge, Mass.

MSI is a nonprofit research organization. The Institute is supported by business "to contribute to improved marketing performance by developing objective, factual information about marketing practices and their effectiveness; by devising and testing new methods for analyzing these facts; and by appraising social and economic issues related to markets." Its research program covers a variety of areas including significant changes in marketing institutions and functions; marketing management problems susceptible to scientific solution; international marketing developments; the development of marketing theory; marketing education, etc. The results of this research are published as books, technical reports, and working papers. In addition to these, MSI publishes a quarterly newsletter and *Research Briefs,* also quarterly.

Similar organizations exist in allied fields. Cited here are a number of institutions with continuing programs in business and economics.

National Bureau of Economic Research (NBER). Cambridge, Mass.

NBER is engaged in impartial determination and interpretation of important economic facts. The Bureau is well known for its pioneering work in the study of business cycles and for its research programs in economic growth, productivity, employment, price levels, national income, public finance, financial institutions, money, international economic problems, human resources, social security, social institutions, and economic performance.

The results of its research are published in books and conference proceedings. Among its continuing publications are the *NBER Reporter* and *NBER Digest.* An index to NBER publications has been published as *Publications, 1920–1976.* The NBER Time Series Data Bank provides analysis and forecasting of business conditions.

The Conference Board (CB). New York, N.Y.

Formerly the National Industrial Conference Board, this organization, whose members include business organizations, trade associations, government agencies, libraries, labor unions, colleges and universities, conducts research in many areas including economics, business management, and human relations in industry. The Conference Board publishes a number of reports covering topics such as business trends, sales and marketing, executive compensation, corporate finance, etc. It operates an information service for members; maintains a library of over 25,000 volumes, conducts seminars, conferences and courses for its members.

The published output of the Conference Board is indexed in its *Cumulative Index* and its Conference Board Abstract Database. Among its regular publications are the following:

Economic Times. Monthly.

Economic Road Maps. 15–18/year. ISSN 0884-4887.
Formerly *Road Maps of Industry,* these numbered charts illustrate business trends.

Across the Board. Monthly. ISSN 0147-1554.

A business periodical that contains articles on all areas covered by The Conference Board. Formerly *The Conference Board Record.*

Business Executive Expectations. Quarterly. ISSN 0888-6674.

The views of executives of large and small firms on current and prospective economic conditions and the outlook for their particular industry. A composite measure of business confidence is calculated from the results of the poll.

Consumer Attitudes and Buying Plans. Monthly. ISSN 0547-7204.

A report of the results of an ongoing consumer survey. Both general economic and business topics and specific areas such as plans to purchase major durable goods and vacation and travel plans are reported.

Current Economic Trends. Quarterly.

A graphic summary of business trends and indicators.

International Economic Scorecard. Quarterly/ Supplements. ISSN 0270-045x.

Economic Policy Issues. Irregular.

A series of publications dealing with matters of public economic policy including such topics as the Federal budget process and its impact on the economy.

In addition, the Board produces the following databases of general interest as well as special interest databases:

Conference Board.

This online database of economic time series produced by the Economic Research Department provides access to the Conference Board Economic Forecast and to a variety of economic indicators, including consumer attitudes and buying plans, business executive expectations, capital appropriations for manufacturing and utilities, automobile sales, and discretionary spending. More data and more detail are contained in the database than appear in the various Conference

Board published series. Coverage extends from 1951 (for some series) to date and is updated at varying intervals depending on the series.

Conference Board Abstract Database, 1980-. Conference Board of Canada, Ottawa, Ont., Canada.
   Conducts research similar to that conducted by the U.S. organization, with emphasis on Canada.

   Canadian Business Review. Quarterly.

   Canadian Outlook. Quarterly.
      Charts for Canadian business.

   Index of Business Confidence. Quarterly.

   Index of Consumer Attitude. Quarterly.

   Provincial Forecast is also issued quarterly.

   Survey of Business Attitudes and Investment Spending Intentions. Quarterly.

   In addition, the Conference Board of Canada produces the following databases:

MTFM Canadian Database, which includes trend and forecast data, and Canadian Provincial Database, which includes provincial statistics.

American Management Association (AMA), New York, N.Y.
   A nonprofit educational organization whose membership is composed of managers, university teachers of management, and administrators. AMA maintains programs of original research in executive compensation, executive training, and other management-related areas. Its programs, courses, conferences, and seminars serve every level of management throughout the world. AMA maintains a large library, bookstore, and Management Information Service that includes information on all areas of management practice available in a variety of formats including films, tapes, records, cassettes, etc. The published output of AMA is varied and includes books authored and edited by staff and

outside specialists; periodicals devoted to management topics; and
studies drawn from conference activity or based on original research.
AMA International is the international arm of AMA.

AMA lists its publications in *AMACOM Resources for Professional
Management,* an annual with monthly supplements, and indexes
them in the *10-Year Index of AMA Publications, 1957–1966* and *Index
to AMA Resources . . . ,* issued irregularly.

Regularly issued publications of AMA include the following:

Organizational Dynamics. Quarterly. ISSN 0090-2616.
A review of organizational behavior for professional managers.

AMA Report on Information Centers. Annual.

Management Review. Monthly. ISSN 0025-1895.
Articles, digests, and book reviews relating to management
and business.

Supervisory Management. Monthly. ISSN 0039-5919.
Up-to-date information about the manager's role, geared to
supervisory personnel.

Personnel. Monthly. ISSN 0031-5702.
A review of all aspects of human relations in industry.

Compensation and Benefit Review. Bimonthly. ISSN 0010-4248.
Articles and digests on compensation and fringe benefits at
all organization levels.

Advanced Management Journal. Quarterly. ISSN 0036-0805.
Original articles on management topics of interest to middle-
and upper-level managers.

SRI International. Menlo Park, Calif.
SRI is an independent, nonprofit, research organization with no
official relationship to Stanford University. The Institute focuses its
activity on the solutions of particular problems for industry, government, and foundations as well as on projects of a basic nature.
Included in its principal fields of study are management sciences,
economic development, and industrial economics, plus the physical

and life sciences and engineering. Its projects cover specific industries, size and growth rate of markets, production and distribution, and regional economies. SRI research results are published except where military or commercial classification prohibits. SRI International maintains facilities in countries worldwide and produces SRI Business Intelligence Index, an online database of abstracts of SRI International studies, as well as the following print publications.

SRI Journal. Quarterly.
Covers projects and activities of the Institute.

Chemical Economics Handbook. Looseleaf/ Bimonthly—Supplements.
In chapters periodically revised, provides comprehensive reports including data sheets which, in graphic form, present basic statistics on economic indicators, major industries, chemical and allied industries, organic and inorganic chemicals, chemical product groups. Also available online.

Directory of Chemical Producers. United States of America. Annual. ISSN 0012-3277.
Arranged in four sections. For each chemical product shows its producing companies, plant capacities, locations, processes. For each producer, gives its subsidiaries and divisions, plants, and products made at each location. A State-city listing of plants identifies the owning company and products made. Regional editions are issued for other world areas.

National Planning Association (NPA), Washington, D.C.
NPA draws upon leaders in labor, agriculture, business, and the professions in assessing problems and mapping out goals in every field of national endeavor. In addition to case studies, special reports and planning pamphlets on economic growth, agriculture, various industries, and foreign conditions affecting American industry, the NPA also publishes the following:

Looking Ahead. Quarterly. ISSN 0024-6409.
Articles pertaining to NPA projects and members; planning, national and international; and summaries of relevant literature, NPA and other.

National Economic Projections Series (NEPS). Irregular.

A series of publications on the GNP and its individual components giving basic data and ten-year forecasts.

Regional Economic Projections Series (REPS). Irregular.

Individual publications on States giving long-range projections of key economic indicators for the State and its SMSAs.

Besides publishing its projections and data, NPA also makes them available on tape:

NPA/Econometric (National Planning Association/Econometric).

An online database, updated annually, provides access to time series 1967 to date and forecasts to the year 2000 covering such items as employment, income, earnings, and population for the U.S., regions, States and counties, as well as SMSAs and Bureau of Economic Analysis areas. A separate database, NPA/Demographic, contains demographic data.

Resources for the Future (RFF), Washington, D.C.

RFF is a nonprofit corporation for research and education in the development and use of natural resources. Its works include studies of trends and requirements, together with long-range projections, for water and land use; mineral, forest, and other resources; energy; and outdoor recreation. Among its divisions are the Energy and Natural Resources Division; Quality of the Environment Division and Center for Risk Management.

RFF publishes a number of studies and a periodical entitled *Resources,* quarterly.

Twentieth Century Fund (TCF), New York, N.Y.

TCF, like Resources for the Future, is a nonprofit educational organization. Its research is directed toward major economic political and social indicators and issues.

In addition to the research institutions listed, a number of other nonprofit research organizations (also known as "think tanks") have gained increased prominence. These think tanks germinate impressive amounts of information, including studies, statistics, and expert opinions. Their published output and general experience are sometimes available to researchers. The following is a list of some prominent think tanks that operate in business-related areas.

It is important to keep in mind the fact that "think tanks" are a global phenomenon. In England, the Centre for Policy Studies, the Royal Institute of International Affairs and the National Institute of Economic and Social Research are examples of "think tanks." In Germany, the Friedrich Ebert Foundation is a recognized "think tank," and in Japan the Nomura Research Institute, the Daiwa Research Institute and the Mitsubishi Research Institute are well known. In Russia, the Foreign Policy Association is the pioneer private "think tank."

American Institutes for Research in Behavioral Sciences. Washington, D.C.
Behavioral sciences, urban areas, unemployment, human factors research.

Batelle Memorial Institute, Columbus, OH.
Population, hazardous materials, defense.

The Brookings Institution, Washington, D.C.
Economics, government, social sciences.

Corporation for Enterprise Development. Washington, D.C.
Entrepreneurial studies.

Capital Research Center, Washington, D.C.
Philanthropy.

Institute for Policy Studies, Washington, D.C.
Public policy.

Japan Center for International Finance. Washington, D.C.
Financial policy.

Overseas Development Council, Washington, D.C.
Overseas development, developing countries.

Potomac Institute, Inc., Washington, D.C.
Racial and other minority groups.

Urban Institute, Washington, D.C.
    Urban areas, land development and land use.

Center for Media and Public Affairs. Washington, D.C.
    Monitors news for political and social issues.

Economic Policy Institute. Washington, D.C.
    U.S. and foreign economic policy.

Rand Corporation. Santa Monica, CA.
    Government and private research.

American Enterprise Institute. Washington, D.C.
    Government regulation.

Japan Economic Institute. Washington, D.C.
    Japanese economy and U.S.-Japanese relations.

Center for Strategic and International Studies. Washington, D.C.
    Global problems.

Heritage Foundation. Washington, D.C.
    Area studies and social issues.

Institute for International Economics. Washington, D.C.
    International economic issues.

Urban Land Institute. Washington, D.C.
    Urban issues.

Research Aids

Research Centers Directory.

Government Reports Announcements and Index.

Statistical Reference Index: A Selective Guide to American Statistical Publications from Sources Other Than the U.S. Government.

Databases

The work of research institutes is often based on statistical data generated by onsite databases. In some cases these databases are accessible through online connections to outside users.

Nomura Research Institute. Tokyo, Japan.
Nomura produces databases available through online services which provide information on Japanese economics and finance.

NPA Data Services. Washington, D.C.
NPA provides statistics on demographics and economics through online databases.

PROFESSIONAL AND TRADE ASSOCIATIONS

PROFESSIONAL SOCIETIES

Professional associations exist in many fields of business, science, and technology to promote and promulgate scientific and fundamental advances in their respective disciplines. Through their meetings and publications, researchers can keep abreast of current developments and find solutions to problems through an interchange of ideas.

Professional societies similar to those operating in the U.S. have been established in foreign countries and function in much the same way for their respective geographic areas.

Marketing: General

American Marketing Association (AMA), Chicago, Ill.

The AMA is the leading professional organization in its field. Its some 46,000 members are drawn from both business and educational spheres. Its major publications are the *Journal of Marketing* (quarterly) and the *Journal of Marketing Research* (quarterly). It also issues monographs and bibliographies; fosters research; promulgates standards for professional and ethical conduct; and sponsors seminars, conferences, and student marketing clubs. These activities are carried out at both the national and local-chapter levels.

Professional associations also exist for the specialized areas of marketing such as direct marketing and telemarketing.

Marketing Education Association (MEA). Reston, VA.

MEA includes a wide variety of persons involved in marketing education. *Marketing Educators News* is published three times per year.

National Association of Market Developers (NAMD), New York, NY.

NAMD includes in its membership individuals who are engaged in or are interested in advertising and selling to the minority market.

Sales and Marketing Executives International, Cleveland, OH.

The Sales and Marketing Executives International has affiliated clubs worldwide. It provides its members with a marketing information center; offers programs at the Graduate School of Sales Management and Marketing at Syracuse University; publishes a bimonthly journal; and conducts educational research, publication, conference, and seminar programs. Although dedicated primarily to the advancement of selling and sales management, a large part of its activity encompasses marketing management, techniques, and methods.

Marketing Research Association (MRA), Rocky Hill, CT.

The MRA membership is composed of field research and executive personnel engaged in marketing research for advertising agencies, research firms, and industries. Publishes *Alert,* the *Blue Book Research Services Directory,* and the *Journal of Data Collection.*

Special Libraries Association (SLA), Washington, DC.

SLA is an international organization of professional librarians and information specialists concerned with the organization, management, and utilization of information resources in specialized subject areas for a specialized clientele. Organized originally to serve the professional needs of librarians employed by business and industry, the membership now includes many representatives from government agencies and other public and private nonprofit institutions. Among its subject interest divisions and sections are Advertising and Marketing; Business and Finance; Chemistry; Insurance and Employee Benefits; Environmental Information; Metals/Materials; Petroleum and Energy Resources; Pharmaceuticals. Publications include *Special Libraries* (a quarterly journal), bibliographies, annuals, as well as many subject-interest bulletins and reference handbooks.

Academy of Marketing Sciences (AMS). Coral Gables, FL.

AMS directs its efforts to the social, economic and educational aspects of marketing. The *Journal of the Academy of Marketing Science* is a quarterly.

Marketing: Industry Oriented

There are a number of professional societies concerned with the marketing function in individual industries. In some cases, associations previously associated with advertising and sales interests have expanded their programs to include the total marketing concept. Among these industry oriented marketing groups are the following:

Bank Marketing Association (BMA), Washington, DC.
BMA includes public relations and marketing executives for commercial banks, savings banks, and related agencies such as advertising and market research firms among its members. It maintains an information center; conducts workshops and seminars; and publishes *Bank Marketing Journal* (monthly) and *Information Center Newsletter* (quarterly).

Broadcast Promotion & Marketing Executives, Inc. (BPME). Los Angeles, CA.
An international association of management and marketing professionals in broadcast media. BPME publishes a newsletter, *BPME Image,* and maintains a mailing list.

Food Marketing Institute (FMI). Washington, DC.
FMI is an association of retail and wholesale food distributors.

Information Technology and Marketing Association (ITAMA). Springfield, VA.
ITAMA includes representatives of government agencies and the private sector who utilize government information in machine-readable format.

Life Insurance Marketing and Research Association (LIMRA). Hartford, CT.
The objective of LIMRA is to improve the marketing activities of its member organizations. LIMRA publishes *LIMRA Digest* and *LIMRA's Market Facts.*

International Newspaper Marketing Association (INMA). Washington, DC.
INMA is an association of professionals involved in marketing

related activities related to newspapers. INMA publishes *IDEAS Magazine* and maintains a monthly list.

Photo Marketing Association (PMA). Jackson, MI.
PMA is an association of firms involved in all aspects of retail and wholesale marketing of photo/video products, supplies and services. PMA publishes *Photo Marketing.*

Allied Disciplines

Contributions of professional societies in allied fields bear significant import for market research and marketing. Special interest organizations such as the National Association of Accountants, National Association of Purchasing Agents, and the American Chemical Society (and particularly its Division of Chemical Marketing and Economics) maintain research, publication, and conference programs. All are potential sources of general and specific marketing information. The following list includes those associations upon whose work marketing has drawn most frequently in the past.

American Economic Association (AEA). Nashville, TN.
AEA members are drawn from a variety of professions. The association fosters economic discussion; conducts research in current and past conditions; issues the *American Economic Review* (quarterly), *Journal of Economic Literature* (quarterly), and *Journal of Economic Perspectives* (quarterly), as well as monographs and other publications.

American Statistical Association (ASA). Alexandria, VA.
ASA members are active in promoting the theory, methodology, and application of statistics in all branches of knowledge. Through special committees, the association acts as an adviser on statistical matters to government and to industry. In addition to the *Journal of the American Statistical Association* (quarterly), it publishes *American Statistician* (quarterly), *Technometrics* (quarterly), and *Journal of Business and Economic Statistics,* (quarterly).

Association of Public Data Users. Arlington, VA.
Membership includes academic institutions, profit and nonprofit organizations, and government agencies—Federal, State, and local.

The Association attempts to secure public access data tapes for its members and to keep them informed on current happenings in the field of public access tape activity. A membership list is published annually.

American Psychological Association (APA). Washington, DC.
    APA is a professional society of psychologists and educators. Its Consumer Psychology Division numbers industry, advertising agency, and media people, as well as consultants and other occupational groups among its members. Among the periodicals which it publishes is the quarterly *Journal of Applied Psychology,* which covers research of interest to marketing.

American Sociological Association (ASA). Washington, DC.
    ASA members are professional sociologists and social scientists. Its bimonthly *American Sociological Review* reports on research findings and methodology of value to marketing and opinion researchers.

Operations Research Society of America (ORSA). Baltimore, Md.
    ORSA is composed of professionals active in operations research. The society's official journal, the bimonthly *Operations Research,* is a major news medium for current developments in the field.

Information Industry Association (IIA). Washington, DC.
    IIA includes a wide range of information providers: *Information Times* (quarterly) and *Information Sources,* an annual directory, are issued.

TRADE ASSOCIATIONS

Business competitors operating in the same industry establish and maintain trade associations to research common problems and to assist the membership with information and advice for the achievement of common goals. Many publish international data. Foreign trade associations provide information for their areas similar to that provided by their counterparts in the U.S. Increasingly domestic associations are establishing or externally expanding their international operations.
    Some trade information is not available for general distribution.

Other data, however, are collected and issued for public consumption in association newsletters, journals, studies, releases, convention proceedings, and statistical reports.

In the allied field of media and advertising, trade associations have concentrated their efforts on promoting their primary interests. They research the results of, and the methods for, more effective advertising and marketing and have tailored their programs to include data quality, standardization, and compatibility suitable to the needs created by computer technology. Working collections of marketing information are acquired and maintained to service client, member, and intramural activities. Publications issued are devoted primarily to assessing the medium in terms of audience, revenue, and industry trends. Occasionally a report supplies market data in compact form.

Some media associations act as clearinghouses for market research conducted and published by their membership. Organizations servicing the newspaper industry (Newspaper Association of America [NAA] Washington, DC) and the consumer magazine industry (Magazine Publishers of America, New York) have published guides to member research reports and services. Other media oriented sources include the Association of Business Publishers, New York; Outdoor Advertising Association of America, New York; the Radio Advertising Bureau, New York; the Television Bureau of Advertising, New York; and the Direct Marketing Association, New York.

Such organizations as the American Association of Advertising Agencies, New York; Business/Professional Advertising Association, Alexandria, VA, and the Association of National Advertisers, New York are most immediately concerned with the advertising function and are seldom represented by marketing publications. These organizations do, however, cover a wide range of topics vital to marketing management in their projects and conference programs.

The informational output of other industry and trade associations is rich and varied. Of particular value to research are several types of statistical compilations that provide original data often unavailable elsewhere.

"Facts and Figures"

Statistical factbooks are by far the largest and most useful category because of continuity (usually annual) and comprehensive scope.

Historical and current data for each industry and its markets—from raw materials utilization to end consumption of product—are culled from official government sources, special surveys, and original compilations submitted by the associations' memberships. Text and tables are, in the main, well documented and clearly dated.

Statistical Releases

Forecasts and current data on production, shipments, stocks, sales, etc. are often issued on a more frequent basis in the form of statistical releases. Sometimes these supplement a basic factbook; in other instances they constitute the only source of data published by the association.

Many are not available for general distribution. Others are issued as press releases for the trade press and are obtainable on a mailing list basis.

Operating Cost Studies

A number of retail and wholesale dealer associations issue annual studies of sales, profits, and operating expenses in their business lines. Details usually include inventory turnover, margin data, departmental sales data, with groupings by geographic area and annual sales volume.

Special Reports and Analyses

Less prevalent, although issued by some associations on a continuing basis, are consumer surveys and industry reviews and forecasts.

Occasional publications, such as economic outlook studies, marketing maps, and similar materials, are particularly useful since they often represent the culmination of a broad research program necessitated by the previous lack of and need for such information.

Administrative Publications

Newsletters, membership rosters, conference programs, and attendance lists are a good source of specialists in the field. Annual reports often include product and industry statistics, reviews, and forecasts. Current industry developments are assessed at national conventions, the proceedings of which are usually made available for general distribution.

Official association journals do not differ materially from commercially published periodicals and are treated as such in a subsequent chapter.

RESEARCH AIDS

Associations

Encyclopedia of Associations. Detroit: Gale Research Co. 3 vols. Irregular. ISSN 0071-0202.

> Vol. 1. *National Organizations of the United States.*
> Vol. 2. *Geographic and Executive Indexes.*
> Vol. 3. *Supplement.*

This is the most comprehensive directory of associations in print. All types of commercial associations, including technical and professional societies, commodity exchanges, numerous special interest groups, foreign chambers of commerce and government trade offices located in the U.S. are named. Volume 1 entries, arranged in sections by type of organization and indexed by proper name and by key word, include key personnel, founding date, size, continuing publications, and annual meeting schedule. Volume 2 contains a state and city listing of all organizations (name and address) in Volume 1 and an alphabetical name index of chief executives. Volume 3 consists of an updating inter-edition service for Volume 1.

A series of companion volumes to the *Encyclopedia* is issued and includes *International Organizations,* a one-volume directory, and *Regional, State and Local Organizations,* a multi-volume set. The Encyclopedia is available online and in CD-ROM format.

Associations Yellow Book. New York: Monitor Publishing. Semiannual. ISSN 1054-4070

One of the Monitor series of "yellow books" which provide

telephone directory-arranged listings of organizations. This publication lists trade and professional organizations and in addition to its
detailed administrative listings, lists publications and publication
editors.

National Trade and Professional Associations of the United States.
Washington, DC: Columbia Books, Inc. Annual. ISSN 0734-354x.
    An annual directory limited to nationwide trade and professional
associations and labor unions. Includes key word and geographic
indexes; an executive index; and a budget index. A companion state
and regional directory is also issued.

Directory of Associations in Canada. Toronto: University of Toronto
Press, Annual. ISSN 0316-0734.
    Provides an authoritative listing of associations in Canada. In-
cludes international and foreign associations with offices in Canada;
national, interprovincial, provincial, metropolitan, and selected local
associations. A subject index and guide to the subject index are
included.

Directory of British Associations and Associations in Ireland. Beckenham,
Eng.: CBD Research Ltd. Biennial.
    For national trade and professional associations, this includes infor-
mation activities and publications. Available from Gale Research.

Directory of European Industrial and Trade Associations. Beckenham,
Eng.: CBD Research. Irregular.
    In English, French, and German, this directory provides informa-
tion, including Telex numbers and major publications issued, on
national and selected regional associations in all fields of activity in
all countries of Europe. A detailed subject index is included.
Available from Gale Research.

Japan Directory of Professional Association. Tokyo: Japan Publications
Guide Service. Triennial.
    A directory of organizations classified as associations or institutes
in Japan.

Directory of European Professional & Learned Societies. Beckenham, Eng.:
CBD Research. Irregular.

A directory of professional and scholarly societies. A companion to its *Directory of European Industrial & Trade Associations*. Available from Gale Research.

Pan-European Associations . . . Beckenham, Eng.: CBD Research. Irregular.
A directory of associations which are multinational in Europe. Available from Gale Research.

Publications

Association publications, with the exception of statistical releases, are listed in such conventional bibliographic aids as *Public Affairs Information Service Bulletin* and *Ulrich's* . . . and *Books in Print*.

Business Organizations, Agencies and Publications Directory. Detroit, MI.: Gale Research. Irregular. ISSN 0888-1413.
A comprehensive directory which includes publications issued by associations, chambers of commerce, and similar organizations along with a wide array of government and non-governmental business publishers.

Newsletters in Print. Detroit, MI.: Gale Research. Annual. ISSN 0899-0425.
Includes newsletters published by trade and professional associations.

Statistical releases can usually be located only by direct inquiry to the respective organizations or by checking *Statistical Reference Index: A Selective Guide to American Statistical Publications from Sources Other Than the U.S. Government*.

Databases

Trade and professional associations have been active producers of machine readable databases for many years. A number of these databases contain information strategic to the trade or profession and are available to members of the association only. A second category of machine-readable databases produced by trade or professional associations includes statistical, index or directory databases created for internal use but available to non-members through "hot lines" or similar information services. A number of databases created by trade and professional associations are available to non-members through commercial online services. Some examples of commercially available online databases are:

American Economic Association. Pittsburgh, PA.
    Economic Literature Index.

American Petroleum Institute. Central Abstracting and Information Services. New York, NY.
    APIBIZ.

American Psychological Association. Arlington, VA.
    PsycINFO.

Bank Marketing Association. Chicago, IL.
    FINIS: Financial Industry Information Service.

British Standards Institution. England.
    BSI STANDARDLINE.

Foundation Center. New York, NY.
    Foundation Directory and Foundation Grants Index.

Information Industry Association. Washington, DC.
    Friday Memo.

Motor Industry Research Association.
    England Automotive Business Index.

Research Libraries Group. Mountain View, CA.
    RLG Research-in-Progress Database.

Royal Society of Chemistry. Information Services. Cambridge, England.
    Chemical Business NewsBase.

SERVICES

The term "service" has been defined as an agency that supplies information, especially current data, in easily accessible form, which is not readily available otherwise. The word is also applied to such information supplied regularly and/or by request on computer tape, in printed, photocopy, looseleaf, microform, floppy disc, CD-ROM, video or other format.

The types of agencies so categorized range widely. The sole output of some consists of publications conveying specialized and /or advisory information. Others are consultant and contract firms that engage exclusively in special assignment work on a fee basis. Between the two lie a number of companies, and even nonprofit institutions, that complement their basic programs with special order work based on individual needs.

Published services, regardless of considerable variation in format and content, are characterized by timeliness and immediate applicability in daily business activity and planning. As a rule, they are the product of continuing research and reporting programs geared to the specific needs of a specialized clientele. Because of this definition, mailing list services, commercially published newsletters and directories, abstract journals, indexes, and other publications are often classed with services. Here, however, they are treated in the respective chapters devoted to such sources.

Selected for this chapter from a field well supplied with both agencies and publications are services chosen for their basic usefulness, for their general interest to business and marketing research, and as illustrations of this type of source.

ECONOMIC SERVICES

Economic services, an outgrowth of statistical compendia, are a comparatively recent development spurred by the advent of computerization. Sophisticated data bases and econometric models offer the researcher quick access to basic data, projections and forecasts.

DRI/McGraw-Hill, Washington, D.C.

This econometric forecasting firm offers access to computerized economic data and supplies forecasts and projections of the U.S. and foreign economies and economic indicators. Additional services provide data and forecasts for industry and market analysis.

The DRI/McGraw-Hill services are available in a variety of formats on a subscription basis and on a fee-for-use basis through their Forecast Plus or Information Plus units. In addition to their national and regional economic services, which cover Africa, Canada, Europe, Latin America, Japan, South East Asia, China, Australia, the Middle East and the United States, DRI offers a county and metropolitan service for the United States. The specialized industry services include the energy, chemical, coal, oil, transportation, aviation, housing, automobile, natural gas, health care and steel industries. The financial services offered by DRI include fixed investments, commodities, finance and credit, U.S. bonds and cost and price indicators. A service is available for text and statistics of economic news releases, Federal contract announcements and awards and consumer market forecasts.

WEFA Group, Bala Cynwyd, PA.

The WEFA Group databases are available to subscribers and on a fee-for-use basis through their Dimensions unit. The individual services of WEFA cover economic forecasts and time series for the world, the United States, Canada, Australia, Germany, Asia, the Middle East and Latin America. A service is also available for the centrally planned economies. Subnational services for the States, counties, MSAs of the United States and the Canadian provinces are also produced. Separate services covering financial indicators and specific industries such as iron and steel, food and agriculture, fertilizers and lead and zinc are available.

Interactive Data Corporation, New York, N.Y.

Formerly Chase Econometric Associates, this organization provides access to a number of data bases of a financial nature on a subscription basis and on a for-fee basis through its Interactive Data Service unit and through commercial online services.

Evans Economics, Inc., Washington, D.C.

Evans Economics offers a full-text narrative and statistical economic forecasting service through Quotron Systems and through Mead Data Central as a Lexis/Nexis database.

Citicorp Database Service, New York, N.Y.

Through a variety of commercial online services Citicorp offers its economic time series monthly and weekly databases. On a subscription basis Citicorp offers access to its International Interest and Exchange Rate Database.

Columbia University, Columbia Business School, Center for International Business Cycle Research, New York, N.Y.

As a Haver Analytics database through General Electric Information Services (GEIS) Columbia offers access to its International Economic Indicators database and to its two business cycle databases.

The Economist Publications, Ltd., New York, N.Y.

On a subscription basis, the Economist offers a quantitative and qualitative service which reviews the economies of over 93 countries. Through a variety of commercial online services, the Economist is offered full-text as is its statistical time series database on non-OECD countries.

Haver Analytics, Inc., New York, N.Y.

Through General Electric Information Services, Haver Analytics offers several economic time series databases including the composite United States Survey of Forecasters which includes forecasts from the major forecasts services.

Helsinki School of Economics, Helsinki, Finland.

On a subscription basis provides access to its bibliographic and statistical databases.

High Tech Verlag GMBH, Munich, Germany.

Through a variety of commercial online services offers access to its time series database on the German economy.

Institut National de la Statistique et des Etudes Economiques, Paris, France (INSEE).

Through GSI-ECO, an online service vendor in Paris, access to all the database of INSEE is available on a subscription basis. The databases provide time series and forecast data for France.

Institut für Wirtschaftsforschung, Munich, Germany.
Through a variety of commercial online services, offers access to its time series and forecast databases on the German economy.

Istituto Centrale Statistica, Rome, Italy (ISTAT).
Through its own online service ISTAT offers access to its databases of forecast and time series data on the Italian economy.

Japan External Trade Organization, Tokyo, Japan (JETRO).
JETRO Ace is a subscription database of economic data from JETRO reports which is available through the Herwa Information Center.

Kyodo News International, Inc., New York, N.Y.
Through a variety of commercial online services offers access to its databases of full-text narrative and statistical information on Asia and Japan.

Mead Data Central, Inc., Dayton, Ohio.
Through its NEXIS service, Mead offers access to a wide variety of full-text and statistical databases on the national and global economy and on business.

Organization for Economic Cooperation and Development, Paris, France.
OECD offers a number of databases containing economic indicators and financial data for OECD member countries and for developing countries.

Reuters, Ltd., London, England.
Econline is offered as a part of the subscription service from Reuters. It includes economic and financial statistics.

U.S. Department of Commerce, Office of Business Analysis and Economic Affairs, Washington, D.C.

The Economic Bulletin Board, which is offered by the Office of Business Analysis, provides full text of U.S. economic indicators.

World Bank, Washington, D.C.
The world debt tables are available through General Electric Information Service.

BUSINESS AND FINANCIAL SERVICES

Business data most commonly appear in compilations dealing with specific industries. The following service is unique in its field:

Dun & Bradstreet Corporation.
Through a number of subsidiaries and divisions, Dun & Bradstreet provides access to financial and credit information on more than five million companies worldwide through its Business Information Reports service. This confidential rating service is available to authorized subscribers in a variety of formats, and the non-confidential financial and directory components of these reports form the basis for a wide variety of directories and financial services available in print, microform and machine-readable formats. In the past, the ratings themselves have been available only to subscribers, but Dun & Bradstreet now makes these available on a wider basis. Some of the more useful Dun & Bradstreet services are:

D & B Dun's Business Locator. Dun's Marketing Services, Parsippany, N.J.
A directory database available through commercial online services which includes eight million domestic (U.S.) businesses. Additional services available for fewer companies but including personnel and financial data are: D & B Market Identifiers, a group of online databases each covering a country or world region; and D & B Dun's Financial Records Plus, which is produced by Dun & Bradstreet Business Credit Services and includes detailed financial and operations information for 750,000 U.S. companies Perhaps the best-known D & B product is the D & B Million Dollar Directory, which is available both through online services and in hard copy.

Financial services issued for the guidance of professional and lay investors range from specific recommendations on individual securities to statistical analyses of companies and industries, as well as forecasts for these and for the national economy. Those listed below indicate the scope of directory and statistical information available for research. Excluded are securities trading services and purely investment advisory publications.

Moody's Investors Service, a subsidiary of the Dun & Bradstreet Corporation, New York, N.Y.

The Moody's series of manuals cover American and foreign companies and agencies whose securities are publicly traded. Listings include location, history, nature of business, officers and directors, subsidiaries, financial and other business information. The supplements update the manuals.

Moody's manuals are available online and in CD-ROM format as well as in microfiche format. A selective CD-ROM database is also available.

Standard & Poor's Corp., New York, N.Y.

The firm collects, analyzes, and publishes corporate and industry data in a number of services.

S & P makes its wide array of services available in a variety of arrangements. The Standard & Poor's Corporate Descriptions service, available online and in print, provides financial and business information and news updates for over 9,300 publicly traded companies; a CD-ROM version is also available. Other important S & P services include:

Standard & Poor's Trade and Securities Statistics. Looseleaf.

Current and historical statistics on banking and finance, production and labor, commodity price indexes, income and trade, building and building materials, transportation and communications, electric power and fuels, and a variety of other areas. The "Security Price Index Record" is published annually as a section of this service. Data also available online.

Industry Surveys. Looseleaf/Quarterly supplements.

Major industries are analyzed in individual sections containing a lengthy basic industry analysis, current analysis, and trends and projections supported by statistical data. In addition, leading companies in each industry are covered with basic information and comparative data. Also available in quarterly bound edition.

Stock Reports. Looseleaf.

A series of single-page reports on individual companies updated at specified intervals. Each contains current company and securities information similar to that above. The reports are assembled in three sets: New York Stock Exchange; American Stock Exchange; Over the Counter and Regional Exchanges. Also available in a quarterly bound edition.

A similar service, *International Stock Reports,* covers top foreign companies.

The Outlook. Weekly.

Investment advisory letter containing data, analyses, and assessments of developments affecting industries and individual companies. Statistical series also available online.

Standard & Poor's Industry Financial Data Bank.

An online data base produced in collaboration with McGraw-Hill. Coverage, from 1946 to date, is updated continuously. Over 1,800 monthly, quarterly, and annual time series provide key data for over 100 industry groups. Corresponds to Standard & Poor's *Analyst's Handbook* (which provides composite corporate per share data for major industries), *Standard & Poor's Trade and Securities Statistics,* and *The Outlook.*

Standard & Poor's Compustat Services, Inc., Englewood, Co.

This organization maintains two financial databases which are available on a subscription basis. Compustat contains financial statement and market data for U.S. and non-U.S. companies and subsidiaries, and Global Vantage contains domestic and foreign corporate information, stock price information and foreign exchange information.

In addition to the above services, S & P also publishes its *Directory,* which provides biographical information on corporate executives and is also available online and in CD-ROM format.

Disclosure, Inc., Bethesda, MD.

Besides supplying copies of company reports filed with the Securities and Exchange Commission, the firm maintains Disclosure, an online data base. Updated weekly and covering 1979 to date, the file provides directory information and extracts of financial data from the 10-K or 20-K reports, filed by U.S. publicly owned companies with the SEC. Disclosure/Spectrum Ownership is a second database which contains corporate ownership information. Both databases are available on CD-ROM.

EPONLINE, a division of the Financial Post Information Service, Toronto, Canada.

The Financial Post Information Service maintains a variety of databases containing financial data on Canadian companies and Canadian securities. These financial databases are available through commercial online services with, in some cases, a contractual arrangement with the Financial Post Information Service.

In addition to the financial databases, there are two specialized database services available on subscription with the Financial Post. The Directory of Directors database contains directory information on over 16,000 Canadian directors and is comparable in part to the print edition of this directory and The Financial Post Electronic Edition is a full-text version of the news and feature articles in the print edition of the Financial Post.

Center for International Financial Analysis and Research (CIFAR), Princeton, N.J.

Worldscope, a database of financial data on major corporations worldwide, as well as industry statistics, is available through commercial online services.

Data-Star, London, England.

Although primarily an online service company, Data-Star produces Tradstat World Trade Statistics, a database of trade statistics for 16 major countries and their trading partners.

Deloitte, Haskins & Sells, Brussels, Belgium.

EC 1992 is a subscription database which provides full text of Deloitte, Haskins & Sells research reports on EC 1992.

Dow Jones & Company, Princeton, N.J.

On a subscription basis, Dow Jones & Company provides access to a large family of financial business and economic databases through its Dow Jones News/Retrieval service. The Dow Jones Master Menu database identifies and describes each of these units.

Extel Statistical Services, Ltd., London, England.

A variety of online databases available through commercial online services includes Extel financial and company information with the emphasis on Europe, the U.K. and Japan.

Financial Times Electronic Publishing, London, England.

The Financial Times produces a large number of databases on individual industries and global markets which are made available through commercial online services under the general title of Financial Times Business Reports.

German Business Information, Munich, Germany.

German Business Information provides subscriber access to a wide variety of databases containing business, market and product information relating to Germany.

ICC Information Group, Ltd., Hampton, Middlesex, England.

ICC produces a number of country-specific as well as general databases on financial and company information for the U.K. and Europe.

Reuters Information Services, Inc., New York, N.Y.

On a subscription basis, Reuters offers full-text access to its company and country databases. Through commercial online services, access to Reuters business news databases is available.

SRI International Business Intelligence Program, Menlo Park, CA.

As a subscription service through DIALOG, this online database, which corresponds to the *SRI Research Reports,* provides forecast and evaluation data on international business.

STM Systems Corp., Ottawa, Ontario, Canada.

The online databases produced by STM are available on a subscription basis and provide detailed directory and ownership data for Canadian businesses. Two databases of note are Canadian Trademarks and Canadian Bankruptcy File.

Teikoku Databanks, Ltd., Tokyo, Japan.
On a subscription basis, Teikoku provides access to its Cosmos databases which contain detailed financial and directory information on Japanese companies and biographical information on Japanese business executives. A credit rating database for Japanese companies is also available.

Telerate Systems, Inc., New York, N.Y.
On a real-time basis, Telerate provides business, financial and investment news and its statistical databases provide time series data on financial instruments. All Telerate databases are available on a subscription basis.

Thomson Financial Networks, Boston, MA.
Investext, The Source for Company and Industry Analysis, is the database produced by Thomson. This database, which provides in full text the analyst research reports from major investment banks and securities firms, is a major source of business and marketing information and is available through commercial online services.

U.S. Department of Labor, Bureau of Labor Statistics, Washington, D.C.
In conjunction with private database producers, the Bureau of Labor Statistics provides access to consumer and producer price data. Subscription to the co-producer service is required.

U.S. Department of the Treasury, Office of Thrift Supervisor, Washington, D.C.
Through commercial online services, the Treasury Department provides access to its savings and loan institutions financial database.

CONSUMER MARKETING SERVICES

For consumer market research a number of firms offer area demographics; continuous reporting programs on retail distribution, product acceptance, brand awareness; and special assignment facilities for custom investigations of various marketing factors.

Cited here are a number of basic services available to consumer goods marketers. Specifically excluded are purely audience measurement and readership services as well as those rating advertisements and reporting advertising volume. Media services such as those listed for Simmons Market Research Bureau provide a significant amount of marketing data, including product and brand usage, purchase information, intentions to buy advertised products, and demographic characteristics. Relevant data from such reports are supplied by individual publications and stations as part of their advisory and marketing assistance, an information category that is treated in the following chapter.

Demographic Data

A recent development, demographic data services are being offered by a new type of company, the demographic data firm, and by other organizations specializing in this field. Based on the Census Bureau's decennial census public-use machine-readable files and other resources, the services range from providing tape copies, special files on tape and printouts, to the compiling of analytic reports, area profiles and comparisons, computer graphics, address matching and geocoding. Though some firms have a specialty, others offer the full range. In addition, a number of organizations offer consultation on Census Bureau data interpretation and applications, assistance in file use, training programs, and seminars.

Those public and private organizations that notify the Census Bureau of the services offered are registered with the National Clearinghouse for Census Data Services. In the public sector similar services are also available through the State Data Centers. Taken as a whole, all supplement the user services provided by the Census Bureau staff.

Sales & Marketing Management, New York, N.Y.

Sales & Marketing Management is published monthly by Bill Communications. The magazine is directed to marketing managers and includes articles on all aspects of sales and marketing. The features which have made this periodical fit the service category are its special issues, which include the "Survey of Buying Power" and the "Survey of Buying Power, Part II," detailed statistical studies of consumer products and industrial products and of buying power potential, the "Survey of Media Markets" and the "Survey of Selling Costs." On an annual basis, a separate *Survey of Buying Power Data Service* is issued. It contains detailed demographic and economic statistics for geographic market areas down to metropolitan market level, as well as retail sales data and television market data.

Glimpse Corporation, Alexandria, VA.

As a subscription service, the Statistical Analysis and Retrieval System is produced by Glimpse Corporation. This database service provides demographic and market potential data for U.S. demographic areas including zip code areas.

Donnelly Marketing Information Services: A Company of the Dun & Bradstreet Corporation, Stamford, CT.

The following Donnelly databases are available through commercial online services:

American Profile, a database which contains decennial census data from 1970 and 1980 along with relevant updates and forecasts.

ClusterPlus, a database which groups households from block groups in the 1980 Census of Population and Housing and provides marketing and demographic information for these clusters.

Donnelly Demographics, the most widely available Donnelly database, provides demographic estimates and projections based on the 1980 Census of Population and Housing.

Market Potential, a database which provides consumer expenditure data based on the 1980 Census of Population and Housing.

Target Scan provides demographic data based on the 1970 and 1980 Census Population and Housing for a wide variety of areas including SAMIs.

CACI, Inc., Fairfax, VA.

CACI is a full-service demographic data firm which offers a wide range of census-related products. In addition to its census activities, CACI maintains the following databases:

DORIS (Demographic Online Retrieval Information System), a database of 1980 census information with updates and projections, is available through commercial online services.

Site-Potential, a database available through commercial online services, includes forecast and historical data on sales potential within geographic areas for specific types of retail stores and for finance-related institutions.

Supersite, a database available through commercial online vendors, provides access to demographic data based on the 1960, 1970 and 1980 census reports. The advantage of this particular service is the access it provides to defined geographic areas using latitude and longitude coordinates for projectors of economic and demographic indicators: ACORN (a classification of residential neighborhoods) is a subset of Supersite.

Urban Decision Systems, Inc Los Angeles, CA.

Urban Decision Systems is a demographic data firm which provides a wide range of census related services. In addition to its census related services, Urban Decision Systems maintains the following databases.

Onsite is a subscription database which includes lifestyle data and marketing data.

UDS Business Database is a subscription service which contains economic and demographic data for a wide range of areas including zip code and ADI areas.

Marketing Intelligence Service, Ltd., Naples, N.Y.

On a subscription basis, Marketing Intelligence Service provides access to its Productscan database which lists and describes new products introduced worldwide and identifies their manufacturers. Through commercial online services access is provided to the full text of new product newsletters from marketing intelligence.

Mediamark Research, Inc., New York, N.Y.

Mediamark Research, Inc. (MRI) provides subscription based services which measure media audiences and audience demographics. The databases are available through a variety of online service vendors and in CD-ROM format. Individual services measure business to business and affluence.

NPA Data Services, Inc., Washington, D.C.

NPA is the data service arm of the National Planning Association. The two databases produced by NPA and available through commercial online services are NPA/Demographic, a timeseries and estimates demographic database, and NPA/Economy, an economic indicator database.

National Planning Data Corporation, Ithaca, N.Y. (NPDC)

NPDC is a demographic data company which provides subscription access to MAX Demographic Data Management and Reporting System, a database of projections and forecasts based on population census data. Also available on CD-ROM.

Strategic Intelligence Systems, Inc., New York, N.Y. (SIS)

SIS provides access to a large number of industry databases which contain indexed and abstracted citations to market information for the industry. The databases are provided on a subscription basis.

Teenage Research Unlimited (TRU), Lake Forest, IL.

The Teenage Market/Attitudinal Study is a market survey database which focuses on the teenage (12–19) market and is available on a subscription basis.

Consumer Behavior

Harvest Marketing Information Services, Ltd., London, England.

On a subscription basis, Harvest Marketing Information is available as a database containing consumer profiles and marketing information for products and services in the U.K. Additional files in this database provide abstracts of current articles and government statistics relative to consumer marketing.

Henley Centre for Forecasting, London, England.

The Henley Centre provides access to its forecasting databases for consumer markets through Profile Information online service.

Information Resources, Inc., Washington, D.C.

InfoScan Panel, available through PROMPT, is an online service from Information Resources which provides demographic and marketing information for consumer purchases of drug and grocery store items. Includes statistics taken from UPC scanning.

Interactive Market Systems, New York, N.Y.
Media Index Survey, a media survey database available through Interactive Market Systems, provides demographic and consumer information for Thailand, Hong Kong, Indonesia, Malaysia and Singapore.

Marketing Intelligence Corporation (MIC), Tokyo, Japan.
On a subscription basis, Marketing Intelligence Corporation makes available the Shakaichosa Kenkyujyo Consumer Index, a database which contains consumer statistics for Japanese households.

Mendelsohn Media Research, Inc., New York, N.Y.
The Survey of Adults and Markets of Influence is available through commercial online services on a subscription basis.

Nikon Kezai Shimbun, Tokyo, Japan.
The NEEDS-AMD database, available on a subscription basis from Nikon Kezai Shimbun (NIKKEI), contains demographic and consumer behavior statistics for Japan. Other NIKKEI databases provide financial and corporate data for Japanese firms.

Research Services, Ltd., London, England.
The Pan European Survey available through Interactive Market Systems contains demographic, consumer and travel statistics for business executives in European Countries. Research Services also produces a similar database covering financial executives.

Scarborough Research Corporation (SRC), New York, N.Y.
The Birch/Scarborough Multimedia Consumer Profile database is offered by SRC on a subscription basis. This database contains for major U.S. cities audience measurement statistics for print, radio and TV as well as demographic and consumer data for persons within those cities.

The Planning Economics Corp., Boston, Mass.
The company provides users with an online model, IMPAS (International Markets Potential Assessment System), which permits them to evaluate the market size, market growth, and market quality

of each of 71 countries, to rank and sort countries, and to generate reports. The data consist of 40 to 50 key demographic, social, and economic indicators for each country, with input obtained from international agencies. The countries selected were those deemed to have multinational corporation suitability.

Store Audits

Nielsen Marketing Research, a company of the Dun & Bradstreet Corporation, Northbrook, IL.

The Nielsen Retail Index is a subscription service which monitors food and drug product sales, both national and regional. Includes information by nature of store, geographic area, brand name, consumer purchases, retailer inventories, etc. Includes historical data and current data.

Nielsen Media Research, a company of the Dun & Bradstreet Corporation, Northbrook, IL.

The Nielsen Station Index is a subscription service which monitors local television viewing in more than 200 TV markets. Includes historical and current data. Also available on CD-ROM. A separate service, CODE (cable on-line Data Exchange), provides information on cable television systems. The Nielsen Syndication Service measures syndicated, local and network audience in over 200 markets and the Nielsen Television Index measures national network viewing.

SAMI, Cincinnati, OH.

SAMI is a subscription service which provides access to a database of information on supermarket withdrawals from warehouses of grocery, household, cosmetic and health products. Includes historical and current data.

DATA Group, King's Lynn, Norfolk, England.

DATA Group is a subscription service which provides access to an online database which contains consumer, industry and product information for the U.S. and foreign countries. Published information is available from Database/Datascan.

Product Use

Simmons Study of Media and Markets, New York, N.Y.

The Study of Media and Markets is a subscription service which provides media audience statistics for print and non-print media, and market statistics including consumption and brand information for a wide range of goods and services. The service also contains lifestyle indicators. A CD-ROM version of the service is available, as are print equivalents. In addition to its annual study, Simmons produces the following subscription services:

> Top Management Insights, a database of demographic and consumption statistics for management level personnel. Includes both personal and business consumption indicators.
> Simmons Teen Age Research Study, a subscription service which provides media, market and demographic statistics for the 12–19 age group.

INDUSTRIAL MARKETING SERVICES

In addition to the services listed here, area, industry and company information of interest to industrial marketers is supplied by some of the economic forecasting, business and financial services cited above, as well as by individual industry and product services such as those that follow. As in the consumer category, media and advertising services have been omitted.

Dun's Marketing Services, a company of the Dun & Bradstreet Corporation, Parsippany, N.J.

This company, a subsidiary of the Dun & Bradstreet Corporation, offers industrial marketers a wide variety of custom research services. A description of the database services is given under Dun & Bradstreet.

Decision Resources, Inc., Burlington, MA.

The research reports produced by Arthur D. Little, a major industrial marketing consultant firm, are available from Decision Resources through the DIALOG database. These reports are full text and are available 1977-.

Trinet, Inc., Parsippany, N.J.

The Trinet Company Database and The Trinet U.S. Business databases are directory databases for U.S. business locations and provide an excellent source of information for industrial marketers.

INDIVIDUAL INDUSTRY AND PRODUCT SERVICES

Specialized industry or product services emanate from a wide variety of agencies; single-industry oriented publishers; general business service firms; consulting firms; trade associations; or from research institutes. The data supplied are extremely detailed and valuable to the analyst concerned with the particular industry.

Although most publishers in the field limit themselves to services for a single industry, some do provide services for a variety of industries:

McGraw-Hill Information Systems Company, Dodge/DRI Construction and Real Estate Information Service, Lexington, MA.

This McGraw-Hill subsidiary is responsible for maintaining a database of information on construction projects under the name Dodge Construction Analysis System, and a database of information on the use of materials and supplies in the residential construction sector under the name LSI Database. Both of these databases are subscription services.

F.W. Dodge Group/McGraw-Hill, Inc., New York, N.Y.

In keeping with Dodge's expertise in the construction field this group maintains a database entitled Dodge Bidscan which monitors in directory fashion bidders on construction contracts. A monthly minimum charge is required for access to this information and a microform equivalent, *Dodge scan,* is available. Dodge Dateline, another database offered by this unit on a subscription basis, monitors costs and other parameters of current projects.

IMS America, Plymouth Meeting, PA.

This company provides a number of services for the U.S. drug and health care industries. Similar services for Canada are available from its Canadian affiliate.

Product services covering the market, including size and composition, are available for pharmaceuticals in hospitals and drug stores; diagnostics in hospitals and private laboratories; toiletries and beauty aids; and animal and poultry feed additives. These are issued primarily on a monthly or quarterly basis.

Ongoing audits report on prescriptions in drug stores and on laboratory tests in hospital and private and combined laboratories.

A monitoring service surveys federal government contract awards for pharmaceuticals, medical supplies and laboratory diagnostics.

IMS America maintains a database containing the results of its audits of the pharmaceutical industry. The database entitled IMSPACT requires a subscription to the print service for access.

Arbitron Ratings Company. New York, N.Y.

Arbitron Radio and Arbitron TV are subscription databases which provide audience measurement for individual stations in specified radio and TV markets. Broadcasters Audience Research in London provides a similar service for the U.K.

RESEARCH SUPPORT SERVICES

Computer Services

Computer applications, widely adopted by marketing research, form the basis of a large number of services that provide a variety of computer programs and systems. Developed by market research and computer service firms such as Market Science Associates, Inc. and Telmar Group, Inc., both in New York, these systems and programs permit clients to retrieve or to manipulate commercial and intramural data to fit specific needs.

Data Base Brokers

The widespread use of computerized data bases, statistical and bibliographic, is a major factor in current business research. For most of these, database brokers, by arrangement with producers, provide users with online access service for a fee.

Since theirs is a dynamic business, the roster of databases serviced by an individual broker will vary from time to time. Researchers interested in accessing a particular database may identify the organization(s) supplying online service by consulting the *Directory of Online Databases* or by querying the database producer.

On-Demand Information Services

Some libraries, information centers, clearinghouses and government agencies provide information on a fee basis. In addition, there are the on-demand services of independent firms and individuals that specialize in gathering information from published sources and contacts in the field, wherever they may be. Research assignments accepted range from location of single facts to compilations of published data and document delivery.

Organizations offering on-demand services can be located through the *Information Industry Directory,* the *Burwell Directory of Information Brokers* or the *FISCAL Directory of Fee-Based Information Services in Libraries.*

Some on-demand services are listed below:

N.W. Ayer, Inc., Ayer Information Center (AIC), New York, N.Y.

In addition to providing on-demand services in the area of business, advertising and marketing information AIC develops customized market research studies.

FIND/SVP, New York, N.Y.

This custom research service for business information gathers secondary data on demand and issues product and industry market studies compiled from published information and industry interviews. The firm also distributes company and industry reports prepared by selected research and consulting organizations and by securities analysts at investment firms, if they are judged of value for business research. A list of available research reports is issued in print, online and in CD-ROM.

Packaged Facts, New York, N.Y.

The data gathering facilities of this commercial information center include extensive newspaper and magazine clipping files. It performs historical research, 1900 to the present, on marketing and advertising topics and publishes market studies primarily on consumer products.

AT&T Easy Link Services, Executive Briefing Service, Upper Saddle River, N.J.
The Executive Briefing Service that provides SDI service by mail, FAX or E-mail.

Minneapolis Public Library and Information Center, INFORM, Minneapolis, MN.
INFORM is an on-demand service with particular emphasis on business and marketing.

New York Public Library, The Research Libraries, Corporate Services, New York, N.Y.
This unit of the New York Public Library provides a wide array of on-demand services to corporate subscribers.

Rice University Library, Regional Information and Communication Exchange (RICE), Houston, TX.
RICE is an on-demand service which accesses information worldwide.

SVP (S'il Vous Plait) Network.
A network of independent on-demand service located in countries throughout the world. FIND/SVP Inc. is a member in the United States.

SRI International Research Information Services, Electronic Database Services, Menlo Park, CA.
SRI is an on-demand service which emphasizes business, science and technology.

Washington Researchers, Washington, D.C.
In its research for individual clients, this information service organization utilizes the resources of the federal government as well as private sources. It also issues a variety of research aids geared to the researcher seeking information generated by the federal government.
In addition to its publications listed in other chapters, it issues a

monthly newsletter, *Washington Researchers,* which provides suggestions for finding information and listings of sources and documents.

Washington Service Bureau, Inc., Washington, D.C.
    The Washington Service Bureau, which is a company of the Commerce Clearing House, Inc., provides a wide variety of on-demand services related to Federal government information.

Field Research

Data lacking in publicly available sources may be developed with the assistance of independent contractors. Some such organizations offer complete research services, from study design through interpretation of results; others specialize in certain aspects such as interviewing and tabulating. Marketing services, similar to those provided by service organizations in the U.S., are offered by marketing service organizations in foreign countries. Some of these organizations may be affiliates of U.S. organizations; others may have subsidiaries of affiliates in the U.S.; and still others may be independent organizations. Detailed information on these firms is included in the directories of market research organizations listed below.

DIRECTORIES OF SERVICES

Information Industry Directory. Detroit. Gale Research. Irregular/ supplements. ISSN 1051-6239.
    Formerly the *Encyclopedia of Information Systems and Sciences,* this directory lists organizations, systems and services within the information sector. Included are database producers, publishers, consultants, on-demand information brokers, E-mail applications, optical publishing applications, software producers, library and information networks, abstracting and indexing services, mailing list services, Videotext and teletext services, and similar information sources. Includes a master index, database index, publications/microforms index, software index, function classification, personal name index, telegraphic index and subject index. The directory is international in scope and is available on magnetic tape or diskette as well as in print.

The Information Industry Directory Supplement updates the base directory.

Published Services and Data Bases

Directory of Online Databases. Detroit, MI: Gale Research. Quarterly. ISSN: 0913-6840.

A descriptive list of databases which gives for each its content, conditions to be met for use, name of producer, and list of online service suppliers. Indexes are by subject, by online service, and by producer.

ADAPSO Membership Directory: ADAPSO the Computer Software and Services Industry Association. Arlington, VA. ADAPSO. Annual.

A directory of organizations which are members of ADAPSO. Each listing describes the software services available from the organization.

Berkman, Robert. *Find it Fast . . .* New York, NY: Harper & Row, 1990. 333p.

An updating of an earlier work which discusses the use of libraries, government agencies, and specialists in business research. Includes coverage of Federal, State, local and foreign sources.

Datamonitor Market Research/Euromonitor Market Research. London: London Euromonitor. [Online database].

These two files constitute the Marketfull online service available through DIALOG. These files cover full-text market research reports for consumer products worldwide.

Directory of Portable Databases. Detroit: Gale. Semiannual. ISSN 1045-8352.

A companion to the *Directory of Online Databases,* this directory lists publicly available databases on CD-ROM, magnetic tape and diskette.

Findex: the Directory of Market Research Reports, Studies and Surveys. Bethesda, MD: Cambridge Information Group. Annual/supplement.

A listing of published market reports and surveys. Arrangement is by subject/industry. Also available online.

Frost & Sullivan Research Reports Abstracts. New York: Frost & Sullivan. [Online database].
A database of abstracts of market research reports from Frost & Sullivan. The database is available through Data-Star and On-line Research and is updated monthly.

Industry Data Sources. Foster City, CA.: Information Access Company (IAC). [Online database].
An online database available through commercial online services which includes citations and abstracts of market research reports by industry.

Marketing Surveys Index. London: Heathmans House/Atlanta, GA: Mac-Farlane. Base book with monthly supplements.
An international listing of published market research reports. Also available online.

Marketsearch. London: Arlington Management Publications. Annual. ISSN 0737-4992.
An international listing of published market research reports. Previous title: *International Directory of Published Market Research.* Also available online.

Mintel Market Intelligence Reports. London, England: Mintel Publications, Ltd. [Online databases].
The Mintel Market Intelligence Reports database is a full-text service online which includes the published Mintel reports. Other Mintel databases cover the leisure market financial services and retailing. The reports emphasize Europe and the U.K. All are available through Profile.

MSI Market Report Series. Surrey, England: Marketing Strategies for Industry. [Online database].
A subscription database which contains full text of the U.K. industry studies published by MSI. The database is available through Profile.

Firms and Individuals

Bradford's Directory of Marketing Research Agencies and Management Consultants in the U.S. and the World. Centerville, VA: Bradford's Directory of Marketing Research Agencies. Biennial. ISSN 0068-063x.

Lists domestic firms and consultants by state and city, and foreign firms by country. Entries define scope and activity and usually list key personnel. Includes a list classified by type of service provided.

U.S. Bureau of the Census. *National Clearinghouse for Census Data Services: Address List.* Washington, DC: Bureau of the Census. Irregular.

A directory of public and private organizations that can assist users in obtaining and utilizing Census Bureau data. The first part, arranged by State, gives for each Clearinghouse registrant its address, name of contact, telephone number, and which types of services are offered.

European Industrial Marketing Research Contact Directory. Brixham, Devon, England: European Marketing Association. Base volume with updates.

A directory of marketing research departments and personnel of industrial firms worldwide.

International Directory of Marketing Research, Companies and Sources. New York, NY: American Marketing Association, New York Chapter. Annual.

A directory of domestic marketing research services with limited international coverage.

Best 100 Sources for Marketing Information. Ithaca, NY: American Demographics/Dow Jones. Annual.

A directory of market research and allied firms arranged by product or service. Includes a product/service index and a company name index.

Directory of Research Services Provided by Members of the Marketing Research Association. Rocky Hill, CT: Marketing Research Association. Annual.

Also known as the MRA Research Services Directory, this provides a listing of market research firms and their services.

International Association for Business Research and Corporate Development—EVAF Membership Directory. West Wickham, Kent, England: International Association for Business Research and Corporate Development. Annual.

A members-only directory of worldwide market research companies.

European Directory of Marketing Information Sources. London: Euromonitor. Biennial. ISSN 0950-656x.

A directory of market research firms and information sources in Europe. Available in the U.S. from Gale Research.

International Directory of Market Research Organizations. London: Market Research Society. Biennial.

An international directory of market research companies arranged by country with a name and service index. Available in the U.S. from MacFarland.

Market Research and Analysis Directory. Omaha: American Business Directories. Annual.

This is one of a series of directories published by American Business Directories and based on "Yellow Pages" advertising. Listings include number of employees and name of directory. Other directories include *Marketing Consultants Directory.* Also available online.

Marketing News—Directory of Software for Marketing Research. Chicago: American Marketing Association. Annual/Supplements. ISSN 0025-3790.

A feature of *Marketing News,* this listing identifies market research software firms.

Quirk's Marketing Research Review. Richfield, MN: Quirk's Enterprises. 10/yr. ISSN 0893-7451.

A trade journal for the market research field, this publication includes special issues of a directory nature for focus groups, software suppliers, market research products and services, and interviewing facilities.

Research Alert. Long Island City, NY: Alert Publishing. Biweekly. ISSN 0739-358x.

A newsletter which provides consumer marketing research reports and also includes directory information for consumer marketing research firms.

ADVERTISING MEDIA

Media provide marketing information primarily to inform the advertiser and to promote the medium. Many also offer their clients and prospects advisory services on marketing problems within their geographic or product areas. Thus, for example, media that conduct product surveys, store checks, and similar studies may be requested to include specific brands, products, or attitude questions in regularly scheduled fieldwork. Media representatives, too, furnish primarily media information and, at times, parallel marketing information for the medium for which they act as selling organizations.

Published data are usually of two types: digests or compilations of extant information, and presentations of original fact based on independent research. A large proportion of both types, subject as it is to the promotional efforts of the sponsor, of necessity varies in content and, with few exceptions, lacks continuity.

Most research produced by media is done by in-house research departments or by outside research organizations working on a contract basis. Some idea of the range of the continuing marketing data distributed by media may be gained from the following examples of such reports. Some of these publications may be found in the research aids listed at the end of the chapter. Other data compilations and marketing services can be located by regular scanning of the trade press or by direct approach to the pertinent medium. Relevant media associations, such as the Magazine Publishers Association, are also important sources of information research published by their members.

As an information source, the media retain their importance, although the published output from this source has decreased significantly during the last decade.

NEWSPAPERS AND NEWSPAPER SUPPLEMENTS

In addition to supplying data for multi-market compendia, many individual papers publish general marketing information for their city or trading areas. These reports vary greatly in the nature and extent of data provided. For some of the larger markets detailed guides are issued from time to time.

Pocket Guide to the Chicago Market. Chicago: Chicago Sun Times. Annual.

Contains selected data on population, income, economic, and retail trade characteristics of the Chicago market. Includes data for Chicago city, SMSA, Chicago-Gary Standard Consolidated Statistical Area, Chicago Area of Dominant Influence, and component communities. Indexed in SRI.

Journal-Bulletin. Rhode Island Almanac. Providence, RI: Providence Journal. Annual. ISSN: 0364-2909.

A compendium of political, social, economic and business information for Rhode Island with time series to 1730.

A number of newspapers sponsor distribution checks and surveys of brand preferences, product use, buying habits, and buying intentions for a broad range of consumer products. Some newspapers have established uniformity in research methods and reporting that add to the advantage of continuity. Among the major types of recurring surveys are these:

> Consumer Analysis studies, patterned on the pioneer *Milwaukee Journal* survey of that name and conducted annually, cover grocery, drug and other consumer products.
>
> Top Ten Brands surveys, also conducted annually, rank the leading brands of foods, household products, appliances, toiletries, etc. on the basis of household use.
>
> Continuing Home Audits, published at varying intervals depending on the nature of the product, provide buying pattern data, in some cases documented with demographic profiles of user households, for a variety of consumer products.

Route lists are compiled by many newspapers, most commonly for drug and grocery stores, and are issued as aids to advertisers' salesmen in making calls.

Newspaper representatives, Sunday supplement publishers, and newspaper sales/service organizations also provide local market data. Marketing aids from these sources quite often deal with local markets collectively and against a background of national data.

Quantitatively, grocery and drug store products receive the greatest emphasis.

CONSUMER MAGAZINES

Research publications produced by consumer magazines deal with both the national market as a whole and selected segments of the national market. These publications provide data on the social, economic, and geographic characteristics of the national market and its segments. The greatest amount of information falls into three general types: marketing guides; surveys; industry or product digests and fact sheets.

Marketing Guides

Statistical studies of the national market usually combine compilations of original data with special tabulations derived from benchmark statistics. Below is an excellent example of this type of report:

American Public's Hopes and Fears for the Decade of the 1990's. New York: Hearst Corporation, 1989. 51p.

A survey conducted by Research & Forecasts under the direction of the Hearst Corporation. Includes social, economic, marketing and related findings and statistics.

Surveys

Many magazines conduct surveys among their subscribers on every type of product or service that could be bought by consumers or, in the case of management publications, by businessmen and their companies.

Along with brand preferences, such studies provide more information than newspaper reports on buying influences, place of purchase, package size, frequency of use, product features liked and disliked, and related aspects of ownership and purchase. Many findings are related to reader characteristics and projected to national totals.

Although numerous, few of these surveys are continuing. Some are conducted at irregular intervals. More frequently, however, a single product or product group is surveyed on a one-time basis, a few of them through subscriber panels such as those maintained by *Good Housekeeping* and *Better Homes and Gardens.*

Digests and Fact Sheets

Infrequent, but very helpful, are the miscellaneous industry and product digests issued by some of the consumer magazines. Fact sheets citing national data are issued occasionally as the sponsors' promotional efforts warrant. These, however, do not constitute a source for market research unless they present well-documented special tabulations of basic statistics that are not easily available otherwise.

FARM PUBLICATIONS

The output of national farm publications, like that of the regional and State papers, closely resembles the surveys, industry digests, and fact sheets issued by consumer magazines.

Regional and State farm papers offer a variety of data (many with geographical breakdowns and comparisons for their areas) on farm population, equipment saturation, cash income, crop production, acreage harvested, livestock population, etc.

Particularly numerous are surveys of equipment ownership, product use, buying intentions, and brand preferences. A large majority of these are one-time studies. Some are repeated at irregular intervals and a few are published on a continuing basis.

TRADE PERIODICALS

Hundreds of trade periodicals, published by commercial organizations or trade and professional associations, service the nation's economic activities. Each is devoted to a particular industry or business function. The number of trade journals servicing a particular field can vary from one to several. Each represents a source of marketing information within its area of specialization. These publications are particularly useful in researching commercial and industrial market facts.

The editorial content of trade journals and special issues supplied with subscriptions is treated in the chapter on periodicals. However, it is well to note here that in many instances statistical analyses, forecasts and industry reviews, originally published in these magazines, are reprinted for more general distribution among interested marketers. To this the publishers add a tremendous volume of special studies compiled either by their research departments or their editorial staff.

Among these the most prevalent are industry "studies," which outweigh in number and scope their counterparts supplied by other media. Many are products of original research or of information obtained from private sources. Some are valuable abstracts of benchmark statistics. Others represent "educated guesstimates" of specialists.

In format these reports vary from single-page data sheets to voluminous sales and marketing guides. Some are revised at irregular intervals; others are issued regularly—usually on an annual basis. In addition to the material available in printed form, vast quantities of machine-readable data are being offered either as substitutes or as data banks complementary to the printed data.

Like the publications, the information supplied is varied: industry censuses indicating branches, primary and secondary producers; plant sizes; number of establishments by geographic location, sales volume, number of employees and other breakdowns; production, shipments, sales; distribution patterns and techniques; consumption, expenditures and needs for supplies, equipment, and services; progress reviews, technical developments, expansion plans; economic forecasts, production and sales estimates; short-range projections and long-range forecasts for industries and their markets.

The trade journals are well indexed by the Predicasts family of indexes; hardcopy and machine-readable and many trade journals are indexed and abstracted in *Statistical Reference Index* (SRI).

McGraw-Hill Book Co., New York, N.Y.

McGraw-Hill is a publisher of trade publications for business and technology-related activities. Subsidiaries of McGraw-Hill such as the Construction Information Group and Data Resources compile annual forecast publications. Many of the McGraw-Hill trade publications are available full-text online.

The Chilton Co., Radnor, Pa.

Like McGraw-Hill, Chilton is a leading publisher of business magazines. Besides the automotive field, they cover iron and steel, hardware, instruments and controls, food, jewelry, optometry, and product design. Reflecting this specialization, the company offers an assortment of marketing services including several industry censuses.

Fairchild Publications, Inc. New York, N.Y.
Like its trade magazines and trade newspapers, the publisher's directories and statistical studies are important information sources for the textile and apparel industries and the retail trade carrying their products.

Fairchild Fact File. Annual/Biennial/Irregular.
A series of statistical reports which present production and marketing data on specific lines of apparel and textiles and other consumer groups.

Time, Inc., New York, N Y.
Although not a publisher of trade periodicals, Time, as an adjunct to its business publication, *Fortune,* publishes many monographs of interest to the business and marketing researcher.

Bill Communications, New York, N.Y. *Survey of Buying Power Data Service.* New York, N.Y. Sales and Marketing Management, Sales Building Division. Annual.
An expansion of the Survey of Buying Power feature of *Sales and Marketing Management.*

Surveys sponsored by trade journals fall into two general groups. Those conducted among industry executives probe expenditures and buying influences, patterns, and needs for a variety of supplies, equipment and services. Dealer, wholesaler, distributor surveys produce "statistical profiles" covering such activities as products handled; sales volume; buying, selling and servicing practices; budget allocations; and, in certain instances, customer needs, buying habits and characteristics.

In addition, a number of publications issue house organs or newsletters on industry trends and marketing developments. Many provide mailing list services and aid on individual problems, including the mounting of field surveys.

A number of the trade periodicals are indexed in SRI and some are available in the companion microfiche service. An increasing number are available full-text online.

AIR MEDIA

Coverage maps, audience measurements and demographic characteristics produced by such services as A. C. Nielsen Marketing Research, Arbitron Ratings Co. and Simmons Market Research Bureau, Inc., trading area information drawn from standard statistical sources and tailored to station coverage, are usually available from individual stations, their networks and station representatives. These sources, too, can also supply findings of product and brand preference surveys if developed for individual stations by intramural research.

RESEARCH AIDS

Standard Rate & Data Service. Wilmette, IL: Standard Rate & Data Service, Inc. Monthly, Bimonthly, Quarterly, Semiannual depending on edition/Supplements.

Primarily a media service providing full directory information, including names of advertising managers and sales representatives, official statement of editorial content, circulation breakdowns, and other detail necessary for media buying. Issued in a series of editions each devoted to a specific advertising medium, including newspapers; consumer magazines and farm publications; business publications; medical/paramedical media; community publications; weekly newspapers; spot radio and spot television; direct mail lists, Hispanic media. The new special issues edition is particularly helpful.

The business publications edition, arranged by industry, identifies and gives scheduled publication dates for feature, directory and other special issues. Also includes semiannuals, annuals and biennials published by the business and trade press.

The service also issues several media editions, each devoted to the media of one of a selected number of foreign countries. A useful new service lists special issues of periodicals, and another combines demographics with consumer behavior.

International Media Enterprises, Inc., South Norwalk, CT.

A series of directories listing print media publications and providing advertisers and descriptive information for each title, these are published by international Media Enterprises under the title *Internal Media Guide,* issued in separate editions for newspapers, consumer magazines, business and professional publications and by region of the world. This series provides media data on an international scale. Similar to SRDS.

College Newspaper Directory and Rate Book. Seattle, WA: American Passage. Annual.
A listing of college periodicals with advertising rates. Also available as mailing labels.

Gale Directory of Publications and Broadcast Media. Detroit, MI: Gale Research. Annual. ISSN 1048-7972
A comprehensive directory of print and broadcast media in the U.S. and Canada. Includes advertising information. Also available as mailing labels. A similar directory is available for areas other than the U.S. and Canada.

Oxbridge Directory of Newsletters. New York, NY: Oxbridge Communications. Annual. ISSN 0163-7010
A directory of newsletters which includes advertising information; also available in machine-readable formats and as mailing labels.

Senior Media Directory. Reno, NV: GEM Publishing. Annual.
A directory of print and broadcast media which service the senior citizen population. Includes advertising information. Also available in machine-readable format.

Advertising-Newspaper Directory. Omaha, NE: American Business Directories. Annual.
An annual directory of newspaper advertisers. The directory listings, as with other titles from American Business Directories, are taken from the "yellow pages".

Burrelle's Media Directories. Livingston, N.J.
Burrelle's publishes a series of guides to media which serve as directories. At present, the series includes guides to black media, Hispanic media, and New England Media.

CAB Cable Spot Advertising Directory. New York, NY: Cabletelevision Advertising Bureau. Annual.
This directory identifies regional and national cable advertising personnel.

College Media Directory. New York, NY: Oxbridge Communications. Biennial. ISSN 1046-4255.

This directory lists colleges and the periodicals published under student airspaces. Includes advertising data. Also available as mailing labels.

Statistical Reference Index: A Selective Guide to American Statistical Publications from Sources Other than the U.S. Government.

What's New in Advertising and Marketing.

BUSINESS FIRMS

Private business organizations are a rich source of information, much of which originates in the course of the firms' own business activity and is offered free for the asking to customers and prospective clients. In a few instances, companies commercialize the results of their compilations and research and, in a case such as Citicorp's, Citicorp Database Services, New York, information services have become a full-fledged subsidiary operation.

Brokerage houses and investment bankers issue industry studies, company analyses, and prospectuses. Banks, railroad industrial departments, and utilities provide local and regional data as well as individual assistance to facilitate business expansion in their areas. Commodity exchanges supply commodity prices and trading volume. Manufacturers and other business enterprises compile statistics and conduct original research, principally to guide their own development or to service the interests of their clients.

Characterized below are categories of information supplied by business firms and examples of their publications that are more generally available.

PRODUCT AND COMPANY INFORMATION

Despite the number of commercially published product and company directories, detailed research, particularly in the industrial field, relies to a great extent on company-issued information.

Product Literature

Company product catalogs, specification sheets, sales literature, technical bulletins, press releases, as well as advertisements in trade and technical journals, provide considerable detail on product properties, uses, and applications.

Some of this literature is available from local distributors. Much of it may be requested directly from the companies. Many firms maintain mailing lists for such materials. Journals publish articles and announcements on new developments in processes and products. Both means can be used to maintain a current flow of this type of information. In recent years company information has been made available in machine-readable and video formats.

Corporate Literature

House organs are also an excellent source for learning about a company's products, research activities, expansion plans, etc. More than 4,000 corporations, mostly manufacturers, issue such magazines and newsletters. But service firms, too, are represented. Well known to marketers, for example, is the *Nielsen Researcher,* which covers many aspects of marketing food and drug products.

The other important source of company information is the financial report. Issued by publicly owned firms, these annual and quarterly documents vary in scope and detail. Many, however, provide in text a corporate profile of progress and plans unavailable in the services that abstract from them only the basic directory and financial facts. Closely related to financial reports are the prospectuses issued by the investment banks and brokerage houses whenever corporations call upon their services for public financing. Uniform in format and disclosure, prospectuses present in detail the company's history, product line, purposes for financing, management profiles, and balance sheet data. SEC filings are available in machine-readable and microfiche formats and Disclosure, Inc. produces an imaged format service.

A selection of useful house organs may be made from the directory listed at the end of this chapter. Financial reports are mailed regularly to stockholders and to interested individuals and organizations upon request. Disclosure, Inc., located in Bethesda, Maryland, offers these reports in CD-ROM and microfiche in a variety of "package" plans. Microfiche and Imaged copies of these reports are available in many large public and university libraries and in offices of the U.S. Securities and Exchange Commission in Washington, D.C., New York, Chicago, and Los Angeles. Prospectuses are advertised in the business press. A favorite medium is the *Wall Street Journal*. Since a limited stock is printed, it is advisable to request them on the day of announcement.

Investext, a machine-readable database available through a variety of online services, offers full-text versions of these reports.

Advisory Literature

A large amount of corporate and product literature is digested in the research departments of large brokerage houses and investment banks. Thus, these firms provide in turn company analyses based on information from corporate and other sources.

INDUSTRY INFORMATION

Brokers, banks, manufacturers, and service organizations also publish a surprising number and variety of industry facts and aids. Probably the most widely known are the industry appraisals issued by the major security dealers. Other publications may be categorized loosely as advisory, statistical, and marketing. The following examples have been selected to illustrate each type.

Advisory

Many house organs and newsletters, including those issued by service firms, some advertising agencies, and research organizations, are advisory in nature. Bank letters, too, although predominantly devoted to business conditions, carry articles on trends in specific industries.

Nielsen Researcher. Northbrook, IL: Nielsen Market Research. 3/yr. ISSN: 0885-6206.
Reports on marketing research.

Statistical

The World's Telephones. Whippany, NJ: American Telephone & Telegraph Co. Annual.

Statistics on the number of telephones in all countries and all principal cities of the world. Includes data on number of conversations, telephones per 1,000 population, etc.

Lilly Hospital Pharmacy Survey. Indianapolis, IN: Ely Lilly & Co. Annual.
   A review of hospital pharmacy operations.

Statistical Bulletin. Baltimore, MD: Statistical Bulletin. Quarterly.
   Vital statistics data and trends based on published and intramural research. A Metropolitan Life publication.

RMA Annual Statement Studies. Philadelphia: Robert Morris Associates. Annual. ISSN 0080-3340.
   Composite or "average" balance sheets and income statements for over 300 different lines of business—manufacturers, wholesalers, retailers, services, and contractors.

Annual Grant Thornton Manufacturing Climates Study. Chicago: Grant Thornton. Annual.
   A report on the level of each state's quality factors for manufacturing industries.

KSA Perspective: Textile. New York, NY: Kurt Salnor Associates. Annual.
   A report on the financial performance of publicly owned textile companies. Other K.S.A. publications cover the apparel industry, footware industries, and retail industry.

National Trend of Business. Lodging Industry. Philadelphia: Laventhal and Horwath. Monthly.
   A periodical providing statistics on the lodging industry market. Other Laventhal and Horwath publications deal with the gaming industry and specialized housing industries.

Who's Buying Houses in America. Chicago: Chicago Title and Trust. Annual.
   A report on the makeup of the first-time home buyer market and the repeat home buyer market.

Marketing

A large amount of research is sponsored by manufacturers for their own guidance in product development and in market planning. Some findings are published primarily to promote the end use of the company's products among their industrial customers, retailers, and other interested marketers. The bulk of these studies is done on a one-time basis and differs considerably from those produced by media. A number of industry studies are done in cooperation with university research centers and other research organizations. Many of these reports are not available for general distribution.

Chivas Regal Report on American Business Leaders: Executive Attitudes in a Time of Upheaval. New York, NY: Ruder-Finn, 1990. 3,179p.
A survey of business leaders with statistics on social and economic factors for the 1990s. An earlier (1985) report entitled *Chivas Regal Report on Working Americans* included comparative data.

BUSINESS CONDITIONS

Bank and brokerage newsletters offer a continuing source of data on economic conditions and the business and political climate affecting them. Large banks in major metropolitan areas provide economic analyses of national and international scope. Others are a good source for regional and local information. In addition, major foreign banks frequently issue financial and economic data that reflect business conditions in their countries. Accounting firms publish a variety of guides for businesses operating abroad.

The changes in corporate structure which took place in the 1980s, coupled with economic considerations, have had a significant impact on banks' publishing activity.

International

World Financial Markets. New York: Morgan Guaranty Trust Company of New York. 3/yr.
Provides statistics by country for a variety of financial series such as

Eurocurrency deposit rates, money market rates, commercial bank deposits.

International Business Series. New York: Ernst & Young. Irregular.
   A series of separate guides on how to do business in each of over 20 countries.

Information Guide for Doing Business in {country}. New York: Price, Waterhouse & Co. Irregular.
   Series includes separate guides for over 60 countries as well as several special volumes devoted to income tax and other business topics.

National

Forecast. Los Angeles, CA: First Interstate Bancorp. Annual.
   An economic survey with an emphasis on Western states; includes foreign country data.

Economic Report. New York, NY: Manufacturer's Hanover Corp. Bimonthly. ISSN: 0885-4149.
   A survey of the U.S. economy with forecast information.

Regional

Economic Outlook: California Report. San Francisco: Bank of America, Specialized Services Dept. Annual.
   An annual forecast of California's economy, business activity, etc.

Economic Indicators. Honolulu: First Hawaiian Bank. Bimonthly/Annual summary.
   A survey of business activity, labor, population, income, etc. in Hawaii.

SERVICES

In addition to publications, many firms offer advice and assistance on many aspects of business.

Suppliers of packaging equipment and materials maintain laboratories for testing their products and customers' package designs. Many manufacturers offer a variety of marketing aids and technical assistance to their clients.

Banks are a good source of unpublished credit information and data on business conditions and local industries. Some banks maintain special departments to service particular industries.

RESEARCH AIDS

There are many area, industry, and product directories that can be checked for names of companies that can supply the kind of information and advice discussed here. These can be supplemented by the following sources:

Business Organizations, Agencies, and Publications Directory. Detroit, MI: Gale. Irregular.

A guide to publications and services available from businesses and other agencies.

Asian Markets: A Guide to Company and Industry Information Sources. Washington, DC: Washington Researchers. Irregular.

A directory of sources of information about Asian business which includes banks and other business organizations among its sources.

Industry Data Sources. Foster City, CA: Information Access Company (IAC). [Online database].

An international database which provides listings of sources of information for specific industries. Included among the sources are private companies.

Investext, the Source for Company and Industry Analysis. Foster City, CA: Information Access Company (IAC). [Online database].

A full-text database which contains the research reports produced by investment firms and banks. A European database providing similar information for European markets is available on Dialog as Marketfull.

European Markets: A Guide to Company and Industry Information Sources. Washington, DC: Washington Researchers. Irregular.

A directory of sources of information about European business which includes among its sources banks and other business organizations.

Marketing Surveys Index. London: Marketing Strategies for Industry. Monthly updates.
A listing of U.K. market research reports and other business research.

PTS Prompt Predicasts. Foster City, CA: Information Access Company (IAC). [Online database].
The Prompt database includes full text and abstracts of research reports from business organizations along with its other data. A current version is available.

Wall Street Transcript. New York: Wall St. Transcript, Inc. Weekly. ISSN 0043-0102.
Reproduces the text of selected brokerage house reports on specific companies and industries, in addition to providing a wealth of other information useful for investment analysis.

Working Press of the Nation: Volume 5, Internal Publications Directory. Burlington, IA: National Research Bureau. Annual. ISSN 0084-1323.
Lists house magazines issued by over 3,500 companies, clubs, government agencies, and other groups throughout the U.S. and Canada.

Findex.
Publications of business firms are announced in the trade press and listed in the regular bibliographies of business materials. Unique in the coverage of statistical publications issued by business firms is the *Statistical Reference Index.*

DIRECTORIES AND MAILING LISTS

DIRECTORIES

Directories constitute a unique group. Compiled and published by a variety of public and private agencies, they serve a dual purpose. Some, like the directories of services, associations, periodicals, and specialists, are guides to information and as such are listed in the chapters relating to those sources. The larger number, however, are marketing tools—aids in identifying prospective customers and in directing sales strategy for a wide variety of goods and services.

The type of information in these directories varies from simple name and address listings to complex analyses of company operations and detailed product classifications. Coverage, too, ranges from multi-industry compilations to lists of specific commodities; from comprehensive enumerations of local residents and enterprises to selective or topical lists of national scope. Familiarity with the content and special features of these and of local and specialized directories indicates, however, a usefulness beyond such precise classification. Thus, too often overlooked in the search for specifics are the ubiquitous telephone directory and the equally common and useful city directories.

The introduction of the CD-ROM as an end-user tool has greatly expanded the accessibility of directory information. Companies such as Standard & Poor's and Dun's have introduced a variety of CD-ROM products based on their large directory databases. The telephone directories have also proved a fertile field for CD-ROM publication: these range from discs produced by the telephone companies themselves, such as the NYNEX CD-ROM products, to commercially reproduced information based on "yellow pages" listings. The greatly improved access provided by the CD-ROM format may justify the relatively high cost of these products; however, care should be taken, particularly with "yellow pages" compilations, that the listings are based on current information.

Telephone Directories

Alphabetical and classified subscriber directories for every community serviced are frequently updated and easily available from the local telephone companies. Collections of out-of-town directories are often maintained by local telephone offices, public libraries, or chambers of commerce. Particularly useful are the classified sections, not only for their specific product and business listings but also for the local firms. The reverse, or criss-cross, directory, which lists telephone subscribers by street addresses, may be leased or purchased commercially. University Microfilms, Inc. supplies both alphabetical and classified directories for major cities on microfiche through its Phonefiche service.

As mentioned earlier, the availability of telephone directory information, both white and "yellow" pages, on CD-ROM has greatly enhanced the use of these directories as marketing aids. The CD-ROM discs supplied by NYNEX in its NYNEX Fast Track Digital Directory service provide access to white pages listings in all NYNEX locators; a companion "yellow pages" service is available. American Business Directories, located in Omaha, Nebraska, produces a series of directories compiled from various "yellow pages." These cover a wide range of businesses, services, and not-for-profit activities, and are also available in print format.

City Directories

City directories, usually compiled by private companies specializing in this type of publication, are available for all but the largest metropolitan areas on a current basis. Standard information includes names of residents with telephone, address, occupation and home ownership indicated; local businesses classified by type of activity; government officials and other city information. Businesses arranged by street address and special listings of manufacturing firms are frequent features.

The International Association of Cross-Reference Directory. Publishers located in Detroit, MI. Publishes a membership list which lists the directories published by each member. The CD-ROM and other machine-readable format telephone directories also function on a cross-reference basis.

Telephone Directory-Format Directories

The telephone directory format has been adopted by several publishers for the publication of directories listing individuals or organizations. The use of this format for government agencies is particularly prevalent. Some of these directories are listed below.

AT&T Toll Free 800 Directory—Business Edition. Bridgewater, NJ: AT&T Communications. Annual.
An authorized listing of business 800 numbers nationwide. A consumer edition is also published for FAX numbers.

National Fax Directory. Detroit, MI: Gale. Annual. ISSN: 1045-9499.
A national listing of FAX numbers for business, government agencies and other institutions.

Electronic Mail

Any directory published for this area of telecommunications would of necessity be subject to the need for constant updating. Persons and organizations involved in E-mail transmission have developed personalized directories. A trade association involved in various aspects of electronic mail activity is Electronic Mail Association, Arlington, VA.

Government Agencies

At the Federal level and for some State-level agencies internal telephone directories are published and distributed. A classic example is *Telephone Contacts for Data Users,* produced by the United States, Bureau of the Census. Some commercially produced telephone directory-format guides to government agencies are listed below:

Federal Fast Finder: A Key Word Telephone Directory to the Federal Government. Washington, DC: Washington Researchers. Biennial. ISSN 0278-4580.
This directory covers government agencies at the Federal level and includes information lines and electronic bulletin boards.

Congressional Yellow Book: A Directory of Members of Congress Including Their Committees and Key Staff Aides. Washington, DC: Monitor Publishing. Quarterly. ISSN 0191-1422.

This is one of a series of directories published by Monitor in this format. Other parts of the series cover executive agencies, associations, sub-national government agencies, etc. The frequent updating of these publications makes them particularly useful.

Biographical Directories

Biographical directories of prominent men and women, such as *Who's Who in America* and its companion volumes, are universally familiar. Local and regional directories in this category are comparatively few. Numerous, however, are the specialized directories of trade and professional people. Many are issued by commercial publishers; some are rosters of trade and professional societies. Some associations provide lists of conference attendees, which lack biographical detail but are a particularly good source of prominent and active professionals. Executive listings are also commonly included in firm and product directories.

The availability of a wide variety of reports and periodicals in full-text format on CD-ROM and on services such as NEXIS has greatly expanded the universe of available biographical information. In addition, traditional profiles of business persons in the news are available in full text on sources such as:

ABI/Inform. UMI/Data Courier.

An index to over 800 business periodicals which may be accessed on CD-ROM or online. The full-text service available with ABI/Inform is called Business Periodicals on Disc and covers over 400 periodicals.

Business Dateline. UMI/Data Courier.

Full text of business sections from regional newspapers and regional business periodicals. Available in CD-ROM format or online. The *Wall Street Journal* is also available fulltext on CD-ROM from UMI/Data Courier.

Business Wire. Business Wire.

A full-text online database which includes press releases of a business nature. The traditional press release databases such as AP News, Reuter News Reports, and UPI Database are also valuable.

Dow Jones International News. Dow Jones News/Retrieval (DJINS).

A full-text current online service which includes major business newspapers and periodicals. A historical companion database is Dow Jones Text Search Service.

NEXIS Service. Mead Data Central.

This large family of databases, described elsewhere, includes as one of its "libraries" full text of major business newspapers and periodicals.

PTS Prompt. Predicasts/IAC.

This database, available online and in CD-ROM format with some full-text availability, is particularly important for its coverage of the trade journal universe.

In addition to the specific sources noted here, a wide variety of other databases and CD-ROM products such as the Disclosure database can serve particular biographical information needs.

Who's Who in Finance and Industry. Wilmette, IL: Marquis. ISSN 0033-9523

A directory of prominent American business executives and other persons impacting on business activities.

U.S. Congress. *Official Congressional Directory.* Washington, DC: Government Printing Office. Annual. ISSN 0160-9890

Outlines the organization and membership of the legislative, executive, and judicial branches of the Federal government. Particularly useful for its detailed roster of sources of supply for copies of certain bills, congressional documents, hearings, and reports. Also lists foreign delegations and consular officers in the U.S. Also available on magnetic tape and diskette.

Standard & Poor's Register of Corporations, Directors and Executives. New York: Standard & Poor's Corp. Annual/Cumulative supplements.

Comprised of three volumes. Volume 1 lists U.S. and Canadian companies with their officers, products or lines of business, SIC numbers, sales, and number of employees. Volume 2 is a directory of executives and directors with brief biographic data. Volume 3 includes a list of companies by SIC number; a list of companies by geographic location; a list of new companies; a list of new executives; and an obituary section. Also available in CD-ROM format and online.

Dun & Bradstreet Reference Book of Corporate Managements. Parsippany, NJ: Dun's Marketing Services. Annual. ISSN 0070-7627.

A biographical directory of management personnel in public and private business organizations. In addition to line management officers, this multi-volume set includes persons in management level positions, personnel, credit and computer operations. Also available online and in CD-ROM formats.

Business Directories

Information on products and firms, helpful in locating markets for goods and services as well as sources of supply, is interwoven in numerous general and specialized business or trade directories: purchasing directories or buyers' guides; general industrial directories—national, State, regional, local; directories of given manufacturing or business lines.

Business directory information is not limited to simple listings of company and product names. Commonly included are data on employment, plant location and capacity, executive personnel and equipment, as well as general statistics for the industry.

There has been a tendency for State industrial directories to be issued by commercial publishers in place of State agencies or business schools, and a further move to the consolidation of this effort in the hands of single publishers such as MacRae's or Colt.

Although many product and special industry directories are issued by commercial publishers, a larger number are issued by trade associations or compiled by trade journals servicing the field. Those directories compiled by trade journals may be special issues of the journals, inclusion within journal issues, or separate publications. Regional and local directories of manufacturers are compiled by State or local government agencies, by chambers of commerce, by university bureaus of business research, or commercially published. Some national or local publications of all types in this group are also issued by trade associations.

Route lists of retailers and wholesalers, most numerous for drug and grocery outlets, are provided as a service to advertisers by newspapers in many large cities. These directories are arranged by street address in a sequence convenient in guiding a salesman's calls.

Some generally useful business directories are listed below. Others may be located through the bibliographies given at the end of this chapter.

Products

MacRae's Blue Book. New York: MacRae's Blue Book, Inc. Annual. ISSN 0886-9189

Primarily a purchasing guide for engineering, production and purchasing executives. Manufacturers are listed alphabetically by company name, by products, and by trade names. Listings include company credit ratings. A separate section contains catalogs provided by manufacturers.

Thomas Register of American Manufacturers and Thomas Register Catalog File. New York: Thomas Publishing Co. Annual. ISSN 0362-7721.

A multi-volume set in which the first volumes are an alphabetical listing of manufactured products, giving their manufacturers or distributors. Succeeding volumes contain alphabetical indexes of companies, products and trade names. The company index entries include address, branch offices, subsidiaries/affiliates, products, asset range classification and, occasionally, officers. The Thomcat section, a multi-volume collection of catalogs arranged alphabetically by company name, completes the set. Also available online and in CD-ROM format.

MacRae's Industrial Directory Connecticut and Rhode Island. New York: MacRae's Blue Book, Inc. Annual. ISSN 0740-2937.

MacRae's is a publisher of industrial directories for several States and regions including the New England States and Maryland, Delaware, the Carolinas, and Virginia. Each follows the pattern of listing companies by county of location. Each listing includes plant size, sales volume and number of employees.

Standard Directory of Advertisers. Wilmette, IL: National Register Publishing Co. Annual/Monthly cumulative supplements.

Lists by industry: national advertisers together with their officers; advertising, marketing and sales executives; products and trade names; and advertising agencies. Includes alphabetical company and trade name indexes, and a separately bound geographic list of advertisers. A separate biweekly, *AD Change,* is available, as is an international edition.

Companies and Their Brands. Detroit: Gale Research Co. Annual. ISSN 1047-6407.

One part of a multi-volume set, the other part of which is a reverse approach entitled *Brands and Their Companies.* The set identifies the source of consumer and some industrial brand names. An update entitled *New Brands and Their Companies* is issued as a supplement.

Kelly's Business Directory Including Industrial Services. East Gunstead, England: Reed Information Services. Annual. ISSN 0269-9265.

Alphabetical company and product list of British manufacturers and merchants. Also lists, by product, British importers and European companies manufacturing for export.

ABC Europe Production. Darmstadt, Germany: Europ Export Edition GMBH. ABC Publishing Group. Annual. ISSN 0065-003x.

A directory, arranged by product, which covers European exporters. Other volumes from this publisher cover German manufacturers. Also available in machine-readable formats.

Manufacturers' catalogs, as well as catalogs from wholesalers and retailers, are important sources of product data. Because catalogs change frequently, they are often issued in looseleaf format with supplements added as changes occur. Manufacturers' catalogs are maintained by their representatives and agents and in some instances by the relevant trade association. In addition to the catalog section of *Thomas Register,* collected catalogs are also available for product groups.

Sweet's Engineering & Retrofit Mechanical Electrical Civil/Structural and Related Catalog File. New York: Sweet's Group, McGraw-Hill. Annual. ISSN 0884-058x.

A multi-volume set of bound manufacturers catalogs. Sweet's publications cover engineering and architectural products.

Productscan. Naples, N.Y.: Marketing Intelligence Service. [Online database].
A consumer products database that is updated weekly. Coverage is worldwide.

PTS New Product Announcement. Foster City, CA: Predicasts/IAC. [Online database].
A products database which is based on press release information. Other Predicasts databases and publications are excellent product sources.

Plants

Plant directories are available in three forms: custom computer printouts from data banks maintained by services and some directory publishers; multi-industry plant directories which cover major manufacturing companies; and single-industry plant directories. Special issues of trade magazines are an important source of single-industry plant directories. State industrial directories provide plant location data for the State covered.

Marketing Economics: Key Plants. Jamaica, NY: Marketing Economics Institute. Biennial. ISSN 0098-1397.
A directory of plants with 100 or more employees. Part I is a geographic listing of plants by State and county. Within county, plants are arranged by SIC product code. Part II lists plants by SIC code broken down by state and county.
In addition to the national edition, regional editions are available. Also available online.

Dun's Industrial Guide: the Metalworking Directory. National ed. Parsippany, NJ: Dun's Marketing Services. Annual. ISSN 0278-8799.
This directory, which covers plants which utilize metals and their suppliers, provides directory information and location data including size of facility.

Companies

Dun & Bradstreet Million Dollar Directory. Parsippany, NJ: Dun's Marketing Services. Annual.

Also available online and in CD-ROM format. This is the Dun's publication which has historically been available in hard copy. A variety of other directories modeled on this list, but with many more listings or added information, are available online only. Some of these additional directories are:

D & B—Dun's Business Locator.

A directory of basic address information for over eight million domestic businesses. Quarterly updates.

D & B. Dun's Market Identifiers.

A directory which includes directory information, executive names, sales volume and number of employees for domestic businesses with five or more employees. Over six million companies are included. Updated quarterly.

D & B. Dun's Financial Records Plus.

A directory which includes extensive financial information in addition to directory information for over 700,000 domestic businesses. Updated quarterly.

Fortune World Business Directory. New York, NY: Time. Annual. ISSN 0197-7792.

A reprint edition of the separate special issue rankings of the largest companies which appear in *Fortune* industrial (500), U.S. June.

Ward's Business Directory of U.S. Private and Public Companies. Detroit, MI: Gale. Annual. ISSN 1048-8707.

Rankings of the largest corporations, private and public, in a large number of manufacturing and non-manufacturing SIC industries. Data are also available on magnetic tape and diskette.

Directory of American Firms Operating in Foreign Countries. New York: World Trade Academy Press. Irregular. ISSN 0070-5071.

Lists companies in two sections: alphabetically by name; and under country of operation. Besides company name, entries give address and name of officer in charge of operations in the country. A reverse volume is also available.

Macmillan Directory of Multinationals. Basingstoke, England: Macmillan. Irregular.
A directory of multinational businesses, primarily industrial, with over $1 billion in sales. Includes information on subsidiaries and executives, administrative structure, products, etc.

Principal International Businesses . . . Parsippany, NJ: Dun's Marketing Services. Annual. ISSN 0097-6288.
A worldwide directory listing major businesses alphabetically under country. Gives company name; address; sales volume in currency of the country; number of employees; importer, exporter or import-export agent (where applicable); SIC codes and product or service designation. Also includes parent company name in listings of subsidiaries. Companies with their addresses are also listed alphabetically and by SIC code. Also available online. In addition, a series of regional volumes is also available.

Directory of Corporate Affiliations. Wilmette, IL: National Register Publishing Co. Annual/Bimonthly supplements.
Lists American parent companies with their divisions, subsidiaries and affiliates. Alphabetical name index. An international edition is also available. Both volumes are available online. A master index to both volumes is available.

America's Corporate Families: Billion Dollar Directory. Parsippany, NJ: Dun's Marketing Services. Annual. ISSN 0890-6645.
A listing of parent companies in the U.S. along with their subsidiaries both in the U.S. and overseas. A CD-ROM version is available and an international volume is also available.

Key Business Information File. New Providence, NJ: Dun & Bradstreet International. [Online database].
A subscription database which provides directory and financial information for domestic and foreign companies.

Disclosure. Bethesda, MD. [Online database].
A database of SEC documentation which includes company and subsidiary information. Also available in CD-ROM format.

Who Owns Whom. Parsippany, NJ: Dun's Marketing Services. Annual.
A series of regional directories which list parent companies and their subsidiaries. Also available in machine-readable format.

Company Thesaurus. Cleveland: Predicasts, Inc. Annual.
Lists company and subsidiary names for all corporations appearing in the publisher's databases and index publications. Besides company relationships, includes country and modified SIC codes used. Also available online.

More detailed data on the organization, finances, and credit ratings of individual companies are published by such services as Moody's, Standard & Poor's, and Dun & Bradstreet.
Closer study of a business enterprise, if it is a publicly owned corporation, may call for an analysis of such primary sources as 10-Ks, annual reports, proxy statements, etc.
The Dialog database service has added a company name search capability to its service.

Research Aids

Directories in Print. Detroit, MI: Gale Research. Irregular/supplements. ISSN 0899-353x.
An international listing of directories published in all formats. The volume is arranged by subject with a separate index volume which indexes by title, alternate format and subject. Also available in machine-readable formats.

Top 3,000 Directories and Annuals. Reading, England: Armstrong, Ltd. Dawson Book Service. Annual.
A ranking of directories and other serials based on "value." The emphasis is on U.K. but other areas are covered.

Current British Directories: A Guide to Directories Published in the British Isles. Beckenham, Kent, England: CBD Research. Triennial. ISSN 0070-1858.
Available in the U.S. through Gale Research, this is a directory of directories for all subjects for Great Britain and Ireland.

Trade Directories of the World. Jericho, NY: Croner Publications. Looseleaf/Monthly supplements. ISSN 0564-0482.

Business and trade directories arranged by title under country of publication. Includes a country index and an index to trades and professions.

In addition, *Guide to Special Issues . . .* includes many directory issues of periodicals and their scheduled publication dates, as does *Standard Rate & Data Service: Business Publication Rates and Data.*

Business Periodicals Index cites under "Directories" and under specific subjects those directories that appear in the magazines covered by the service. Similar indexing of such directories appears in the *PAIS International* which also includes separately published directories.

City and State Directories in Print. Detroit, MI: Gale. Biennial. ISSN 1043-8939.

A guide to all types of directories published for particular geographic areas such as cities and States.

Directory of Directory Publishers. Philadelphia, PA: Morgan-Rand. Irregular. ISSN 1053-4210.

An international directory of directory publishers.

Directory of Industrial Directories and Annual Buyers Guides. New York, NY: Industrial Directory Association. Annual.

A directory of publishers of industrial directories and buyers guides.

Phonefiche. Ann Arbor, MI: University Microfilms International. Irregular.

A collection of telephone directories in microfiche format for U.S. areas with a population of over 15,000. A guide which locates individual cities and tours is included.

Directories: Successful Advertising Media. Brussels: European Association of Directory Publishers. Annual.

A listing of directories published by European directory publishers. Includes publishing and price information.

Yellow Pages Industry Sourcebook. Larchmont, NY: Communications Trends. Irregular.

A directory of "yellow pages" publishers.

MAILING LISTS

Directories and original records are the primary sources used in the compilation of specialized mailing lists for all lines of business and all types of individuals. The lists are of two general types. Mail order lists consist of names that originated in sales or responded to promotion appeal mailings similar to those of the list buyer. Compiled lists consist of names, individual or corporate, culled from many sources to tap a specific market.

The quality and selectivity of mailing lists have always been of major consideration to list buyers. Both are becoming more attainable through improved processing and control techniques. Computerization has greatly improved the process of selection and offers list buyers highly sophisticated products kept almost continuously current. Lists are available of businesses classified by SIC classification, sales size, geographic location; of individuals by age, sex, occupation, and spending for air transportation, travel, department store purchases; etc.

Some mailing list houses offer national or local lists in a limited number of lines. A number of large firms issue catalogs of those that are readily available. Since these price lists indicate the number of names per list and are often revised annually, they also serve as useful guides to the number of prospective customers.

All mailing lists, either ready-made or custom compiled, are either sold or rented. In the latter case, the mailing house itself addresses, inserts, and posts the outgoing literature. As a rule, these services are also available for lists sold in lieu of the normal list format, preprinted labels and tapes. In addition, some houses offer to supply copy, design, and production facilities for the mailing pieces themselves.

Trade journal publishers, trade and professional associations, newspapers, magazines, and chambers of commerce are also useful sources of mailing lists and mailing list services.

Although not the best substitute, current catalogs of general-line houses and the classified telephone directories may be used for lack of the following guides.

The availability of telephone directories in CD-ROM format has greatly expanded the practicality of creating a mailing list for specific needs.

Standard Rate & Data Service: Direct Mail Lists Rates and Data. Wilmette, IL: Standard Rate & Data Service, Inc. Semiannual/ Supplements. ISSN 0038-9463.
Business, consumer, and farm lists classified and indexed by industry, product, or consumer demographics. In addition to description of list, this reports list source, size, rental rate, delivery time, etc. Also lists brokers and custom compilers.

Edith Roman Direct Mail Encyclopedia. New York: Edith Roman. Annual.
A directory of mailing lists arranged by SIC code and alphabetically.

Direct Mail Producers Association, Services and Specialities of the Member Companies. London, England: Direct Mail Producers Association. Annual.
A directory of U.K. mailing list suppliers which indicates types of lists available.

Directory of Mailing List Companies. West Nyack, NY: Todd Publications. Triennial.
A directory of suppliers of mailing lists and related services, with information on the types of lists available.

The List Directory. Armonk, NY: Karl Business Lists. Annual.
A directory of available mailing lists for business, medicine and law.

Mailing List Companies and Categories. Mitchellville, MD: Enterprise Publishers. Annual. ISSN 1043-4372.
A directory of available mailing lists by type.

Mailing List Directory. Omaha, NE: American Business Directories. Annual.
A title within the "yellow pages" series from American Business Directories. Also available in machine-readable formats.

National Directory of Mailing Lists. New York, NY: Oxbridge
Communications. Irregular.
   A directory of mailing list suppliers and sources.

Who's Who in Mailing: A Professional Buyers Guide. Alexandria, VA:
Mail Advertising Service Association. Annual. ISSN 1058-9201.
   A directory of mailing services which includes list suppliers.

PERIODICALS

The advent of full-text machine-readable versions of periodicals and the expanded coverage provided by document delivery services have revolutionized research by business researchers utilizing these resources. Major publishers such as University Microfilms International, Mead Data Central, Dow Jones & Company, Information Access Company and McGraw-Hill have made hundreds of business periodicals and newspapers instantly available in full text, either through online services such as NEXIS or through CD-ROM services such as ABI/INFORM Business Periodicals on Disc.

The revolution in access to business periodicals has not happened without related problems, such as high direct cost per article and copyright restrictions; however, it seems clear that full-text machine-readable access is the direction which researchers in business areas prefer.

Up-to-date facts are a prime necessity. The business sections of such newspapers as *The New York Times* report local and national events of business significance as they occur. In addition, from time to time they publish review articles on individual products and industries. More detailed and equally timely are the business dailies, *Wall Street Journal* and *Journal of Commerce and Commercial.*

Supplementing the current and straight reporting of the daily press is the interpretative reporting of periodicals with their deeper, more analytic, more specialized coverage.

New developments of interest to marketers range through many areas, from new product announcements to basic research and methodology. The mainstream of such information courses through a great variety of periodicals whose responsiveness to trends in the field creates a constant flux in their editorial content. Thus, the current focus on marketing has been reflected not only in the introduction of new periodicals but also in an increasing editorial emphasis on this subject, particularly in the business and trade press.

Consequently, each practitioner must select and update his or her own reading list, including, if necessary, foreign newspapers, magazines and professional journals, on the basis of their timeliness and editorial policy which would supply him with the coverage necessary for his immediate needs or for research on specific problems.

Grouped below are those periodicals that offer a continuing flow of marketing information, plus only a sampling of specialized magazines. A larger selection of the latter is available in the directories cited at the end of this chapter.

Statistical magazines of Federal agencies, newsletters of banks and services, periodicals issued by colleges and universities, research institutions, and other corporate bodies have been treated in the chapters devoted to those sources. Further information on such publications can be located in the directories and catalogs covering those organizations.

TABLE OF CONTENTS

Tables of contents have long been a staple of SDI systems, either selectively reproduced by in-house personnel or provided by information brokers. In keeping with the movement toward machine-readable access to business periodicals, the traditional tables of contents publications listed below are also available online. The newest trend for tables of contents information is being pioneered by the Colorado Alliance of Research Libraries (CARL), which is making available to member and associate member libraries a database of citations to articles listed in the table of contents of thousands of periodicals held by these libraries. This system, called CARL UnCover, is being added to the machine-readable public access catalogs of many of these institutes.

Current Contents Search. Philadelphia: Institute for Scientific Information. [Online database].

The traditional hard copy *Current Contents* is a by-product of this database. The rapid updating of the database and the broad coverage of the broad universe of the sciences, social sciences and humanities render this an excellent contents tool. Some abstracts are included.

PROFESSIONAL JOURNALS

Journal of Marketing. Chicago: American Marketing Association. Quarterly. ISSN 0022–2429.
Leading journal devoted exclusively to all phases of marketing. Full text available on NEXIS.

Journal of Marketing Research. Chicago: American Marketing Association. Quarterly. ISSN 0022–2437.
Initiated in 1964 as a medium for technical articles on marketing research. Full text available on NEXIS.

Marketing and Research Today. Amsterdam: Elsevier Research. Quarterly. ISSN 0923–5957.
Devoted to articles which review current marketing research in individual European countries. Full text available on NEXIS.

Research methods and techniques, statistical and technical problems of survey research, developments in sociology and applied psychology, and allied areas of interest to marketing are covered in a number of journals. Most of these are issued by professional societies. Among them, for example, are the following:

Journal of Advertising. Athens, GA: University of Georgia, College of Journalism and Mass Communications. Quarterly. ISSN 0091–3367.

Journal of Advertising Research. New York: Advertising Research Foundation. Bimonthly. ISSN 0021–8499.
Full text available on NEXIS.

Journal of Consumer Research. Evansville, FL: Journal of Consumer Research. Quarterly. ISSN 0093–5301.
Full text available on NEXIS.

Public Opinion Quarterly. Chicago, IL: University of Chicago Press. Quarterly. ISSN 0033–362x.

American Economic Review. Nashville, TN: American Economic Association. Quarterly. ISSN 0002–8282.
Full text available on NEXIS.

JASA Journal of the American Statistical Association. Alexandria, VA: American Statistical Association. Quarterly. ISSN 0162-1459.
   Full text available on Trade and Industry ASAP.

Journal of Applied Psychology. Washington, DC: American Psychological Association. Bimonthly. ISSN 0021–8847.
   Full text available on NEXIS.

American Sociological Review. Washington, DC: American Sociological Association. Bimonthly. ISSN 0003–1224.

Marketing Research: A Magazine of Management and Applications. Chicago, IL: American Marketing Association. Quarterly. ISSN 1040–8460.
   A journal devoted to the practical and applied aspects of market research. Emphasizes professional issues and trends.

Public Relations Journal. New York, N.Y.: Public Relations Society of America. Monthly.
   Available full text on NEXIS.

Quirk's Marketing Research Review. Minneapolis, MN: Quirk Enterprises. 10/year. ISSN 0893–7451.
   A journal which emphasizes the applied aspects of market research. Includes case histories and instructional articles.

BUSINESS MAGAZINES

Business Week. New York: McGraw-Hill. Weekly. ISSN 0007–7135.
   Articles on industries, individual companies, technological advances, new product developments, and national events of interest to business management. Includes the magazine's business and financial statistics series in each issue; periodic financial analyses of banks and leading corporations, domestic and foreign; annual report on executive compensation. Special issues include *Industry Outlook* (January); *Business Week 1,000* (April); *Hot Growth Companies* (May); *Global Finance* (October). Full text on NEXIS.

Fortune. New York: Time, Inc. Biweekly.

Detailed analytic treatments in nontechnical language of economic and marketing factors, industries, and individual companies. Special issues include: *Fortune 500* (April); *Fortune Service 500* (June); *50 Largest U.S. Exporters* (July); *Fortune Global 500* (July); *Fortune Global Service 500* (August); *Billionaires* (September). Available full text on NEXIS.

Harvard Business Review. Boston: Harvard University Graduate School of Business Administration. Bimonthly. ISSN 0017–8012.

Presents analytic articles, written by academic and business specialists, on all phases of business management, including marketing. Available as a full-text database and on NEXIS.

Nation's Business. Washington, DC: Chamber of Commerce of the United States. Monthly. ISSN 0028–047x.

Mainly of interest for its occasional forecasts of general business conditions and individual industry outlook.

Crain's New York Business. New York, N.Y.: Crain Communications. Weekly.

One of a family of regional business magazines each of which emphasizes business news and issues important to the business executives in the region. A separate Crain publication entitled *City and State* covers regulatory and other information. Available full text on NEXIS.

The Economist. New York, N.Y.: The Economist Newspaper. Weekly. ISSN 0013–0613.

A North American edition of this international business magazine is available. Available full text on NEXIS.

Inc: the Magazine for Growing Companies. Boston, MA: Goldhirsh Group. Monthly. ISSN 0162–8968.

A business magazine directed to middle-size companies. Special issues include profiles of America's leading growth companies. Available full text on NEXIS.

Although directed at investors, financial magazines such as *Forbes* and *Barron's* publish valuable background material not available elsewhere, on industries, companies and products.

NEWSLETTERS

In the last decade, there has been a major change in access to newsletter format publications. The availability of databases such as NEXIS, NewsNet, Inc. and PTS Newsletter Database has made it possible to retrieve, full-text, newsletters of every type. It is important when utilizing this database resource to keep in mind that retrieval may be costly and that the publishers' blackout period may preclude currency.

Databases

News Net, Inc. Bryn Mawr, PA.
    An online service which includes business as well as general interest newsletters.

PTS Newsletter Database, Predicasts, Cleveland, OH.
    A business newsletter database available on commercial online services.

NEXIS, Mead Data Central, Dayton, OH.
    Newsletters are a component of the NEXIS libraries.

National Affairs

Kiplinger Washington Letter. Washington, DC: The Kiplinger Washington Editors, Inc. Weekly.
    Analysis and some forecasting of political and economic events.

Special Interest

Kiplinger Tax Letter. Washington, DC: The Kiplinger Washington Editors, Inc. Weekly. ISSN 0023–1762.
    News and advisory service on Federal tax legislation and administration.

Government Contractor. Washington, DC: Federal Publications, Inc. Biweekly. ISSN 0017–2596.

Reports and analyzes significant Federal contract rulings from the Federal courts, the Comptroller General, Congress, executive agencies and other sources.

Business International. New York: Business International Corp. Weekly. ISSN 0007–6872.
Covers developments in international trade and investment. The publisher also issues similar newsletters for Europe, Eastern Europe, Latin America, Asia and China.

Mideast Markets. New York: Chase World Information Corp. Bi-weekly.
Reports new developments of interest to companies doing business in the Middle East and North Africa.

Quarterly Economic Review. London: Economist Intelligence Unit Ltd. Quarterly.
Published in a large number of country editions that present news analyses and data on economic and business activity within individual countries worldwide.

Fedwatch. Belmont, CA: MMS International. Weekly. ISSN 1052–6471.
A service which monitors Federal Reserve activity.

Acquisition/Divestiture Weekly Report. Santa Barbara, CA: Quality Service. Weekly. ISSN 0279–4160.
A news service on corporate change.

Consumer Confidence Survey. New York, N.Y.: Consumer Research Center, The Conference Board. Monthly. ISSN 0547–7204.
A news service which reports on all aspects of consumer confidence.

Affluent Markets Alert. Long Island City, N.Y.: Alert. Monthly. ISSN 1041–7508.
A report on upscale market trends.

Business Information Alert. Chicago, IL: Alert. Monthly. ISSN 1042–0746.

A news service directed to the business information professional on new information products and services.

Individual Industries

Unlike the national newsletters, many of those serving individual industries tend to report facts rather than interpret or predict news. Their format, however, and timeliness relate them more to this category than to services that place a greater emphasis on reference use. The following examples were selected to illustrate variety in content, frequency, and source. A significant number of these newsletters is produced by trade and professional associates.

Doane's Agricultural Report. St. Louis: Doane Agricultural Service, Inc. Weekly. ISSN 0093–5271.
Reports on all phases of farm management and farm economics including price forecasts.

Kiplinger Agricultural Letter. Washington, DC: The Kiplinger Washington Editors, Inc. Biweekly. ISSN 0023–1746.
Forecasts, advises on, and interprets political and economic news of interest to farmers.

Applied Genetics News. Stamford, CT: Business Communications Co. Monthly. ISSN 0271–7107.
For biotechnology, reports on all developments, from research to applications, and on company activity in the field.

Platt's Oilgram News. New York: McGraw-Hill. Daily. ISSN 0163–1284.
Reports petroleum industry and related news, worldwide. Available fulltext on NEXIS.

Ward's Automotive Reports. Detroit: Ward's Communications, Inc. Weekly.
Reports automotive industry news, events impacting the industry, and motor vehicle statistics.

CIO: the Magazine for Information Executives. Framingham, MA: CIO Publishing. 18/year.

An information executives professional journal which covers the issues and trends in information management.

TRADE PUBLICATIONS

Much marketing information appears in the numerous magazines that service individual industries and trades. Scope and editorial coverage expand in direct relationship to the specialized interests of each magazine's audience.

Some publications support their own research programs and report statistical data on the products and services of their industries as regular features of their editorial content. Larger projects are incorporated in special issues distributed regularly to subscribers. A number of such compilations serve as basic handbooks in their respective industries and in market research. Data banks maintained by a great number of trade magazines have greatly expanded their potential for producing statistical compilations and directories.

Editorial staffs, well versed in their highly specialized fields, can supplement published data with information drawn from experience. The availability of indexing and full-text versions of these publications online and in CD-ROM format is a significant advance.

Advertising and Marketing

General advertising magazines carry news and articles on marketing developments, plans and case histories, and announcements of research sources as they become available. Much of their material is topical and pertinent to the study of individual products, companies and industries. A few titles follow and others may be located through the research aids listed.

Adweek/East. New York, N.Y.: A/S/M Communications. Weekly. ISSN 0199–2864.
One of a series of regional editions which present the issues important to the advertising and marketing executive with a regional focus. Available full-text on NEXIS.

Adweek's Marketing Week. New York, N.Y.: A/S/M Communications. Weekly. ISSN 0892–8274.

A news and update journal for professionals engaged in marketing activities. The focus is on large-scale marketers and major brands. Special issues include topics similar to and with similar timing to the Adweek special issues.

Advertising Age. Chicago: Crain Communications, Inc. Weekly. ISSN 0001–8899.
Timely and broad news coverage of all events of interest to marketers as well as advertisers. Available full text.

American Advertising. Washington, DC: American Advertising Federation. Quarterly.
A trade journal with news of the activities of the American Advertising Federation.

Direct Marketing. Garden City, N.Y.: Hobe Communications. Monthly.
A journal devoted to all aspects of direct marketing including the creative and business aspects of telemarketing and mail marketing. Includes a detailed "what's new" section. Available full text on NEXIS.

International Journal of Advertising. New York, N.Y.: Haworth Press. Quarterly. ISSN 0265–0487.
A new title for the journal of the Advertising Association of England. Stresses U.K. interests with international emphasis. Available fulltext on NEXIS.

International Journal of Research in Marketing. Amsterdam, Netherlands: Elsevier Science. Quarterly. ISSN 0167–8116.
The official journal of the European Marketing Academy. Available fulltext on NEXIS.

Journal of Global Marketing. Binghamton, N.Y.: Haworth Press. Quarterly. ISSN 0891–1762.
A journal which focuses on the opportunities and challenges of international marketing.

Marketing News. Chicago, IL: American Marketing Association. ISSN 0025–3790.

A news and current update journal for professionals engaged in marketing and sales. Includes special issues devoted to marketing software; consultants; marketing education; international marketing and marketing research. Available fulltext on NEXIS.

Marketing Research. Chicago, IL: American Marketing Association. Quarterly. ISSN 1040–8460.
A journal of articles written by marketing research professionals and academics on new directions in marketing research.

Media Guide. Morristown, N.J.: Kampmann. Annual.
A review of the editorial and reporting standards of major U.S. newspapers and general periodicals.

Mediascope. Wilmette, IL: Standard Rate and Data Service. Annual.
A series of regional planning aids devoted to the media and the market within the region.

Mediaweek. New York, N.Y.: A/S/M Communications. Weekly.
A news and update journal for professionals engaged in media buying and planning. Special issues similar to those for *Adweek.*

Business Marketing. Chicago: Crain Communications, Inc. Monthly. ISSN 0745–5933.
News and articles directed to advertising and marketing executives in business and industry. Available on Dow Jones.

Sales & Marketing Management. New York: Bell Communications. 15/year.
Informative articles on all phases of marketing, selling and distribution. Three major marketing aids are published annually as issues of the magazine: *Survey of Buying Power* (August); *Survey of Media Markets* (October); *Salesmanager's Budget Planner* (June).

Other Industries

Industry trade journals are one of the most important information sources available, particularly to the industrial market researcher. Their awareness of trends generally precedes actual events. It also permits them to forecast the effect of technological progress and economic conflicts on products and industries. Advertisements in these magazines, as mentioned previously, are important indicators of product properties, end uses, and applications, as well as of new developments. Regular issues, in many instances, carry current statistics compiled by trade associations, government agencies and, in some cases, by their own research efforts. Comprehensive data are usually featured annually in the magazine or published separately. In addition to these statistical factbooks, trade papers issue handbooks, manuals, and by far the largest proportion of all buying guides and directories published. A brief sampling, purely illustrative, follows.

Alcoholic Beverage Industry

A major publisher in this field is The Jobson Beverage Group. New York, N.Y. which publishes several statistical annuals as well as *Beverage Dynamics* and *Cheers.*

Other relevant titles include:

Modern Brewery Age. ISSN 0076–9932
Wines & Vines. ISSN 0043–583x

Apparel Industry

A major publisher in this field is Fairchild Publications, New York, N.Y. Two important Fairchild titles are:

DNR (Daily News Record). ISSN 0011–5460
WWD (Women's Wear Daily).

Appliances Industry

Appliance. ISSN 0003–6781

Automotive Industry

Automotive News. ISSN 0005–1551
Automotive Marketing. ISSN 0193–3264

Aviation Industry

Aviation Week & Space Technology. ISSN 0005–2175

Banking

Bank Marketing Magazine.

Chemical Industries

Chemical Marketing Reporter. ISSN 0090–0907

Entertainment and Sports Industries

Broadcasting. ISSN 0007–2028
Playthings. ISSN 0032–1567
Variety. ISSN 0042–2378
Sporting Goods Business. ISSN 0146–0889

Food Processing Industry

Food & Beverage Marketing. ISSN 0731–3799
Frozen Food Age. ISSN 0016–2191

Health Care

Healthcare Marketing Report.
Medical Products Sales. ISSN 0279–4802

Home Furnishings Industry

HFD. ISSN 0162–9158
Interior Design. ISSN 0020–5508

Insurance Industry

The A.M. Best Co. (Oldwick, N.J.) is a major publisher in this field. Other important journals include:

National Underwriter (Life, Health/Financial Services Edition). ISSN 0028–033x

National Underwriter (Property & Casualty/Risk & Benefits Management Edition). ISSN 0163–8912

Office Equipment Industry

Computerworld. ISSN 0010–4841
The Office. ISSN 0030–0128
Office World News. ISSN 0164–5951
PC Magazine.
PC Week. ISSN 0740–1604

Retail Industry

Modern Grocer. ISSN 0026–7805
Stores. ISSN 0039–1867
Supermarket News. ISSN 0039–5803

Travel & Lodging Industry

Hotels.
Successful Meetings. ISSN 0148–4052
Travel Weekly. ISSN 0041–2082

DIRECTORIES OF PERIODICALS

The source lists which are included in the databases produced by the major machine-readable indexing services such as IAC, ISI, CIS, PAIS, and UMI are excellent listings of periodicals for business research. A listing of published directories of periodicals follows.

Gale Directory of Publications and Broadcast Media. Detroit, MI: Gale. Annual. ISSN 7048–7927.
    Formerly the "Ayer" directory, this directory lists newspapers, periodicals and broadcast stations.

Standard Periodical Directory. New York: Oxbridge Communications, Inc. Annual. ISSN 0085–6630.

Arranged by numbered subject categories that are indexed alphabetically. For each title gives name and address of publisher, name of editor, editorial coverage, frequency, and other detail. Title index.

Standard Rate & Data Service. Wilmette, IL: Standard Rate & Data Service, Inc.

Provides detailed and up-to-date directory information in a series of editions of varying frequency updated by inter-issue supplements. Periodicals are limited to those carrying a substantial amount of national advertising.

Ulrich's International Periodicals Directory. New Providence, NJ: R.R. Bowker Co. Biennial/Supplements. ISSN 0000–0175.

Provides directory information on over 120,000 periodicals published throughout the world. The publications are grouped by detailed subjects arranged alphabetically, preceded by a listing of abstracting and indexing services. In addition to general directory information, each entry indicates the presence of abstracts, bibliographies, statistics, and other editorial features. Services that abstract or index the periodical are indicated. A title index; an organization name index to publications of international organizations; and a cross-index to subjects are provided. *Ulrich's Update* serves as a supplement. Also available in CD-ROM format.

Oxbridge Directory of Newsletters. New York: Oxbridge Communications, Inc. Annual.

Entries, arranged by subject, give name of publisher or editor, circulation and distribution (national, international, State, local), whether indexed or abstracted and where. Title index.

Newsletters in Print. Detroit: Gale. Biennial.

A directory of newletters arranged by subject.

International Media Guide: Business/Professional Publications. South Norwalk, CT: International Media Enterprises. Annual.

This is part of a series of guides patterned after *Standard Rate and Data Service.* This part of the series is issued in separate regional editions covering Asia/Pacific; Europe; the Americas and the Middle East/Africa. Other parts of the series cover general periodicals and newspapers.

INFOSERV. Westwood, MA. [Online database—daily update].

A machine-readable list of serial publications in all formats available from FAXON.

ABSTRACTS AND INDEXES

The search for current data can be greatly expedited by the knowledge and use of general and specialized indexes and abstracting services. The major difference between the two is that indexes supply only bibliographic citations and page references whereas abstracts briefly summarize a publication, or, in specialized services, extract relevant facts or data in addition to carrying complete bibliographic identification for easy reference to the original source. Consequently, abstracts, if topically arranged or subject indexed, are more immediately informative than indexes.

Some abstracts appear as regular features of professional journals. More common are collective abstracting services and indexes issued on a subscription basis by professional societies or commercial publishers. These cover many publications but, of necessity, not in exhaustive detail. For broader and more thorough coverage some periodicals index or abstract their own editorial content. A number of large city dailies maintain either unpublished indexes or "morgues" which consist of full texts of their news and other articles filed by subject. Many individual magazines, too, either publish their own editorial indexes as part of the publication or separately, or maintain them on cards or magnetic tape as a service to their staff and readers.

Computer technology has greatly expanded the capacity and value of abstracting and indexing in the business field. Most important indexing and abstracting services are now available online and many are available in CD-ROM format. The quality of the abstracts in such services as ABI/Inform and Predicasts has made them in many cases an end product.

A major expansion of the index and abstract service has been the addition of full-text information to the online database and the introduction of accelerated on-demand document delivery service. A further advance has been the introduction of full-text CD-ROM services such as those offered by IAC, Mead Data and UMI and, at this writing, the latest development, which is a full-text imaged service such as ABI/Inform, Business Periodicals on Disc. Such advances, coupled with software that is increasingly end-user-friendly, has greatly expedited the retrieval of business facts and data.

Selected for inclusion here are a number of published services and bibliographic data bases that index and abstract business information, marketing literature, and statistical data, as well as current events and technological developments of interest to business and market research. For those concerned with academic areas related to these applied fields, a group of services covering allied disciplines has also been included.

Omitted are abstract features of journals; services that cover a single industry; and indexes of individual magazines. Such published and computerized indexes and abstracts, as well as other services similar to those included, may be found by consulting the directories listed at the end of this chapter.

Like periodicals, some other types of publications have their own indexes or abstracting services. These may be continuing, such as the abstracts to dissertations, or one-time, such as the special indexes to some of the decennial censuses. Both types are highly specialized and are grouped with the sources to which they pertain.

Not usually classed with traditional indexes are the index features of annuals, bibliographies, guides, publications catalogs, and check-lists. In business research, however, these are important keys to facts and figures and are found in such publications listed throughout this guide and in the chapter on research aids.

Current Events

Yet another example of the tremendous improvement in the availability of information in a greatly improved access mode is the entire area of current events. The introduction of full-text newspapers, press releases, newsletters and research services in machine-readable format, often with full-text indexing, has revolutionized current events research. The adoption of broadcasting techniques via satellite or cable for the real-time transmission of capturable information represents the current cutting edge of current events research. The future of research in this area will encompass the indexing and storage of information in visual, audio and narrative media.

The researcher using current events information on a current basis should focus on the source best suited to his or her needs from a subject and geographic point of view. In addition, the researcher should determine for the sources used how comprehensive the "full text" is (does it include classified advertisements, short news items, etc.). The researcher of current events information on a retrospective basis should determine the time span covered by the sources used.

The sources listed below represent major current events tools for business research and, as with most current events resources, they have particular value in locating information about persons (press releases, newstories), places (companies) and things (products). Special consideration should be given to press release information which is available through many of the sources listed below and also directly from AP, Reuters, UPI, etc.

Advertising and Marketing Intelligence. New York, N.Y.: New York Times Company. [Online database].

Available as a NEXIS database, this service abstracts a wide variety of publications which focus on advertising and marketing. Included are *Advertising Age; ADWEEK; Ad Day; American Demographics;* along with relevant articles from such national newspapers as the *New York Times* and the *Wall Street Journal* updated weekly.

Burrelle's Broadcast Database. Norwalk, CT: Business Communications. [Online database].

An online database of transcribed radio and television news and public affairs programs. Includes business news programs. Updated daily.

Business Dateline. Ann Arbor, MI: University Microfilms International. [Online database].

This database contains the full text of regional business journal articles as well as the full text of the business sections of major metropolitan daily newspapers including the *Washington Post.* The service is updated weekly. A CD-ROM version is also available.

Courier Plus. Ann Arbor, MI: University Microfilms International. [Online database].

A database of abstracts of articles in newspapers and periodicals. The scope of the indexing covers general interest subjects, but business articles appearing in general interest newspapers and magazines would be included. Updated weekly. A CD-ROM version is also available. This is the current service for the former *Newspaper Abstracts.*

DataTimes. Oklahoma City, OK: DataTimes Corporation. [Online database].
A full-text service with daily updates which covers major metropolitan newspapers including some which focus on business news. Provides access to newspapers not available full-text on other databases.

Information Bank Abstracts. New York, N.Y.: New York Times Company. [Online database].
An abstract database which includes news and features in the *New York Times, The Wall Street Journal* and a wide variety of domestic and foreign newspapers and periodicals. The database is available as a NEXIS database and is updated daily.

McCarthy Online Press Cuttings Service. London, England: McCarthy Information Ltd. [Online database].
A subscription database which provides full-text business articles from European newspapers and business magazines worldwide. Updated daily.

National Newspaper Index. Foster City, CA: Information Access Company. [Online database].
This database indexes the *Christian Science Monitor,* the *Los Angeles Times,* the *New York Times, The Wall Street Journal* and the *Washington Post.* The subject coverage is universal. Updated monthly with daily updates in a related database, *Newsearch.* Also available in CD-ROM format.

NewsNet. Bryn Mawr, PA: NewsNet. [Online database].
A full-text database which includes a wide variety of newsletters. Updated daily with varying time delay factors for individual newsletters.

Newspapers Abstracts. Ann Arbor, MI: University Microfilms International. [Online database].
Indexes with abstracts a number of major metropolitan newspapers including the *New York Times, USA Today,* and the *Wall Street*

Journal. This is a historical database covering 1984–1988. The current service is *Courier Plus.* A CD-ROM version is also available.

Dow Jones Text Library. Princeton, N.J.: Dow Jones & Company. [Online database].
A database of business news on financial information. Includes full text of *Barron's, National Business and Financial Weekly* and the *Wall Street Journal,* along with the full text of a number of business journals. The database is updated daily. Dow Jones also provides a continuously updated business news service, Dow Jones Business and Finance Report, and an international news service, Dow Jones International News.

Federal Register Abstracts. Gaithersburg, MD: National Standards Associations. [Online database].
An online database updated weekly which indexes and abstracts the *Federal Register.* Includes notices, hearings, etc. and references *Federal Register* pages.

Newsearch. Foster City, CA: Information Access. [Online database].
The initial database used by IAC for current indexing. Included in this database are press releases and regional business news.

NEXIS. Dayton, OH: Mead Data Central. [Online database].
A full-text database which contains the *New York Times* along with a wide variety of business periodicals and newspapers. NEXIS is also a gateway to a variety of online business services.

Business News and Business Policy

The services listed below are indexing and abstracting periodicals and newspapers from a management perspective. Business news stories will be covered by the current events services in a more timely fashion, and in the trade literature, which will reflect industry, company and product information covered more intensively by the industry services.

Wall Street Journal Index. Ann Arbor, MI: University Microfilms International. Quarterly/annual cumulation. ISSN 0099-9660.

An index of all articles in the 3-Star Eastern Edition of the *Wall Street Journal.* A microfilm edition and a CD-ROM edition of the WSJ are available from UMI.

The Wall Street Journal is available as an indexed and abstracted publication on a number of machine-readable indexes and is available full text from Dow Jones Text-Search Services. The *Wall Street Journal* (Europe edition) is indexed and abstracted by PTS Prompt.

Business Periodicals Index. New York, N.Y.: Wilson. [Online database].
The print version of *Business Periodicals Index* continues to be published; however, along with the other Wilson indexes, it is now available online and in CD-ROM format. The additional access in machine-readable formats is a great advantage.

PAIS International in Print. New York, N.Y.: Public Affairs Information Service. Monthly/Annual. ISSN 0898-2201.
The print version of the online database. This new title combines the domestic and foreign editions formerly published by PAIS. The new title continues to provide indexing for a variety of publications in English and in French, Portuguese, German, Italian and Spanish. The items in non-English languages are grouped under English subject headings. A CD-ROM version is available.

ABI/Inform. Ann Arbor, MI: UMI/Data Courier. [Online database].
An online database which indexes and abstracts over 800 business periodicals in English. A full-text service including 450 business periodicals is also available. Both services are available on CD-ROM.

Management Contents. Foster City, CA: Information Access Company. [Online databases].
An online database covering 1974 to date which indexes and abstracts English-language periodicals dealing with business. Updated monthly.

Canadian Business Index. Toronto: Micromedia. [Online database].
The print equivalent of this database continues to be published monthly. The service indexes over 200 Canadian English-language business periodicals including financial newspapers.

SGBD DataBank. Brussels: Générale Bank Business Informat Services.

Online database, updated monthly, provides citations to business and economic literature from 1974 to date and abstracts from 1979 to date. Emphasis on Europe.

Index to Business Reports. Yorkshire, England: Quarry Press. 2/year. ISSN 0266-0180.

An abstract service which covers business reports, primarily U.K.

Business Information Alert. Chicago, IL: Alert Publications. 10/year. ISSN 1042 0746.

A newsletter for information professionals which identifies and evaluates new or revised business information sources and services.

Financial Times Abstracts. London: Financial Times Business Information. [Online databases].

An index and abstracting service for the *Financial Times.* The service is available on Data-Star with daily updating and on DIALOG with weekly updating.

Info Trac. Foster City, CA: Information Access Company. [CD-ROM Service].

Info Trac is the IAC service on CD-ROM which indexes and abstracts a wide variety of business periodicals, newspapers and, with the addition of *Investext,* research reports.

Trade & Industry Index. Foster City, CA: Information Access Company. [Online database].

A database of business-related articles culled from the IAC index pool of general and business publications. Updated weekly with daily input into Newsearch.

F & S Index of Corporate Change. Cleveland, OH: Predicasts, Inc. Quarterly/Annual Cumulation.

Provides extracts covering corporate identity developments in the U.S., including acquisitions, bankruptcies, foreign operations, joint ventures, liquidations, mergers, name changes, formation of new companies, reorganizations, and subsidiary changes.

Industry, Product and Company

In addition to the coverage given to industry and company information in the general business press and general business magazines, the trade journal literature and the research reports issued by investment banks and securities dealers are a major source of such information. The following services are of particular importance in these areas:

Predicasts. Cleveland, OH.
Predicasts, now a part of the IAC group, has a long tradition of indexing trade literature. Over time, Predicasts has developed a numeric identification scheme based on the SIC codes, and on its own developed a variety of identifying codes for location, organization, activity, etc. This streamlined approach to online searching makes the Predicasts databases ideally suited to industry, product or company searches. The most important parts of the Predicasts service for general or marketing research are:

PTS Marketing and Advertising Reference Service (MARS).
An industry specific database which focuses on advertising, marketing, public relations and sales. Includes coverage of major trade journals such as *Advertising Age* and *Adweek,* along with specialized newsletters such as *Jack O'Dwyer's Newsletter* for public relations, and the advertising/marketing information in major newspapers.

PTS New Product Announcement/Plus.
A press release database which concentrates on releases dealing with new products or new processes.

PTS Newsletter Database.
A full-text database which includes a wide variety of newsletters published throughout the world.

PTS Prompt.
This is the major Predicasts database and as such covers the broadest spectrum of trade literature. Print and CD-ROM versions are available.

PTS U.S. Forecasts and PTS International Forecasts.
This database culls forecast data from the trade literature. A print version is available.

F & S Indexes.
This is the print product output from Predicasts. Separate editions cover the United States, Europe and the international area.

Investext. Boston: Thomson Financial Networks. [Online database].
A full-text service which covers research reports from investment bank and securities firms. These reports provide detailed information on companies, industries and products.

A useful new addition to the company and product research process is the development of cross-file search databases such as the DIALOG Company Name Finder and a similar product finder which was developed by DIALOG to search across files where the databases permit.

Arthur D. Little Online. Burlington: M. Decision Resources. [Online database].
A full-text database which contains a transcript of research done by Arthur D. Little and Decision resources. Includes industry and company profiles.

In addition to the multi industry services listed above, many industries are covered by individual abstracting and indexing publications devoted to their particular business interests including marketing, as well as by single-industry scientific and technical abstracting services, significant tools for the industrial market researcher. These may be located by consulting the research aids listed at the end of this chapter.

Computers and Technology

The use of computers in information research has made it essential that the researcher be aware of new hardware, software and related products, and new systems of information storage and retrieval.

In addition to the need to be aware of new developments in information technology, the researcher is frequently called upon to do research on the scientific and technological aspects of a business problem. The indexes listed below cover the literature of the computer or of technology in a manner useful to the business researcher.

Computer Database. Foster City, CA: Information Access Company. [Online database].
A database which indexes and abstracts articles covering the technology and business of corporations. A full-text subset is available as is a CD-ROM version.

Microcomputer Index. Medford, N.J.: Learned Information. [Online database].
A database from which the quarterly *Microcomputer Index* is produced. Includes information in abstracts about hardware and software. Updated monthly.

PTS Prompt. Cleveland, OH.: Predicasts. [Online database].
A database which focuses on technologies, markets and companies. Also available in print and in CD-ROM format.

Applied Science and Technology Index. New York: H. W. Wilson Co. 11/year. Cumulative to annual. ISSN 0003-6986.

Biological and Agricultural Index. New York: H.W. Wilson Co. 11/year. Cumulative to annual. ISSN 0006-3177.

Government Reports Announcements and Index. Springfield, VA: Notal Technical. Semiweekly. ISSN 0097-9007.

Information Science Abstracts. Alexandria, VA: IFI/Plenum Data. [Online database].
A database of abstracts which relate to all aspects of information research. A paper version is available. Updated 11 times per year.

DATAPRO. Delran, N.J.: Datapro Research. [Service].
A series of looseleaf publications each of which covers a portion of the information industry segments—hardware, software, systems and services.

Statistics

Statistics are the basis for quantitative research and are integral to almost every resource listed in this work. Two publishers, Predicasts and the Congressional Information Service, have been the backbone of business-related statistical research from the perspective of statistics generated by the Federal government, trade associations, companies, etc. as part of articles, reports or studies. The major services from these publishers are listed below.

American Statistics Index: A Comprehensive Guide and Index to the Statistical Publications of the U.S. Government. Bethesda, MD: Congressional Information Service, Inc. [Online database].

Indexes and abstracts in detail social, economic, demographic, and natural resource statistics contained in all types of Federal agency publications including recurrent and one-time reports, periodicals, annuals, etc. Also covers selected publications for scientific and technical data. Each issue consists of an abstracts section arranged by government structure and a section containing indexes by subject and name; categories (i.e., economic characteristics, demographic characteristics, and geographic areas ranging from city to foreign country/world area); title; agency report number. A guide outlining the major standard classification systems used by various federal agencies to arrange and present social and economic data is included.

As a separate service the publisher supplies microfiche of the indexed publications, either single items or on a subscription basis. Also available in CD ROM format and in print.

CIS/Index. Bethesda, MD: Congressional Information Service.
Also available in CD-ROM format and in print.

Statistical Reference Index: A Selective Guide to American Statistical Publications From Sources Other Than the U.S. Government. Bethesda, MD: Congressional Information Service, Inc. [Online database].

Complements the American Statistics Index, listed above, by indexing and abstracting statistics, including survey findings, issued by such sources as trade, professional, and other nonprofit associations and institutes; media; business organizations; commercial publishers; independent research centers; State government agencies;

and university research centers. National data, State-wide data, and limited coverage of data on foreign countries and of local or narrowly focused data are included. Also available in CD-ROM format and in print and a selective microfiche service is available.

Index to International Statistics. Bethesda, MD: Congressional Information Service, Inc. [Online database].

Designed to index and abstract the statistical publications of the United Nations, other international intergovernmental organizations, and their subsidiary regional and specialized bodies; the Asian, African, and Inter-American development banks; and principal international commodity exchanges. Microfiche of indexed publications are offered as a separate subscription service. Also available in CD-ROM format and in print.

"Index." In: U.S. Bureau of the Census. *Statistical Abstract of the United States.* Washington, DC: Government Printing Office. Annual.

Minutely detailed subject index to the statistical tables abstracted from the Federal and private sources cited in the headnotes, footnotes and bibliographic appendix.

Predicasts. Cleveland, OH.

Among the online services available from Predicasts, the following are particularly useful for statistical research.

- PTS PROMPT
- PTS U.S. Forecasts
- PTS International Forecasts
- PTS U.S. Time Series

Marketing

Topicator. Clockamas, OR: Labemoor. Bimonthly. ISSN 0040-9340.

An index covering articles in the advertising, marketing, and communications fields appearing in leading magazines. Also available in microfiche format.

Advertising and Marketing Intelligence (AMI). Parsippany, N.J.: New York Times—Times Online Services (TOLS). [Online database].

PTS Marketing and Advertising Reference Service (MARS). Cleveland, OH.: Predicasts. [Online database].

An index with abstracts of articles in the trade journals, newspapers and industry publications dealing with advertising and marketing. The PROMPT service from Predicasts is also important for information on marketing and technologies.

Market Research Abstracts. London: The Market Research Society. Semiannual. ISSN 0025-3596.

Abstracts articles from British and American periodicals selected from the fields of research, statistics, psychology, sociology, economics, marketing, advertising, and business management. Arranged by broad subject groups; specific subject index. Also available online.

MSI Market Report Series. London, England: Marketing Strategies for Industry. [Online database].

A full-text service which contains the industry reports from MSI.

Market Search. Tokyo, Japan: JMA Research Institute. [Online database].

An index with abstracts to Japanese market research reports. In Japanese with daily updates.

Allied Disciplines

Current Index to Statistics: Applications, Methods, Theory. Alexandria, VA: American Statistical Association. Annual. ISSN 0364-1228.

Indexes a variety of publications in addition to relevant articles in over 3,000 journals. Also available online.

International Abstracts in Operations Research. Amsterdam, Netherlands: Elsevier. Bimonthly. ISSN 0020-5804.

Compiled under the auspices of the Operations Research Society of America. Covers English-language journals published worldwide. Abstracts of over 1,000 papers per year in the field of operations research and management sciences are classified by topic and indexed by author and subject.

Journal of Economic Literature. Nashville, Tenn.: American Economic Association. Quarterly. ISSN 0022-0515.

Lengthy abstracts of economic articles arranged by broad subject. An author index is provided. Also available online and in CD-ROM format.

Psychological Abstracts. Washington, DC: American Psychological Association. Monthly. ISSN 0033-2887.

Covers a broad range of psychological research with frequent references to publications of value in market research. Brief subject and author indexes.

The publisher's corresponding online data base, updated monthly, covers 1967 to date. A CD-ROM version is also available.

Sociological Abstracts. San Diego, CA: Sociological Abstracts, Inc. Bimonthly. ISSN 0038-0202.

In addition to sociology, abstracts cover methodology, research technology, statistical methods, communications and related subjects. Annual cumulative index.

The publisher's corresponding online database, updated quarterly, covers 1963 to date. Also available in CD-ROM format.

Social Sciences Index. New York: H.W. Wilson Co. Quarterly/Annual Cumulation. ISSN 0094-4900.

An author/subject index to the more widely available English-language periodicals in economics, environmental sciences, sociology, psychology, medical sciences, public administration, and other social science fields. A separate author listing of citations to book reviews appears in each issue. Also available online and in CD-ROM format.

Social Sciences Citation Index. Philadelphia: Institute for Scientific Information. 3/year including annual cumulation. ISSN 0091-3707.

A comprehensive index providing access by author, specific subject and source to all materials with substantive information published in the social sciences and related fields worldwide. Periodical coverage includes editorials, letters, and book reviews. The publisher's corresponding online data base, Social Scisearch, covers 1974 to date and is updated weekly. Also available in CD-ROM format.

Research Aids

As existing index services move more rapidly into production in machine-readable formats, new features are added and existing ones are enhanced. A regular review of the following aids will help to keep the user currently informed about these changes.

Books and Periodicals Online. Ann Arbor, MI: Books and Periodicals Online. Irregular.
A directory with brief descriptions of books and periodicals available online and in CD-ROM format.

Computer-Readable Data Bases: A Directory and Data Sourcebook. Detroit, MI: Gale. Irregular.
Published for the American Society for Information Science, Washington, D.C. Describes publicly available bibliographic and textual databases produced in the free world. Arranged by database name with subject, name/acronym/synonym, producer, and processor indexes.

Directory of Online Databases.

DIALOG Bluesheets. Palo Alto, CA: DIALOG Information Services. [Online database].
Each bluesheet is a description of a database available on DIALOG. Print versions and CD-ROM are available. Other online services offer similar aids.

Directory of Periodicals Online: Indexed, Abstracted & Full-Text News, Law & Business. Washington, DC: Federal Document Retrieval. Annual.
A directory of periodicals in the fields of business, law and news which are available online.

Directory of Portable Databases. Detroit, MI: Cuadra/Gale. Semiannual. ISSN 1045-8352.
A directory of databases available in CD-ROM, diskette and other portable formats.

Ulrich's International Periodicals Directory.

Standard Periodical Directory.

INFORMATION CENTERS AND SPECIALISTS

Publications, information and advice are available through a number of channels, many of them close at hand, and are often free for the asking.

NETWORKS

The 1980s saw a rapid acceleration in the concept of access to information in the broadest sense. This concept was actualized in the development of computer and library networks which permit the sharing of information between institutions and between researchers. Traditional library networks sharing catalog information, such as the Research Libraries Group's (RLG) RLIN system and the OCLC system, took a giant step at the end of the decade by introducing, in the case of OCLC, subject searching via the EPIC system and end-user friendly access to a variety of databases via its First Choice system, while RLG made similar moves with its CITADEL service.

The widespread acceptance of electronic mail systems and FAX machines created a new universe of networking. The use of CREN, Inc.'s BITNET international network has made worldwide sharing of collegial information at over 600 institutions of higher education an established fact. Commercial online services such as DIALOG have implemented electronic mail equivalents for their subscribers. The future of computer and library networking holds in the as yet planning stage National Research and Education Network (NREN). Information about networks is available from:

EDUCOM, 112-16 St. N.W., Washington, DC 20036.

U.S. Library of Congress, Network Development and MARC Standard Office, 10 First St. S.E., Washington, D.C. 20540.

LIBRARIES

Numerous public and academic libraries maintain excellent collections of business information. In the larger institutions these materials are serviced by special departments. Smaller libraries can obtain publications which they lack through interlibrary loan.

On a broader scale, computer technology has fostered the growth of cooperative systems, consortia and library networks that attempt to share their resources and provide information through their member bodies. Many of these groups are closed systems that serve only member institutions; others, however, particularly those made up of academic and research institutions, provide assistance to the public. Access to the resources of these networks is generally provided directly or by referral through a local member body. One example of such a network of interest to the researcher is the following:

Research Libraries Group (RLG), Stanford, CA.

This consortium of academic and research libraries includes the Research Libraries of the New York Public Library along with a growing number of leading university libraries. Access to RLG's resources is available to patrons of member libraries through its cooperative bibliographic control system, resource sharing and collection development.

In Washington, D.C., a number of Federal resources are open to researchers. Of broadest scope is the Library of Congress, which also provides certain databases in its collection for searching by the public from the computer catalog center or from terminals in the reading rooms.

Required to be open to the public without charge are Federal Depository Libraries located in every State, the District of Columbia, Puerto Rico, and Guam. These are academic and public institutions that have been designated to receive and maintain certain Federal government publications. Designated Regional Depositories are required to receive and retain one copy of all government publications made available to depositories either in printed form or microfacsimile. Other depository libraries select publications of interest to their communities. The system is administered by the Superintendent of Documents who also issues two periodically revised lists that can be used to determine depository facilities in specific areas:

List of Depository Libraries . . . Washington, D.C.: Superintendent of Documents. Annual.

Arranged alphabetically by State and alphabetically by city under each State. Also usually published once a year in the *Monthly Catalog of United States Government Publications.*

List of Classes of United States Government Publications Available for Selection by Depository Libraries. Washington, D.C.: Superintendent of Documents. Annual.

Publications are grouped by name of issuing agencies and their subordinate divisions.

Although many public, academic, and Federal Depository libraries maintain files of major Census Bureau publications, the Bureau itself has designated over 100 institutions as Census Bureau Depository Libraries. These supplement the Federal Depository system and are meant to serve local needs more conveniently. Each Census Bureau Depository receives a small number of basic Bureau publications and copies of reports for reference and research. Each can select the reports it needs and many choose only those that pertain to areas within their home and contiguous States. Space limitations, clientele needs, and other factors influence not only the volume but also the length of time these materials are retained. Without regard to size of collection, the Bureau lists those libraries which have elected to receive Census Bureau publications in its annual *Census Catalog and Guide.*

INFORMATION CENTERS AND CLEARINGHOUSES

Information centers, more than libraries, specialize in narrow areas of subject information for which they maintain in-depth resources and provide specialized services. Given this definition, special libraries, since they function like information centers, are included in this group.

Information centers, or special libraries, exist in all types of private and public organizations, including agencies at all levels of government. In public institutions, information centers generally welcome inquiries and offer services and database searches for a fee. Special libraries maintained to implement the activities of private business organizations—commercial firms, chambers of commerce, trade associations—also cover the organizations' primary and allied subject areas in depth with a variety of documentation formats ranging from books to unpublished materials. Although some are open to the public, most are meant to provide service to in-house personnel. Therefore, practical considerations of limited space and staff and the frequent complexity of the research project would suggest a preliminary contact by phone or letter as a matter of good policy if one hopes to achieve the best results.

Information clearinghouses, a comparatively new development, also function in specialized subject areas. In addition to collecting and servicing their information materials, they also process them for wider dissemination. This activity in some instances produces, in turn, reference publications and databases for general access or distribution. Like information centers, a number of clearinghouses function within the departments and agencies of the Federal government; others operate privately. The following units from the Federal sector may be supplemented by others of similar interest to business research by checking the directories listed at the end of the chapter.

Federal Information Center Program, Cumberland, MD.

The Federal Information Center (FIC) Program is a network of toll-free telephone numbers in key metropolitan areas. The specialists answering these numbers will provide information about Federal programs and services. A complete listing of the locations of FIC centers is included in the *Federal Yellow Book*.

Congressional Clearinghouse for the Future, U.S. Congress, Washington, D.C.

Provides Congress with forecasts and research on the future in any field of congressional interest and maintains a list of experts on futures research. Information and referral service is available to constituents who make requests through their congressional representatives.

National Injury Information Clearinghouse, U.S. Consumer Product Safety Commission, Bethesda, Md.

Maintains a collection of in-house databases relating to injuries associated with consumer products.

National Energy Information Center, Energy Information Administration, U.S. Department of Energy, Washington, D.C.

A public information unit with a staff of subject specialists available to respond to inquiries. Provides statistical information; copies of the Administration's statistical and analytical publications; searches of the FEDEX (Federal Energy Data Index) database; and referral, as needed, to the proper Department office or other Federal agencies.

National Technical Information Service, U.S. Department of Commerce, Springfield, VA.

This agency acts as clearinghouse and central sales source for U.S. and foreign government-funded research, development and engineering reports and analyses. In this capacity it collects, abstracts and indexes, and maintains a computerized database of these materials; issues an indexed abstract journal and other dissemination media; supplies the reports in a variety of formats and offers a standing order service.

Online searches of the NTIS data base by the agency's analysts are available for a fee, as is a catalog of previously conducted searches.

Commercial CD-ROM versions of the indexes are available.

STATE DATA CENTERS

Initiated under a Bureau of the Census program begun in 1978, State Data Centers now exist in every state, the District of Columbia, Puerto Rico and the Virgin Islands. They constitute a unique network of information centers committed to improving access and use of census data products.

State Data Center structure and services vary from State to State since they are established by joint statistical agreements between the Bureau and the individual States. Typically, however, the State designates a consortium of State organizations (e.g., State planning agency, State library, and major State university) and a network of affiliates in public service agencies throughout the State.

The Bureau of the Census supplies each State Data Center system with all statistical and reference reports, computer and microfiche data, maps and related materials covering all Bureau programs—population, housing, manufactures, agriculture, distributive trades, service industries—for its State and neighboring States. It also provides Center personnel with technical assistance and training.

The Centers, in turn, provide assistance in data retrieval, analysis, tape processing, maps, and other specified services to in-State census data users, and to out-of-State users, if they choose. Within the State, the Centers work under service-sharing arrangements with affiliates providing local assistance or referral to the proper State-level organization. Services are supplied free or at moderate cost.

A directory of State Data Centers listing their lead, coordinating, and affiliate members may be obtained from the Bureau's Data User Services Division. It is also updated from time to time in *Data User News* and in the *Census Catalog and Guide.*

Business/Industry Data Centers (BIDC).

In 1988, the Census Bureau began a pilot project utilizing the State Data Center (SDC) network as a means of fostering economic development within the States. The Census Bureau and other Federal agencies supply economic information and related assistance and training to BIDC participants. A list of participating agencies is included in the *Census Catalog and Guide.*

FIELD OFFICES OF FEDERAL AGENCIES

Publications for distribution and consultation, as well as libraries, information, and advice, are available through a network of field offices supported by a number of Federal agencies. Some are listed in the *United States Government Manual.* More comprehensive coverage is provided in *Federal Yellow Book* and other directories listed in this chapter.

An extensive system of field offices is maintained by the Department of Commerce. Here ready access is provided to the publications of the Bureau of the Census and other Department of Commerce units. Each office maintains a reference library of private as well as official materials, and some act as sales agents for numerous government publications relating to business. Department field personnel are available for individual service on specific problems.

Similarly, the Census Bureau, at its regional and satellite offices, maintains a staff of Information Services Specialists who can, by consultation or referral, answer questions on the Bureau's data products and assist users in obtaining and using data for specific applications. The work of this regional network is further extended by the Bureau's State Data Center program, described above.

The Department's International Trade Administration also maintains field offices, a number of which offer search services on a cost-plus basis. These cover online searches of databases and data generated by the Commerce Department as well as data bases available on the Dialog system, such as those of Predicasts. Information on this service may be obtained from International Trade Administration, U.S. Department of Commerce, Washington, D.C. 20230.

In addition, several hundred official Cooperative Offices of the Department of Commerce (such as chambers of commerce, manufacturers' associations, and similar groups) receive and maintain the Department's publications for consultation. Problems beyond their resources are referred to the nearest field office.

Regional offices of the Bureau of Labor Statistics are located in eight cities. Each distributes its own regional office materials and certain national publications of the Bureau.

Similarly, regional material of the Board of Governors of the Federal Reserve System is offered through the Publications Offices of the twelve Federal Reserve Banks. These also distribute some of the Board's publications other than subscription items. Research departments of the Banks are staffed with personnel conversant with the Board's national and regional data output. And each of the twelve maintains a library whose reference collection includes not only the Board's publications but also a wide selection of sources on domestic business and economy.

The Department of Agriculture maintains field offices and staff in support of its many local programs. Generally, a limited number of "national" publications is available for distribution at these locations as well as from State extension offices, usually located at the State colleges. Agricultural experiment stations and State agricultural colleges distribute their own reports.

The Small Business Administration maintains field offices where small firms are encouraged to seek individual assistance in the solution of business and marketing problems. Regional offices maintain reference libraries of publicly and privately published material of possible value to the small businessman.

An excellent list of regional offices by agency is included in the *Federal Yellow Book.*

SPECIALISTS

Information gathering often requires reliance on the knowledge and skills of two kinds of experts: information specialists and subject specialists.

Information specialists cover broad fields. Their expertise lies in locating published information, identifying unpublished resources and subject specialists, and compiling data gathered from all of these. They are to be found in libraries, information centers and clearinghouses, and government agencies at all levels. A number of independent information specialist firms and individuals undertake special assignment or contract arrangements on a fee basis.

By comparison, subject specialists command in-depth knowledge of a specific product, technology, industry, market area, or aspect of data collection and analysis. Some are expert in the intricacies, potential and limitations of published data. Others can supply unpublished information, first-hand knowledge, personal experience, or assessments of trends in their areas of expertise. Subject specialists may be found in or through trade and professional associations, research centers, chambers of commerce, and business firms.

A major resource for answers not readily available in published sources are the subject specialists in the Federal government. They may be identified through agency programs and functions. For example, researchers concerned with food and food marketing would be led to the Department of Agriculture, specifically to the staff concerned with its nationwide Food Consumption Survey conducted at ten-year intervals, and to the staff of the Economic Research Service because its interests include the convenience food market, fast food industry, food purchases away from home and consumer attitudes about nutrition, food expenditures, food safety regulations, etc.

Also, once an agency's functions have been identified, referral to its experts may be obtained through the agency's public information office. Thus, for information on starting a business abroad, trade policies of foreign countries, etc., the Public Information Staff, Bureau of Public Affairs, Department of State (Washington, D.C.) can direct the inquirer to the appropriate office or country officer in the Department, which monitors more than 200 foreign countries and multinational agencies throughout the world.

Document Delivery Services

The 1980s saw the development of a new information service which was modeled after the traditional interlibrary loan service. This new service—document delivery—provided at first by information brokers such as FIND/SVP and Washington Researchers but increasingly provided by universities and research libraries through fee-based information units such as New York Public Libraries' Corporate Services Division, made rapid delivery of full-text information a reality. The availability of document delivery services from major index producers such as UMI/Data Courier, Information Access and the Institute for Scientific Information greatly expanded the possibilities for the use of such services. A good listing of document delivery services is included in the *Information Industry Directory*.

DIRECTORIES OF INFORMATION CENTERS AND SPECIALISTS

To be supplied with current data on specific industries, products or trading areas frequently requires recourse to library resources, appropriate trade associations, government agencies, chambers of commerce, media, research centers and other sources, and to their knowledgeable personnel. All of these are enumerated in preceding chapters and the list of general and specialized guides to information centers and specialists.

The researcher should keep in mind that scanning indexing and abstracting services can also provide names of individuals and organizations expert on specific products, industries, or practices.

Comprehensive

Directory of Special Libraries and Information Centers. Detroit: Gale Research Co. Biennial. ISSN 0731-633x.

Volume 1, alphabetically arranged and subject indexed, describes U.S. and Canadian special libraries and information centers, their collections and services, and gives names of key personnel. Also includes entries for networks and consortia. Volume 2 consists of geographic and personnel indexes. New special libraries covered in inter-edition supplements comprise Volume 3.

A companion publication, *Subject Directory of Special Libraries and Information Centers,* rearranges the entries into subject volumes: health, business, government and law, social sciences, humanities and education, computer, engineering and science.

American Library Directory. New York: R.R. Bowker Co. Annual. ISSN 0065-910x.

The State-city listing includes special libraries, notes subject collections of general libraries and indicates Federal document depositories. Since ephemeral format characterizes much of the business literature, the number of volumes held should not be taken as a final criterion of scope. *American Library Directory Updating Service* is issued between editions.

World Guide to Special Libraries. New York: K.G. Saur. Irregular. ISSN 0724-8717.

This directory is one volume in the *Handbook of International Documentation and Information* series. A more general title in this series is the *World Guide to Libraries.*

Subject Collections. New York: R. R. Bowker Co. Irregular. ISSN 0000-0140.

Under each detailed subject, arrangement is alphabetical by State, city, and name of collection. In addition to the library, its address and the name of the librarian, some indication is given as to the extent and character of the collection, reproduction facilities, and restrictions on use of the materials.

Research Centers Directory. ISSN 0080-1518.

Federal and Washington-Based Sources

U.S. Office of the Federal Register. *The United States Directory of Federal Regional Structure.* Washington, D.C.: Government Printing Office. Biennial. ISSN 0730-1332. SuDoc: 034.119.

Maps regional structures used by Federal agencies and gives

locations of their regional offices including addresses, telephone numbers and names of officials.

Federal Executive Directory. Washington, D.C.: Carroll Publishing Co. Bimonthly. ISSN 0270-563x.
A nationwide directory of executive managers in Federal offices, including regional and field officials, arranged by Federal government structure. Alphabetical keyword index.

Federal Yellow Book. Washington, D.C.: Monitor Publishing. Quarterly. ISSN 0145-6202.
A telephone-directory formatted directory of the Executive agencies and Independent agencies of the Federal government. Similar directories are published by Monitor Publishing for State, municipal, and Federal Congressional agencies as well as for law firms and associations. A forthcoming directory will cover regional offices of Federal agencies.

U.S. Bureau of the Census. *Telephone Contacts for Data Users, Bureau of the Census.* Washington, D.C.: Bureau of the Census. Irregular.
Bureau administrators and staff specialists located in Washington are listed with their phone numbers by area of expertise under broad subject categories. Also includes phone numbers of Information Services Specialists in the Bureau's regional and satellite offices. Revised several times a year, this leaflet is updated in *Census and You* and is also distributed automatically to its subscribers.

U.S. Energy Information Administration. *Energy Information Directory.* Washington, D.C.: Government Printing Office. Quarterly. ISSN 0278-1581. SuDoc: E3.33:
For specific energy-related information and activities, arranged by broad topic, lists the office of primary interest within the Department of Energy and other federal agencies, together with the names, addresses and telephone numbers of the individuals to contact.

Congressional Quarterly's Washington Information Directory. Washington, D.C.: Congressional Quarterly, Inc. Annual. ISSN 0887-8064.
Gives directory information and contacts for agencies of the

Executive branch, Congress, and private organizations located in Washington, D.C. Subject-arranged section provides extensive coverage of business-related areas. Organization section includes useful lists of Federal committees, offices, departments, agencies, as well as nongovernment contacts. A detailed subject index and agency/organization index are provided.

Who Knows, A Guide to the Washington Experts. Washington, D.C.: Washington Researchers. Annual. ISSN 0740-087x.
Arranged by affiliation, the directory lists specialists in all branches of the Federal government located in the Washington area. Besides name, gives title, specialization, address and telephone number. Indexed by specific topic/agency name.

Who Knows About Industries and Markets. Washington, D.C.: Washington Researchers. Annual. ISSN 1042-0215.
A directory of analysts and their specialities arranged by SIC industry and product codes.

Who Knows About Foreign Industries and Markets. Washington, D.C.: Washington Researchers. Annual.
A directory of specialists on foreign countries, their economies and industries.

Washington Information Workbook. Washington, D.C.: Washington Researchers. Annual. ISSN 0192-8848.
This companion publication to the guide above identifies the major Federal departments and agencies and focuses on such sources as Capitol Hill, Federal document rooms, Freedom of Information offices, libraries and clearinghouses. Also explains how to use these resources when searching for information.

U.S. General Services Administration. *Federal Advisory Committees Annual Report to the President.* Washington, D.C.: Government Printing Office. Annual. ISSN 0091-0040.
Lists Federal advisory committees alphabetically and by Federal agencies which have jurisdiction. Gives committee management officers and staff contact persons, activities, functions, and cost of operation.

State and Local Sources

Association for University Business and Economic Research. *Membership Directory*. ISSN 0360-7402.

The Book of the States.

U.S. Department of Agriculture. *Directory of State Departments of Agriculture*. Washington, D.C.: Department of Agriculture. Annual. ISSN 0500-3024.
Lists addresses and telephone numbers of State marketing service agencies and names of key officials of State departments of agriculture.

————. *Professional Workers in State Agricultural Experiment Stations and Other Cooperating State Institutions*. Washington, D.C.: Government Printing Office. Annual. SuDoc: A1.76:305/
Lists specialists in marketing.

Municipal Yellow Book. Washington, D.C.: Monitor Publishing. Semiannual.
One of the Monitoring telephone-directory formatted directories. Included in this volume are city and county officials. A separate volume is published for State agencies.

World Chamber of Commerce Directory. ISSN 0893-326x.

New ICC World Directory of Chambers of Commerce. Paris, France: ICC Publishing. Annual.
A directory of members of the International Chamber of Commerce.

The Municipal Yearbook. ISSN 0077-2186.
In addition, State and local blue books and manuals are also excellent guides to officials and agencies at the State and local levels. A separate compilation of directories from the *Municipal Yearbook* has been issued.

Specialists and Consultants

Experts affiliated with government agencies and public institutions dominate the directories grouped above. In addition, many specialists and consultants work in private organizations or operate independently.

Associations and their personnel constitute a combined resource of specialists and information centers. Headquarters staff can suggest names of experts willing to offer assistance and advice. Directories useful in finding such contacts are listed in the chapter on associations.

Individuals expert in their industry or profession may also be found in such membership rosters as the following:

American Marketing Association. *The Marketing News International Directory of the American Marketing Association and Marketing Services Guide.* Chicago, IL: American Marketing Association. Annual.

A directory of American Marketing Association members which provide biographical and professional information.

Subject specialists with in-depth knowledge of published and unpublished information are also to be found among the editors, research directors and advertising managers of advertising media. For this purpose the following sources are particularly useful:

Standard Rate & Data Service. Skokie, IL: Standard Rate & Data Service, Inc. Monthly, Quarterly, Semiannual depending on edition/ Supplements.

Service in a series of editions, of which newspaper, consumer and farm magazines, and business publications are most useful in locating editors, advertising managers, and sales representatives acquainted with specific products, industries and markets.

Directories such as *Gale Directory of Publications* and *Ulrich's,* though lacking the specialized information included in the items above, are widely available and can be used to the same end. Consultants in market research and related areas, as well as specialists in supplying data, may be found in the directories listed in the chapter on services. The following titles provide a broader scope of specialties.

Consultants and Consulting Organizations. Detroit: Gale Research Co. Biennial. ISSN 0196-1292.

Directory and descriptive information is provided for individuals, firms and organizations and their offices abroad. Arrangement is geographical. Includes subject specialization index and indexes by name of individual and firm. Kept up-to-date by the semiannual supplement.

Dun's Consultants Directory. Parsippany, N.J.: Dun's Marketing Service. Annual. ISSN 0884-3724.
A directory of consultants who perform business consulting services.

Information Services

FISCAL Directory of Fee-Based Information Services in Libraries. Norwalk, CA: FYI/County of Los Angeles Public Library. Biennial.
A directory of fee-based information services available in libraries.

Burwell Directory of Information Brokers. Houston, TX: Burwell Enterprises. Annual.
A directory of firms and individuals which provide fee-based information services. Updated in the periodical *Information Broker.*

Information Industry Directory. Detroit, MI: Gale Research. Irregular/Supplements. ISSN 1051-6239.
A directory of organizations, systems and services which are included in the information industry.

Information Industry Association. *IIA Telephone Guide.* Washington, D.C.: Information Industry Association. Annual.
A telephone-style directory which lists members of the I.I.A.

Association of Public Data Users (U.S.). *APDU Membership Directory.* Princeton, N.J.: Association of Public Data Users. Annual.
A directory of libraries and other institutions which are public data user associate members.

RESEARCH AIDS

The reference aids included in this chapter are those commonly used as selection tools. These are the comprehensive bibliographies, guides, catalogs, checklists and other less formal media.

Criteria of usefulness are the timeliness, accuracy, scope, bibliographic detail and annotations provided by each aid. Subject arrangements and subject indexing contribute to expeditious fact-finding and back-checks in special project research.

The compilations listed here cover various types of sources or a number of issuing bodies. Research aids that list the publications and other information resources of a single type of source, organization or agency are grouped in the preceding chapters with the source or issuing body to which they pertain.

Although comprehensive bibliographies, guides and catalogs are superior to selected lists in the overall approach to business and marketing information, the latter, when cited in textbooks at the ends of chapters and in the footnotes of reference works, should not be overlooked.

The index and abstract features of bibliographic guides listed in the preceding chapters also can be used in search projects. Such guides, if published on a continuing basis, and the current press constitute excellent selection and current awareness sources.

BIBLIOGRAPHIES AND GUIDES

The number of marketing bibliographic tools remains small in comparison to the number of general guides and bibliographies of business data as a whole. Consequently, relevant citations may also be found in the titles grouped below in the "General Business" and "Statistics" categories. In addition to these general publications, practically every bibliography compiled from the general business or economic aspect of a specific industry or trade includes references important in marketing research.

As for the bibliographic guides themselves, valuable as they are for general orientation, they become dated quickly. Therefore, periodically revised guides and continuing catalogs, checklists, published indexes and abstracts, and the growing and increasingly accessible bibliographic data bases offer more precise tools for the location of current information. Such, moreover, is the interrelation of these groups, that all must be considered in the search for pertinent publications or for the facts themselves. A particularly useful source is the Graduate Business Schools, which produce useful "pathfinders" for research in specialized areas.

To correlate the references cited in this chapter with such groups and with the more specialized bibliographic-type publications classed elsewhere with the sources to which they pertain, it is advisable to use the general index to this manual.

General Business

Strenges, Michael. *Analyzing Your Competition.* 2d ed. New York, N.Y.: FIND/SVP. 1992. 1v.
Includes bibliographic references and indexes.

Annual Index to Legal and Business Related Bibliographies. Studio City, CA: Inform Press. Annual.

Baker Library. *Baker Library Mini-list.* Boston, MA: Harvard Business School. Irregular.
A series of bibliographies covering a wide variety of business-related topics. Other graduate business schools such as those at the University of Michigan or Cornell publish similar series.

Schlesinger, Bernard S. *The Basic Business Library: Core Resources.* 2d ed. Phoenix, AZ: Oryx. 1989. 278p.
A one-volume overview of core business information sources.

Business Sources of Latin America and the Caribbean. Washington, D.C.: Organization of American States, Columbus Memorial Library. Irregular.

Lists publications by type (guides, gazetteers, bank reports, periodicals, etc.) which cover more than one Latin American country, and publications, similarly arranged, for each country of Latin America. Also includes relevant publications of the Organization of American States and describes the information and services provided by the U.S. Department of Commerce regional representative for Latin America.

Business and Economics Books and Serials in Print. New York, N.Y.: Bowker. Irregular. ISSN 0000–0655.
New editions not seen, but useful for retrospective research.

Daniells, Lorna M. *Business Information Sources.* Rev. ed. Berkeley, CA: University of California Press. 1985. XVI, 673p.
An exhaustive guide to business information sources for the business person, student, and researcher. Descriptive annotations are provided for basic business sources as well as for works in the various subdivisions of the management function. A detailed author, title, subject index is included. A new edition is promised and a CD-ROM version is available.

Data Map. Phoenix, AZ: Oryx. Irregular. ISSN 0264–7745.
An index to published statistical tables.

Encyclopedia of Business Information Sources. Detroit: Gale Research Co. Irregular. ISSN 0071–0210.
Covers business activities, products and related fields. Arrangement is by subjects identified in a lengthy table of contents. Sources listed include directories, guides, statistics sources, periodicals and other basics, as well as trade associations, professional societies, commercially available online databases.

International Directory of Non-Official Statistical Sources. London: Euromonitor. Irregular.
A listing of statistical services and information services other than government for countries and regions of the world. A companion volume exists for Europe.

Management Information Guide. Detroit: Gale Research Co. Irregular. ISSN 0076–3632.

A series of bibliographic sourcebooks covering management and business topics, and individual industries.

Small Business Sourcebook. Detroit, MI: Gale. Biennial. ISSN 0883–3397.

A guide to resources useful for small business which includes lists of useful information sources for general business and individual industries.

Source Directory of Predicasts, Inc. Cleveland: Predicasts, Inc. Quarterly/Annual Cumulation. ISSN 0092–7767.

A bibliography of publications abstracted and indexed in the various Predicasts, Inc. indexes and abstracts. Entries are arranged alphabetically by title, geographically by area covered, and by subject. The annual includes a special list, "100 Basic Sources of Business Information." The source list is part of the online service and the CD-ROM product.

Business Information Alert. Chicago, IL: Alert. 10/yr. ISSN 1042–0746.

A topical guide to business information sources. Includes a "what's new" section.

CD-ROM Professional. Weston, CT: Pemberton Press. Bimonthly. ISSN 1049–0833.

A review medium for new CD-ROM products.

Database. Weston, CT: Online. Bimonthly.

An information source for all aspects of electronic information.

Information Today. Medford, N.J.: Learned Information. Monthly. ISSN 8755–6286.

An information source for both CD-ROM and online information.

Business Information: How to Find It, How to Use It. 2d ed. Phoenix, AZ: Oryx. 1991. 499p.

A guide to information sources for business with an emphasis on company information.

Statistics Sources. Detroit: Gale Research Co. Irregular. ISSN 0585–198x.

Covers domestic, foreign and international sources in a dictionary arrangement of specific subjects, including foreign countries. For each subject shows publications and/or government or private agencies that supply statistical data. Includes a selected list of basic compendia of general statistics.

Statistical Reference Index . . . Bethesda, MD: Congressional Information Service. Annual.

A reference list of the information sources cited in the SRI annual.

Washington Researchers Business Research Series. Washington, D.C.: Washington Researchers. Irregular. ISSN 0894–881x.

Guide to corporate documents and information available by direct contact. Identifies types of local governmental units, specific State agencies, individual Federal agencies and congressional committees, and courts at the Federal and State levels with the kind of information they would have and can provide. The series covers private companies, public companies, and service companies. Other series cover international companies, market and industry information and management techniques.

Marketing and Market Research

The assessment of bibliographic guides given above applies equally to the titles cited here. In addition, more specialized bibliographies and guides dealing with subdisciplines of marketing, statistical research sources, and marketing practices of specific industries may also be located by referring to the general business indexes, specialized indexes to marketing and statistical publications, and bibliographic databases which greatly expand the feasibility of extracting extensive and up-to-date marketing literature.

AMA Bibliography Series. Chicago, IL: American Marketing Association. Irregular.

Until 1980, this was a numbered series [1–38]. It is now unnumbered and includes a listing of marketing doctoral dissertations.

Market Share Reporter. Detroit, MI: Gale. Irregular. ISSN 1052–9578.
A listing of brand market share information taken from published sources.

British Library. Science Reference and Information Service. *Market Research and Industry Surveys: a Select List of Reports . . .* 4th ed. London: British Library Science Reference and Information Service. 1986. 160p.
A listing of market research reports and industry surveys held by the British Library.

Financial Sourcebooks. Naperville, IL: Financial Sourcebook. Biennial. ISSN 0892–7812.
A directory and listing of financial research, market surveys and services.

Findex: the Directory of Market Research Reports. New York, N.Y.: FIND/SVP. Annual/Supplement. ISSN 0737–4992.
A listing of market research reports and investment surveys available from FIND/SVP. Also available online.

Marketsearch. London: Arlington Management Publications/British Overseas Trade Board. Annual. ISSN 9066–1605.
A listing of market research reports and surveys published world-wide.

World Sources of Market Information. Cambridge, MA: Ballinger. Irregular.
A multi-volume set arranged by region which lists market surveys and market research services.

Harvey, Joan M. *Statistics Europe: Sources for Market Research*. Beckenham, Eng.: CBD Research Ltd. Irregular.
For each country, lists and describes its general statistical publications as well as those covering mining, agricultural, and industrial production; external trade; internal distribution; population; standard of living. Also includes information on the central statistical office and other principal institutional sources. Organization and title indexes. Separate volumes are available for Africa, America and Asia and Australasia.

What's New in Advertising and Marketing. New York: Special Libraries Association, Advertising and Marketing Division. 10/yr. ISSN 0043–4558.

Lists by subject a variety of publications including special issues of magazines, market guides, studies produced by media.

Market News. Chicago, IL: American Marketing Association. Bi-weekly.

A news source for the marketing researcher.

Population Today. Washington, D.C.: Population Reference Bureau. Monthly. ISSN 0092–444x.

An information source for data on the 1990 Census and other population issues.

Competitor Intelligence Manual and Guide . . . Englewood Cliffs, N.J.: Prentice-Hall. 1990. 376p.

Contains lists of information sources for competitor intelligence.

Industry Data Sources. Cambridge, Mass: Ballinger Publishing Co. [Online database].

Identifies primarily publications carrying information on industries and products in the U.S. and Canada. A listing of general reference sources by type precedes a section of 60 industry categories, each subdivided by type of source. Entries give full bibliographic citations, annotations, and prices. Materials covered include market research reports, government publications, directories, investment banking studies, special issues of trade periodicals, numeric data bases, books. Contains an alphabetical directory of publishers/producers indexed by type of publication and indexes by SIC number, subject, and title.

GOVERNMENT PUBLICATIONS AND DATA FILES

The catalogs and checklists published by the agencies and departments of the Federal government provide broader coverage, greater detail, and timeliness often lacking in comprehensive and topical lists. Two important factors have influenced the availability of these publications: machine-readable formats and Federal cutbacks.

Grouped here are the major comprehensive catalogs of Federally produced sources. Catalogs and checklists issued by specific Federal departments and agencies are included in earlier chapters which deal with the publications of those units individually. Among them, particularly relevant are the purely data-oriented lists issued by agencies whose programs produce a large number and variety of statistical publications and data files.

Similarly, checklists of State and local government publications may be found in the chapter on regional and local sources. In many cases publications lists of individual States are available from the State library, archivist, or other State agency. To a lesser degree municipal libraries render a similar service for their jurisdictions.

In all cases, whether using them for research or selection, it is important to keep in mind those comprehensive privately published indexes that cover publications of governments at all or specific levels.

U.S. Superintendent of Documents. *Monthly Catalog of United States Government Publications.* Washington, D.C.: Government Printing Office. Monthly/Annual and Semiannual Supplement. ISSN 0362–6830. SuDoc: GP3.8.

According to law, the Library of the Division of Public Documents of the Government Printing Office should receive one copy of each publication produced by any branch or bureau of the U.S. government. On this basis each issue lists, by agency, every publication (except administrative and confidential) published during the preceding month. Entries include bibliographic detail but not content annotations. For each it indicates whether the publication is available for sale, distributed by the issuing unit, published for official use only, sent to Federal Depository Libraries, and format in which the item is available. A separate serials supplement is issued annually.

Individual indexes by author, title, title-keyword, subject, series/report number, and stock number covering the month's content are included in each monthly issue. They are also issued in separate semiannual and annual cumulations that include, additionally, an index by Superintendent of Documents classification number. The Monthly Catalog is available online and in CD-ROM format.

―――. *GPO Sales Publications Reference File* (PRF). Washington, D.C.: Government Printing Office. Microfiche. Bimonthly/Monthly Supplements. SuDoc: GP3.22/3:

This inventory of publications for sale by the Superintendent of Documents is arranged in three ways: by Government Printing Office stock numbers; by Superintendent of Documents classification numbers; and in a single alphabetical sequence of authors, titles, subjects, keywords and phrases, series/report numbers. The complete microfiche set is updated and reissued six times a year. The monthly supplement, *GPO New Sales Publications*, records all items added the preceding month. Also available online.

Monthly Catalog Previews: a Monthly Index to U.S. Government Publications Distributed to Depository Libraries . . . Lanham, MD: Bernan. Monthly.

An index to publications which have not yet appeared in the *Monthly Catalog.*

United States. Superintendent of Documents. *Subject Bibliography.* (SB) Washington, D.C.: Government Printing Office. Irregular. SuDoc: GP3.22/2:

A numbered series of several hundred topical acquisitions guides listing Federal publications of general interest. Individual titles devoted to specific subjects (e.g., *How to Sell to Government Agencies*) and to publication groups (e.g., *Statistical Publications*) are added and revised from time to time. Entries, arranged alphabetically by title, give ordering information and price, if any.

Federal Data Base Finder. Potomac, MD: Information U.S.A. Irregular. ISSN 0897–4810.

A directory of databases available from the Federal government. A companion volume is available for States.

Government Publications Review. Elmsford, N.Y.: Pergamon. Bimonthly. ISSN 0277–9390.

An information source for government publications from all jurisdictions.

Guide to U.S. Government Statistics. McLean, VA: Documents Index. Irregular. ISSN 0434–9067.

Publications ranging from one-table releases to compendia are listed alphabetically by title under issuing departments and agencies (extant and discontinued), arranged in a single Federal-structure sequence. Entries include description of the publication (e.g., summary, compendium) and type of statistics, frequency of publication, publication dates, and reference to earlier title(s).

U.S. Bureau of the Census. *Data Finder*. Washington, D.C.: Bureau of the Census. Irregular.

A series of topical pamphlet guides to locating statistics published by the Census Bureau and other federal agencies. Titles issued to date have covered government construction, industrial, business, agricultural, foreign trade, and energy statistics, as well as data from the economic surveys. Each describes and tabulates the major items of data and the current report and survey where they are to be found.

"Guide to Sources of Statistics." In: U.S. Bureau of the Census. *Statistical Abstract of the United States*. Washington, D.C.: Government Printing Office. Annual.

Included in each edition under a slightly different title, this bibliography classifies primary and selected secondary and nonrecurring statistical publications by subject, and cites abstract sections where data from these sources appear.

U.S. National Technical Information Service. *Directory of Federal Statistical Data Files*. Springfield, VA: National Technical Information Service. Annual. ISSN 0731–3504. SuDoc: C51.15:

Over 600 machine-readable Federal statistical data files from 14 departments and 57 agencies are arranged in agency sequence. Besides bibliographic citation, each entry gives file reference number, description and subject coverage, geographic and time coverage, technical characteristics, reference materials, related printed reports and files, agency contacts, and information on availability. Includes an agency index, subject index, and file and keyword index.

————. *Government Reports Announcements and Index*. Springfield, VA: National Technical Information Service. Biweekly. ISSN 0097–9007. SuDoc: C41.21:

Technical reports and other materials of specialized interest in a variety of formats, sent to the agency for distribution, are classified by subject field, including behavioral sciences and business and economics. The indexes (subject, personal author, corporate author, contract number, and accession/report number) referencing the annotated citations are also issued in an annual cumulation.

Coverage includes U.S. government-sponsored research, development and engineering reports, as well as foreign technical reports and other analyses prepared by national and local government agencies, their contractors and grantees. Organizations contributing reports include universities, independent research organizations and trade associations, as well as Federal government agencies and their affiliates.

Indexed materials may be purchased from the agency in paper copy, microfiche, microfilm or magnetic tape form, as indicated in the citation. An additional service (SRIM) supplies microfiche or research reports in specific subject areas on a subscription basis. The corresponding database, NTIS, is available online and is updated every two weeks. A CD-ROM version is also available.

————. *NTIS Alert.* Springfield, VA: National Technical Information Service. Weekly/Monthly depending on individual title. ISSN 0364–6467.

A group of individual checklists, each with its own frequency, that cover technical reports based on Federally funded research. Each is devoted to a specific subject area, including administration and management, business and economics, transportation. Each cites and abstracts reports as they become available from NTIS and includes a detailed subject index as a year-end issue.

Current National Statistical Compendiums . . . Bethesda, MD: Congressional Information Service. Irregular.

A guide to the CIS microfiche series.

Business Serials of the U.S. Government. 2d ed. Chicago, IL: American Library Association. 1988. 86p.

A listing of Federal government business serials.

CURRENT PRESS

Catalogs and checklists can be used most effectively against a background of business and industry trends. And it is the business press—the magazines and newspapers of business and industry—that supply current awareness of events and developments and provide the perspective that directs the successful selection of specific sources for current or future use. Editorial content of periodicals has been treated in a preceding chapter. Reviewed here are the features that, in addition to news notes, make them a useful complement to other selection tools.

Judged by the measure of timeliness, newspapers, particularly the business sections and advertising columns, offer immediate reporting on current studies of general interest. Unlike news notes, however, feature stories in the daily press are more likely to cite data of indeterminate vintage from sources not always clearly identified.

Advertising and marketing magazines, on the other hand, offer timeliness and scope as indicated by the special columns each one features.

Advertising Age. Chicago: Crain Communications, Inc. Weekly. ISSN 0001–8899.
News announcements of privately published books, studies, research materials, etc.

Sales & Marketing Management. New York: Bill Communications. Monthly. ISSN 0163–7517.
"Worth Writing For" is a list of available catalogs, sales aids, publications, etc.

Business Marketing. Chicago: Crain Communications, Inc. Monthly. ISSN 0745–5933.
Lists current publications of interest to the industrial marketer.

Journal of Marketing. Chicago: American Marketing Association. Quarterly. ISSN 0022–2429.
"Book Review" features detailed, authoritative, signed reviews. "Legal Developments in Marketing" and "Marketing Abstracts" report on business, trade and legislative publications.

JMR Journal of Marketing Research. Chicago: American Marketing Association. Quarterly. ISSN 0022–2437.
"New Books in Review": lengthy, signed reviews of academic works, reference tools, and popular books bearing on all aspects of

marketing. Supplemented by an unannotated checklist, "Publications Received."

In addition to the advertising and marketing periodicals listed above, professional and trade journals in other fields, as well as data-oriented periodicals such as those below, contain features, bibliographic citations, and book reviews applicable to business and market research.

American Demographics. Ithaca, N.Y.: American Demographics, Inc. 10/yr. ISSN 0163–4089.
   Covers demographics—population, housing, social trends, lifestyles with emphasis on the American consumer, as well as data sources and analytic techniques.
   "Sources": descriptions of organizations and the data they produce. "Profile": in-depth presentations of demographic publications extended to the "how-to" demographic analysis. "Books": a book review feature. Includes an annual *Directory of Marketing Information Companies.*

Journal of Economic and Social Measurement. New York: Elsevier Science. Quarterly. ISSN 0747–9662.
   Covers all aspects of data production, distribution and use, with primary emphasis on economic and social data.

FSUC Newsletter. Arlington, VA: Federal Statistics Users' Conference. 12–14/yr. ISSN 0014–9225.
   Covers new reports issued by Federal statistical agencies, describes proposed statistical programs, and lists publications of State and local governments, research organizations and associations.

HARDWARE AND SOFTWARE

The enormous expansion in the number of machine-readable information sources for business and market research has created a need for current information on available hardware and software for these resources. Researchers needing advice on computer hardware and software and on other technological advances can follow the source path outlined in this volume. The Federal government, universities, research institutions, trade associations and other information producers, in their development of machine-readable products, have produced a major body of work on the use of these products and the hardware and software required for their use. The following is a list of general sources of information for the user of machine-readable information.

Information Industry Directory. Detroit, MI: Gale. Annual. ISSN 1051-6239.
Includes listings on software producers.

Business Software Directory . . . Medford, N.J.: Learned Information/ Information Sources. Irregular. ISSN 0887-9478.
A directory which describes application software available by industry or business function. Each record provides the name of the producer, the software name, directory information, hardware requirements and technical and other support available. Also available online.

Datapro. Delran, N.J.
Datapro is the most comprehensive source of information on both hardware and software. All aspects of data processing, communication and office automation applications are covered. In a series of looseleaf, frequently updated volumes, Datapro provides descriptions, ratings, cost information, training requirements and other important decision-making information for each product listed.

Periodicals

Macweek. New York, N.Y.: Ziff Davis. Weekly.

Macuser . . . New York, N.Y.: Ziff Davis. Monthly. ISSN 0884-0997.
Both of the above are devoted to Apple Macintosh computer applications.

PC Magazine . . . New York, N.Y.: Ziff Davis. Biweekly.

PC Week . . . New York, N.Y.: Ziff Davis. Weekly.
Both of the above are devoted to IBM pc applications.

The *New York Times,* in its Tuesday section on science, covers new products for the computer user.

APPENDIX: STATE STATISTICAL ABSTRACTS

The statistical abstracts for States identified here are drawn from the annual list published in the *Statistical Abstract of the United States* and from the *Statistical Reference Index,* both of which may be consulted for the latest editions available. In some instances a near equivalent has been listed in substitution for, or in addition to, a statistical abstract. All contain statistical tables on a variety of subjects for the State as a whole, its component parts, or both.

ALABAMA
Economic Abstract of Alabama. Tuscaloosa: University of Alabama, Center for Business and Economic Research. Irregular.

ALASKA
Alaska—Economy Performance Report. Juneau: Department of Commerce and Economic Development.

ARIZONA
Arizona Statistical Abstract. Flagstaff: University of Arizona, Division of Economic and Business Research. College of Business and Public Administration. Annual.

ARKANSAS
Arkansas Statistical Abstract. Little Rock: University of Arkansas, State Data Center. Biennial.

CALIFORNIA
California Statistical Abstract. Sacramento: Department of Finance. Annual.

COLORADO
Statistical Abstract of Colorado. Denver: University of Colorado, Business Research Division. Annual.

CONNECTICUT
Connecticut Market Data. Rocky Hill: Department of Economic Development. Annual.

DELAWARE
Delaware Data Book. Dover: Delaware Development Office. Annual.

FLORIDA
Florida Statistical Abstract. Gainesville: University of Florida. Bureau of Economic and Business Research.

GEORGIA
Georgia Statistical Abstract. Athens: University of Georgia, College of Business Administration, Research Division. Annual.

HAWAII
The State of Hawaii Data Book: A Statistical Abstract. Honolulu: Department of Business and Economic Development and Tourism. Annual.

IDAHO
Idaho Facts Data Book. Boise: Department of Commerce. Annual.

ILLINOIS
Illinois Statistical Abstract. Champaign: University of Illinois. Bureau of Economic and Business Research.

INDIANA
Indiana Fact Book. Indianapolis: Indiana University, Indiana Business Research Center. Triennial.

IOWA
Statistical Profile of Iowa. Des Moines: Iowa Department of Economic Development, Research Bureau. Irregular.

KANSAS
Kansas Statistical Abstract. Lawrence: University of Kansas Institute for Policy and Business Research. Annual.

KENTUCKY
Kentucky Economic Statistics. Frankfort: Department of Existing Business and Industry. Annual.

LOUISIANA
Statistical Abstract of Louisiana. New Orleans: University of New Orleans, Division of Business and Economic Research.

MAINE
Maine: A Statistical Summary. Augusta: Maine Department of Economic and Community Development. Irregular.

MARYLAND
Maryland Statistical Abstract. Baltimore: Department of Economic and Employment Development. Biennial.

MICHIGAN
Michigan Statistical Abstract. Detroit: Wayne State University, School of Business Administration, Bureau of Business Research. Annual.

MINNESOTA
Compare Minnesota . . . Saint Paul: Department of Trade and Economic Development, Analysis Division. Annual.

MISSISSIPPI
Mississippi Statistical Abstract. Mississippi State: Mississippi State University, College of Business and Industry, Research Division. Annual.

MISSOURI
Statistical Abstract for Missouri. Columbia: University of Missouri, Business and Public Administration, Research Center. Biennial.

MONTANA
Montana County Profiles. Helena: Department of Commerce, Economic Information Center. Irregular.

NEBRASKA
Nebraska Statistical Handbook. Lincoln: Department of Economic Development, Research Division. Biennial.

NEVADA
Nevada Statistical Abstract. Carson City: Department of Administrative Planning Division. Biennial.

NEW JERSEY
New Jersey Statistical Factbook. Trenton: New Jersey State Data Center. Annual.

NEW MEXICO
New Mexico Statistical Abstract. Albuquerque: University of New Mexico, Bureau of Business and Economic Research. Annual.

NEW YORK
New York State Statistical Yearbook. Albany: Nelson Rockefeller Institute of Government. Annual.

New York at a Glance. Albany: Energy Association of New York. Annual.

NORTH CAROLINA
Statistical Abstract of North Carolina. Raleigh: Office of State Budget and Management. Annual.

NORTH DAKOTA
Statistical Abstract of North Dakota. Grand Forks: University of North Dakota, Bureau of Business and Economic Research. Annual.

OHIO
Benchmark Ohio. Columbus: Ohio State University School of Public Policy and Management. Biennial.

OKLAHOMA
Statistical Abstract of Oklahoma. Norman: University of Oklahoma, Center for Economic and Managment Research. Annual.

OREGON
Blue Book. Salem: Oregon Secretary of State. Biennial.

PENNSYLVANIA
Pennsylvania Statistical Abstract. Harrisburg: Pennsylvania State Data Center.

RHODE ISLAND
Rhode Island Basic Economic Statistics. Providence: Department of Economic Development. Annual.

SOUTH CAROLINA
South Carolina Statistical Abstract. Columbia: Budget and Control Board, Research and Statistical Services Division. Annual.

SOUTH DAKOTA
South Dakota Community Abstracts. Vermillion: South Dakota State Data Center. Annual.

TENNESSEE
Tennessee Statistical Abstract. Knoxville: University of Tennessee, Center for Business and Economic Research. Annual.

TEXAS
Texas Fact Book. Austin: University of Texas, Bureau of Business Research. Annual.

Texas Almanac. Dallas: Dallas Morning News. Annual.

UTAH
Statistical Abstract of Utah. Salt Lake City: University of Utah, Bureau of Economic and Business Research. Triennial.

VERMONT
Demographic and Economic Profiles. Montpelier: Department of Employment and Training. Irregular.

VIRGINIA
Virginia Statistical Abstract. Charlottesville: University of Virginia, Center for Public Service. Biennial.

WASHINGTON
Washington State Data Book. Olympia: Office of Financial Management. Annual.

WEST VIRGINIA
West Virginia Economic—Statistical Profile. Charleston: West Virginia Chamber of Commerce. Biennial.

West Virginia Statistical Handbook. Charleston: West Virginia Research League. Annual.

WISCONSIN
Wisconsin Blue Book. Madison: Wisconsin Legislative Reference Bureau. Biennial.

WYOMING
Wyoming Data Handbook. Cheyenne: Department of Administration and Fiscal Control, Division of Research and Statistics. Annual.

INDEX

Index

ABOUT THE AUTHOR

John V. Ganly has his B.B.A. from Baruch College, an M.A. in Political Science from the New School for Social Research, and an M.L.S. from Pratt Institute. After a ten-year career in business he joined the staff of the New York Public Library where he is now Assistant Director for the Science, Industry and Business Library Collections, The New York Public Library Research Libraries. Since 1976 he has been a Coadjutant Professor at Rutgers University and has also taught at Columbia University from 1983 to 1986.

Elected to Beta Gamma Sigma, Mr. Ganly has also been honored by the Special Libraries Association, which in 1992 gave him its DISCLOSURE Technology Award, and in 1993, the President's Award. The previous edition of this present book, *Data Sources for Business and Market Analysis* (Scarecrow Press, 1983) was chosen by *Library Journal* as one of its "Business Books of 1983." His *Small Business Sourcebook* (Gale Research, 1983) was selected by *American Libraries* as one of the "outstanding reference sources of 1983."